#82401-1

# POLITICS AS RADICAL CREATION

Herbert Marcuse and Hannah Arendt on
Political Performativity

# Politics as Radical Creation

*Herbert Marcuse and Hannah Arendt*
*on Political Performativity*

CHRISTOPHER HOLMAN

UNIVERSITY OF TORONTO PRESS
Toronto Buffalo London

© University of Toronto Press 2013
Toronto Buffalo London
www.utppublishing.com
Printed in Canada

ISBN 978-1-4426-4488-5

∞

Printed on acid-free, 100% post-consumer recycled paper with
vegetable-based inks.

Publication cataloguing information is available from Library and
Archives Canada

University of Toronto Press acknowledges the financial assistance to its
publishing program of the Canada Council for the Arts and the Ontario
Arts Council.

Canada Council    Conseil des Arts
for the Arts      du Canada

ONTARIO ARTS COUNCIL
CONSEIL DES ARTS DE L'ONTARIO
50 YEARS OF ONTARIO GOVERNMENT SUPPORT OF THE ARTS
50 ANS DE SOUTIEN DU GOUVERNEMENT DE L'ONTARIO AUX ARTS

University of Toronto Press acknowledges the financial support of the
Government of Canada through the Canada Book Fund for its publishing
activities.

# Contents

# Acknowledgments

Thanks above all to Asher Horowitz, Martin Breaugh, and David McNally, who provided me with valuable guidance and feedback throughout the process of producing this book, which was originally a Ph.D. dissertation written for the Department of Political Science at York University. Richard Matthews, Shannon Bell, and J.J. McMurtry also read an early version of the manuscript and supplied highly useful critical commentary. Further criticism was provided by four anonymous reviewers for the University of Toronto Press. The original impetus for writing this book emerged while I was an M.A. student at Trent University, taking a course on the political thought of Marcuse and Arendt with Douglas Torgerson. I am grateful to the latter for suggesting to me the possibility that Marcuse and Arendt could be situated in a potentially productive relation. The final revisions of the manuscript took place while I was a SSHRC postdoctoral fellow in the Department of Philosophy at Stony Brook University. While at Stony Brook I benefitted greatly from conversations with my supervisor, Eduardo Mendieta, as well as various other members of that department. Finally, while a graduate student at York University and Trent University I had the good fortune of encountering numerous faculty members and graduate students who have shaped my thinking in a variety of ways. A partial list of such individuals includes: Caleb Basnett, Jonathan Blair, Jordan Brennan, Elliott Buckland, Karl Dahlquist, Tod Duncan, Jason Harman, Rodrigo Hernandez-Gomez, Arthur Imperial, Rachel Magnusson, Paul Mazzocchi, James McMahon, Sara Mohr, Dana Mount, Stephen Newman, Devin Penner, Daniel Ross, David Sayer, Sasa Stankovic, Elaine Stavro, Andrew Wernick, and Katharine Wolfe.

Some material from chapter 5 first appeared as "Dialectics and Distinction: Reconsidering Hannah Arendt's Critique of Marx," *Contemporary Political Theory* 10, no. 3 (2011).

An earlier version of chapter 6 appeared as "Towards a Politics of Non-Identity: Rethinking the Political Theory of Herbert Marcuse," *Radical Philosophy Review* 16, no. 2 (2013).

# POLITICS AS RADICAL CREATION

Herbert Marcuse and Hannah Arendt on
Political Performativity

# Introduction: Marcuse, Arendt, and the Idea of Politics

For many years political theorists have been pointing to a crisis of contemporary liberal democracy, a crisis that reveals itself primarily in the expression of popular discontent regarding, not just the nonacknowledgment of the voice or opinion of citizens, but the incapacity of citizens to meaningfully participate in activities that aim at determining the political direction of communities. It is within the context of this participatory discontent that we must recall the historical noncorrespondence of the concepts of liberalism and democracy: "On one side we have the liberal tradition constituted by the rule of law, the defence of human rights and the respect of individual liberty; on the other the democratic tradition whose main ideas are those of equality, identity between governing and governed and popular sovereignty."[1] In short, the distinction is between an active and inclusive model of rule, the rule of the *demos*, and a mere limitation of rule, made for the sake of the promotion of individual rights and liberties. This contradiction can in fact be read as reproducing itself even in certain of those new populist modes of activism that implicitly revolt against civic marginalization. Typical in this respect is the American Tea Party movement. Although it is fundamentally concerned with the limitation of the social penetration of government, such concern can be read as arising from the perception that the latter does not serve what are taken to be appropriate human ends. Such is apparently revealed in certain of its popular political forms, which implicitly emphasize, via the utilization of theatrical and carnivalesque techniques, the joy and gratification that can, and perhaps should, accompany political activity. That such political action, though, is not seen as being generalizable, that it is often accompanied by violent forms of marginalization and exclusion, should not be surprising: to redeploy an idea of Horkheimer and Adorno, such is the result when individuals "robbed of their subjectivity are set loose as subjects."[2] In Jeffrey Isaac's words, while liberal democracy "claims to embody the will of the people, it lacks channels of healthy civic participation, and thus tends to promote – or at least is perpetually vulnerable to the emergence of – political alienation and resentment," that which it had originally attempted to repress.[3]

What this book will attempt to do is think a gratifying democratic politics that is capable of universalizing what is taken to be that human capacity for creativity, which is, for example, given a distorted expression in certain of the reactionary political movements that are rightly recognized as symptoms of contemporary liberalism's democratic crisis. It is within the context of this crisis that this book will seek to develop a new theoretical model of democracy, a model of democracy that can be considered radical in Marx's sense, that is, in the sense that it penetrates to the root of the concept. In particular, I intend to develop a model of political action that eschews as partial democratic demands that look toward an eventual overcoming of the political sphere via the establishment of a terminal condition of existence, be this condition associated with, as in traditional socialist theory, the production of positive communism, or with, as in traditional liberal theory, the preservation of abstract right. On the contrary, this model will affirm democratic politics as a potentially performative good-in-itself, undertaken not just to the extent that it is instrumentally aimed at the achievement of a certain extrinsic goal, but also to the extent that its practice is understood to function as a medium for the manifestation of a creative human impulse whose expression brings forth a unique type of public happiness.

This model of democracy will be articulated through a critical juxtaposition of two of the twentieth century's most important theoretical traditions: the Frankfurt School and the Arendtian. The attempt to establish a productive relation between Arendt and the Frankfurt School may initially seem strange. Indeed, it is well known that each shared a strong, mutual antipathy toward one another. Julia Kristeva probably does not overstate the case when she writes that "Arendt had *no respect* for the Marxists of the Frankfurt School."[4] Her distaste for the Frankfurt School was especially prominent with respect to Adorno, whom she objected to not only on a theoretical level, but on a personal one as well. Arendt, for example, would famously remark to her husband after first meeting Adorno, "That one's not coming into our house!"[5]

Adorno, for his part, thought just as little of Arendt, whom he considered to be a member of "the Right."[6] This hostility between Arendt and the Frankfurt School has largely been reproduced in the relationship between those subsequent theorists who have found inspiration in the work of one of the two primary terms. My suggestion will be, however, that Arendt in particular greatly exaggerated the degree to which her project was theoretically opposed to the philosophy of Critical Theory. As a consequence of Arendt's misreading of the work of the Frankfurt School, and indeed of a certain tradition of critical Marxism more generally, two of the most important theoretical tendencies of the twentieth century have not made the effort to seriously engage with one another. This book thus aims at something of a rapprochement between these two traditions, demonstrating the degree to which not only Critical Theorists and Arendtians might find a common ground, but perhaps even more importantly, the degree to which this juxtaposition might allow for the emergence of not only a unique understanding of the meaning of democracy or acting politically, but indeed of being human.

My analysis will be grounded in a rereading of the critical theory of that member of the *Institut für Sozialforschung* who was always the most concretely involved with political matters: Herbert Marcuse. The study of Marcuse may itself require some justification. Over the past thirty years Marcuse's work has become increasingly marginalized, as unlike that of certain of his colleagues, most especially Benjamin and Adorno, it has been identified as excessively positive and identitarian, looking toward historical closure via the elimination of all psychic and social conflict. It is precisely such readings, though, that I will attempt to counter. Most generally, I will demonstrate that Marcuse is a fundamentally negative thinker who has much to contribute to those contemporary theories of radical democracy that emphasize social division, difference, and contingency. In particular, I will attempt to overcome Marcuse's often inadequate approach to the problem of politics through the examination of certain modes of political action that have the potential of affirming the model of essence upon which Marcuse's theoretical project is seen to be based. My analysis will present itself as an immanent critique, specifically as an immanent critique of an apparent contradiction in Marcuse's thought between his theory of human subjectivity and his theory of politics. Regarding the former, it is first of all important not to forget, as is often done, Marcuse's Marxist heritage.[7] Marcuse, however, will treat Marxist theory as a living body of ideas constantly in flux, as a lively bundle of forces and tendencies that recombine and reorganize themselves in various ways, producing through these recombinations a multitude of potential permutations. For Marcuse this malleability is justified by Marx's early conception of *essence*, a conception that refuses to deal in stagnant and impenetrable categories, which refuses to outline the objective contours of human nature but rather understands the human being as that dynamic and creative being endowed with the capacity to sublate objective and subjective reality. What Marx concretizes is the insight of Hegel, which sees essence, in an admittedly bad form, as "praxis, free self-realization, always taking up, superseding and revolutionizing pre-established 'immediate' facticity."[8] Marcuse's Marxism is rooted in this essential structure; he is attempting to construct a nonidentitarian Marxism rooted in a nonidentitarian concept of essence. For Marcuse the principle of nonidentity affirms always the permanent discrepancy between appearance and potential, affirms the immediate's inability to exhaust the actuality of the object. As that being striving always toward the supersession of immediacy, the human being is that which affirms through its life-activity the negative and nonidentical.

However, just as he primarily takes his theory of essence from Marx, so too does Marcuse take from the latter his theory of politics. In doing so, though, he reproduces and intensifies a fundamental tension in Marx's thought. Whereas Marx identifies the institution of true positive communism as being marked by the actualization of all sides of human nature, Marx for the most part denies the political sphere's potential operation as a field for this process of actualization, which is primarily, and perhaps even exclusively, to be realized in the sphere of labour. Whereas Marx considers the actualization of the human essence – the realization of the species-being as the creative and self-overcoming being – as an intrinsic good-in-itself, politics seems to be reduced to a mere means to the extent that it aims only at the instrumental construction of a social formation capable of facilitating the actualization. That the political itself is not intended as a potential sphere for the realization of essence is clearly revealed in the call for the postcapitalist construction of an administration of things. Marcuse defines politics as that activity oriented toward the transformation of the potential into the actual; yet much more clearly than Marx, Marcuse adamantly maintains the nonexistence of a terminal point in historical time when this discrepancy between potential and actual would be overcome. For Marcuse, in other words, the political is a permanent sphere of human existence. If, though, Marcuse defines socialism as the actualization of the human essence in *all* of those human spheres in which the human being is active, which he does, and if the human essence is considered as a spontaneous, creative, and negative process of overcoming, then Marcuse must reject all those models of politics that are exclusively positive and identitarian, all those models that consider politics as a purely instrumental activity oriented toward the achievement of a fixed state of being, Marx's included.

The question, then, is what form of political activity would be capable of affirming Marcuse's particular understanding of the human essence, of realizing the creative impulse in those activities oriented toward the reinstitutionalization of the social formation? In this book I will attempt to think the possibility of a form of politics that corresponds to or affirms Marcuse's understanding of essence and nonidentity. Such a politics would be noninstrumental – that is to say, a politics understood as being not simply practiced within a means-end continuum, but rather as a performative good-in-itself – and nonidentitarian – that is to say, a politics that seeks not the construction of a static condition of existence that is capable of homogenizing the social through the perfect reconciliation of human conflict. The present work will contend that if upon first reading, it is the orthodox Marxian understanding of politics that seems to dominate Marcuse's work, there is embedded within certain of his texts a specific countertendency that can help us think an answer to the above question. It will be argued, though, that this countertendency can be more fully appreciated by reading Marcuse in conjunction with that political theorist who has perhaps gone further than anyone in thinking the possibility of a performative politics: Hannah Arendt.

Specifically, the political lack in Marcuse will be superseded by way of pushing to the extreme certain performative political tendencies in Arendt. What in particular I will be attempting to push to its extreme is Arendt's insight into politics as spontaneous and performative public action concerned with calling forth the radically new, new modes and orders that cannot be traced back to any prior moments in a logically organized causal sequence. I will argue that such radical creation can be interpreted as the affirmation of Marcuse's concept of essence in the sphere of the political. What is more, however, at the same time that Arendt's political ontology opens a space for the critical reconstruction of the meaning of politics in Marcuse, it will be suggested as well that Marcuse's dialectical approach to social being allows for the possibility of superseding Arendt's restriction of performativity to an isolated and singular human realm, thus generalizing the radical emancipatory potential in her thought. As I will attempt to show, Arendt's political thought need not be rejected by those critical theorists who perceive an elitist and nondemocratic strand in her thinking, represented primarily in her neglect of the so-called social question. Just as a certain theoretical deficiency in Marcuse – a seeming nonconcern with the political as a potential sphere for the manifestation of performativity – can be superseded by reading him in conjunction with Arendt, so can a theoretical deficiency in Arendt – a definite nonconcern with the social as a potential sphere for the manifestation of performativity – be superseded by reading her in conjunction with Marcuse. In this text I will not necessarily be concerned with producing a comparative analysis looking toward the identification of conceptual similarities, nor concerned with relating distinct elements to one another on the basis of a shared derivation from a higher conceptual source. It will be suggested, rather, that a specific juxtaposition of the relevant concepts in Arendt and Marcuse is capable of providing a foundation for overcoming a certain lack in each, and the subsequent generation of a new understanding of the possibility of acting democratically in the world. The critical relation of Marcuse and Arendt will ultimately allow for the generation of a unique model of comprehensive democratic being that affirms the values of radical creation in both the political and productive spheres, a double affirmation that neither Marcuse nor Arendt can fully accomplish on his or her own.

Before the specifically political question can be answered, however, we must first examine in some detail Marcuse's critique and reformulation of the philosophical concept of essence. As I have alluded, both Marcuse and Arendt will ultimately be concerned with the affirmation of a negative ontology that defines human beingness in terms of the capacity for radical creation, in terms of the capacity for the spontaneous generation of new subjective and objective actualities. Marcuse most systematically develops his understanding of such an ontology in certain of his programmatic essays from the 1930s, which will be the main object of chapter 1. We will see here how Marcuse criticizes the philosophical concept of essence for dehistoricizing reality through its hypostatization of essence into a variety of fixed and immobile structures of Being. Against such constructions, which attempt to simply reduce essence to an object out in the world ready to be grasped, Marcuse reconceives of essence as a historical process of creative self-overcoming realized primarily through labour. In chapter 2 I analyse Marcuse's philosophical appropriation of the psychoanalytic theory of Freud, in particular Marcuse's reformulation of the Freudian concept of sublimation. Marcuse's concept of nonrepressive sublimation will be seen to be a redeployment of the Marxian concept of nonalienated labour, and hence a restatement of the theory of essence. Here essence is, relative to Marcuse's writings on the subject in the 1930s, much more clearly linked to joy and gratification, nonrepressive sublimation pointing to the possibility of conceptualizing a form of productive human activity that replicates the structure of play.

Chapter 3 articulates what was identified earlier as the fundamental contradiction in Marcuse's critical theory: that between the model of essence that I detail in the first two chapters and his theory of political transformation. Although Marcuse understands the institution of socialism in terms of the actualization of human essence in all human spheres of existence, and although he identifies the permanence of human conflict in society, he fails to consider political activity as an appropriate mode of essential expression, with respect to both action aimed at social transformation and negotiations concerned with the mediation of conflict posttransformation. Specifically, his political theory reveals itself to contradict his theory of essence in a double sense, both to the extent that it considers politics as a merely instrumental activity undertaken according to means-end calculation, and to the extent that it fetishizes technical reason, not adequately distinguishing between the critical deployment of technical reason as an element of a comprehensive reason oriented toward emancipation, and the application of technical reason as a general solution to the conflicts that mark human life in a historical world.

I have suggested, however, that there is embedded within Marcuse's political theory a certain countertendency eschewing all instrumentalist and managerialist political considerations, one that affirms a performative and nonidentitarian form of politics looking toward radical creation. I have also suggested that such a countertendency can be more clearly revealed through reading Marcuse in conjunction with Arendt. Chapter 4 thus details those elements of the Arendtian political theory that could be seen to affirm, within the realm of the political, the fundamental element of Marcuse's ontology. Particularly important here is Arendt's concept of political action as a form of being-with-others that looks toward the performative generation of radically new beginnings, new modes and orders that cannot be identified as mere moments of a rationally discernible causal sequence. Such generation can be seen as producing a unique type of public happiness, rendering the activity an

enjoyable good in itself. Having located those elements of the Arendtian political theory capable of affirming Marcuse's concept of essence,
chapter 5 attempts to overcome what I, and most critics of Arendt, take
to be the major bar preventing her relation to Critical Theory: Arendt's
perception of a need to construct rigorous ontological boundaries between various spheres of human existence, boundaries that ultimately
do not allow for the conjuncture of politics and labour. I demonstrate
the rootedness of this perception in Arendt's failure to adequately comprehend certain twentieth-century heterodox Marxist traditions, and
demonstrate the extent to which it can be dialectically overcome. The
overcoming of this bar, I argue, eliminates the main theoretical obstacle
to the construction of the Marcuse-Arendt relation, thus making it possible to simultaneously affirm the Arendtian political theory and the
Marcusean critical theory.

Finally, chapter 6 reconsiders the political philosophy of Marcuse in
light of what I say about the political philosophy of Arendt in chapters
4 and 5. Here is finally revealed, via a study of Marcuse's early articulation of the theory of the radical act and certain late political writings on
the self-organization of the New Left, a model of political activity that is
capable of affirming, through acting as a medium for the actualization
of a performative creativity, Marcuse's understanding of the particularly human essence. Such a model affirms a politics that is spontaneous, noninstrumental, and nonidentitarian, a politics that functions as
a form of creative reinstitutionalization looking, through the critical
interrogation of existing forms of human self-organization, to always
surpass the limits of social existence. The ultimate suggestion is that if
an isolated reading of Marcuse is not sufficient to bring out this latent
dimension of Marcuse's thought, a reading of Marcuse in combination
with Arendt is. Such a reading provides a ground for the emergence
of a unique understanding of democratic being that affirms the ethics of creation in both the realm of social production and the realm of
political-institutional production.

# 1 Marcuse's Critique and Reformulation of the Philosophical Concept of Essence

If we are to think the possibility of a mode of political action capable of affirming a certain creative human essence, then we must of course first outline the structure, even if it is only possible to do so in a negative way, of this essence. It will perhaps be necessary, however, given the current state of much contemporary social and political theory, to justify the very deployment of any concept of essence. In "The Foundations of Historical Materialism" Marcuse notes his reluctance to use the term *ontology* in his discussion of the critical philosophical anthropology that grounds Marx's speculations in the *Economic and Philosophic Manuscripts of 1844*. He writes that "we would be loath to use the often misused term ontology in connection with Marx's theory, if Marx himself had not expressly used it here."[1] This chapter will be organized around a discussion of Marcuse's concept of essence as presented in certain of his early philosophical works from the 1930s; for the same reason that Marcuse was hesitant about deploying the term ontology, so too are we here with respect to essence. The theoretical disrepute within which the categories of ontology and essence currently lie provides an immediate bar to an adequate understanding of Marcuse's use of both terms. It is of the utmost importance at the outset to recognize that Marcuse, when using the term *essence*, is always speaking of either one of two understandings, understandings that must be kept strictly separate: on the one hand, essence as conceived of traditionally within the philosophical and theological traditions, as a fixed and immobile structure of Being, and on the other hand, essence as the sublation of the former, as a negative process of overcoming. This chapter will, after noting Marcuse's critique of positive essential structures, outline the features of his negative ontology, tracing the latter's origin to his reading of the Hegelian logic, and noting what he takes to be its concrete-sensuous affirmation in the sphere of creative labour.

## Culture and Bourgeois Freedom

The distinction between Marcuse's two understandings of the notion of essence, as well as his critique of one in the name of the other, is made explicit in the essay "On the Concept of Essence."[2] Marcuse defines the philosophical concept of essence as the abstraction and isolation of the one true form of Being from a multitude of changing appearances, and the subsequent transformation of this fragment into an object of authentic knowledge.[3] Essence is in this way the substitution of the partial for the total, and the declaration that this partial alone, now presumed to be a timeless and eternal entity, exists as the whole. For Marcuse the concept of essence first explicitly enters the mainstream of philosophy in Plato's theory of Ideas, but achieves its initial expression in the realm of transcendental subjectivity – the object of Marcuse's critique in this essay – with Descartes. Descartes's theory is anchored in the universally valid reality of the individual consciousness, the observation that the essence of all things lay in the freedom of the thinking individual, the *ego cogito*. The new autonomous ego is presented with the task that had been up to this point metaphysically hypostatized in the doctrine of essence: "realizing the authentic potentialities of being on the basis of the discovery that nature can be controlled."[4] Descartes's philosophy attempts to provide the theoretical preconditions for the practical liberation of the individual subject, the freeing of this subject to such an extent as to allow her to enter the world and shape it consciously according to her will. His was a philosophy "by means of which, knowing the force and the actions of fire, water, air, the stars, the heavens, and all the other bodies that surround us, as distinctly as we know the various crafts of our artisans, we might also apply them in the same way to all the uses to which they are adapted, and thus render ourselves the lords and possessors of nature."[5]

According to Marcuse, however, this newly empowered individual quickly encounters a seemingly insurmountable contradiction – as soon as the ego sets out to shape its life, it finds itself subject to and constrained by the unalterable laws of the newly emerging logic of the market. Whereas the free individual's first step appears dictated by her own reason, all subsequent ones appear dictated by the conditional logic of commodity society.[6] The old medieval relations of visible dependence are replaced by opaque and unknowable relations of dependence. Since the unknowable necessarily escapes the actor's rational intention, empirical reality presents itself to her as a mere externality unconnected to her authentic potential and essence. The individual, seemingly unconnected to the world, comes to the realization that this disjunction militates against her asserting herself by means of conquering and shaping externality; externality is beyond the individual's control. Reason is thus forced to stop at the status quo and become a critique of pure thought. Since the individual is no longer capable of conquering the world, she comes to be concerned only with conquering herself. If we are to preserve the concept of human freedom, the essence of the individual must lie in the autonomous world of consciousness. Freedom thus comes to have meaningful potential only as pure knowledge, reason being incapable of expressing itself in the rational manipulation and shaping of objects by sensuous individuals. Concrete material human relations (e.g., work relations) are henceforth no longer essentially related to the individual's potentialities.

The critique of this fictional internationalization of freedom in bourgeois philosophy is reproduced multiple times throughout Marcuse's writings. In "A Study on Authority" Marcuse maintains that the bourgeois concept of freedom is characterized above all by the union of internal freedom and external heteronomy. The obvious contradiction between freedom and unfreedom is only justified to the extent that the human subject is capable of being bifurcated into a spiritual and material being: "As an 'internally' free being man is born into a social order which, while it may have been posited or permitted by God, by no means represents the realm in which the existence or non-existence of man is decided upon. Whatever the nature of this order may be, the inner freedom of man (his pure belief and his pure will, provided they remain pure) cannot be broken in it."[7] The development of this bifurcation in its bourgeois form is traced in some depth in the essay "The Affirmative Character of Culture." Marcuse will begin his analysis with Aristotle, who separates pure theory from other forms of knowledge to the extent that the object of pure theory, human flourishing, is recognized to be unachievable in a world in which the degree of material satisfaction is essentially contingent: "Insofar as philosophy is concerned with man's happiness – and the theory of classical antiquity held it to be the highest good – it cannot find it in the established material organization of life. That is why it must transcend this order's facticity."[8] We have at this point not yet reached, though, the bourgeois stage in which it is assumed that material conditions can be transcended from above by universal values. For Aristotle only those capable of living outside the sphere of necessity can practice the contemplative life, and through this "practice" transcend the contingency and facticity that mark the sphere of material reproduction. Just as for Descartes, the sphere of necessity is seen as a constraint, but a constraint that cannot be removed, either through social reorganization or through the relocation and internalization of the sphere of happiness. Happiness is certainly contemplative, but it is nevertheless recognized that material freedom from necessity is the prerequisite for contemplation, and this freedom remains the privilege of the few. With the emergence of bourgeois culture the view that universal values could be realized only by a particular social fragment, a privileged minority, is progressively discarded, and there emerges the idea of cultural universality. Just as it is affirmed that each and all are capable of realizing themselves in the market, so too are each and all supposed to realize themselves in culture. The honesty of Aristotle, his brutal observation that freedom is barred to all who labour, disappears, but the nonbelief in the potential for a form of social transformation capable of affirming freedom in labour remains.

For the ancients necessity and material dissatisfaction is a natural fact of human existence. For the bourgeois moderns freedom can in fact be realized within the world of necessity, but just because it is now to be realized only from within. Marcuse defines affirmative culture as

> that culture of the bourgeois epoch which led in the course of its own development to the segregation from civilization of the mental and spiritual world as an independent realm of value that is also considered superior to civilization. Its decisive characteristic is the assertion of a universally obligatory, eternally better and more valuable world that must be unconditionally affirmed: a world essentially different from the factual world of the daily struggle for existence, yet realizable by every individual for himself "from within," without any transformation of the state of fact.[9]

The social fact that blocks the concrete material realization of freedom is overcome through the positing of a spiritual space that is present within each individual, and that each individual is capable of controlling with the utmost autonomy. In a society governed by the law of value the bourgeois ideal of the individual as free, rational, and universal can be sustained only by the concept of the soul: "In the idea of the soul, the noncorporeal faculties, activities, and properties of man (according to the traditional classifications, reason, will, and appetite) are combined in an indivisible unity that manifestly endures through all of the individual's behaviour and, indeed, constitutes his individuality."[10]

What we see in bourgeois philosophy is a reproduction of that level of self-consciousness that Hegel associates with Stoicism. The subject's objective position in the world does not affect the subject's capacity for freedom: whether or not the ego is "on the throne or in chains, in the utter dependence of its individual existence, its aim is to be free, and to maintain that lifeless indifference which steadfastly withdraws from the bustle of existence, alike from being active as passive, into the simple essentiality of thought."[11] As Marcuse sums up the position in his critique of Sartre, "freedom is in the very structure of human being and cannot be annihilated even by the most adverse conditions: man is free even in the hands of his executioner."[12] Marcuse's point, of course, is to show that the idea of such a unity capable of affirming the free potentialities of the individual subject is, not strictly speaking wrong, but utterly partial. "Man does not live by bread alone; this truth is thoroughly falsified by the interpretation that spiritual nourishment is an adequate substitute for too little bread."[13]

Transcendental subjectivity, Marcuse maintains, reaches its apex in the development of twentieth-century phenomenology. Phenomenology's attempt to reorient philosophy as a rigorous science is the culmination of a thought that anchors the absolute and universal certainty of knowledge in the *ego cogito*. It is also represents, however, the liquidation of the critical element we find present in transcendental thought from Descartes to Kant. According to Marcuse, Husserl's critique of Descartes begins with the observation that Descartes erred in viewing the individual ego as the world's primary existing particle, deducing the rest of the world from this. But Cartesian philosophy is linked with the *progressive* trends of the bourgeoisie only at the point where the ego is conceived of as being this existing particle. Only an ego understood as something actually existing as a first principle can provide us with a critical standard of real knowledge and serve as a ground for the structuring of life. Here there is still a connection between consciousness and empirical existence: the goal of consciousness is the ordering of the world. Phenomenology, however, wants to deal with essence only within a sphere of transcendental consciousness purged of all facts intending spatiotemporal existence. The concept of essence is relevant only within the dimension of pure subjectivity that remains a residuum after the phenomenological "annihilation of the world."[14]

The fundamental problem with Husserl's phenomenological reduction is that in its attempt to bracket certain categories of experience, it is simply indifferent to the multiple and variable social and historical contexts of life. Building upon Marcuse's analysis, Douglas Kellner provides the following example: "a phenomenological analysis of a factory 'brackets' from its socio-historical existence and conceives of it, in Husserl's terms, as an intentional object of an act of consciousness, in which the 'phenomenological reduction' excludes its social-material constituents and grasps the 'givenness' of the factory as an 'object of perception,' a thing with the qualities of extension, color, solidity, etc."[15] A machine in a factory, then, is simply the sum of these various latter qualities; no consideration is given, for example, to the specific social relations of production that governed its manufacture and distribution in a particular social formation. Similarly, the subject of perception is equally bare. The subject is not a member of a particular class or social group, and hence there is no recognition that one's subjective position might potentially alter the nature of the form of experience. The same machine will be perceived in precisely the same manner by the owner of the factory as by the workers who operate it. Again, the social relations that define one's interactions with the object of perception, in this case the factory, are deemed irrelevant from the standpoint of phenomenological analysis; all that matters is immediate, apparent existence.

Not only does phenomenology eliminate empirical facts in their empirical relevance from the philosophical field of study, leaving behind only facts of consciousness, but the essential content and organization of these facts of consciousness are themselves further diminished in their being indistinguishable from one another in terms of their essential validity. All contents of consciousness are equally "exemplary": "Essence results as the invariant within the infinitely manifold variations which representational acts undertake with regard to their object."[16] Freedom becomes "a mark of pure fantasy, as the free arbitrariness of ideational possibilities of variation. The constant, identical, and necessary is no longer sought as the Being of beings but as what is invariant in the infinite manifold of representational modifications of 'exemplars'. Possibility is no longer a force straining toward reality; rather in its open endlessness it belongs to mere imagination."[17] The unboundedness of phenomenology functions to eliminate the critical tension previously present in the relation between the essence of the *ego cogito* and factual existence. Once the connection between rational thought and the world has been cut, the "interest of freedom" disappears from philosophy.[18]

The negation of this tension dooms phenomenology to a mere descriptive operation: it can aim only at describing that which already is, not that which could or should be, and it is here that it shows itself as being consistent with positivism. Phenomenology seeks to grasp the common foundation of perception, which requires the elimination of all modes and objects of perception that have the ability to produce alternate forms of experience. Perception must be made identical across contexts, which means that phenomenology cannot pronounce judgment on the immediate form of experience in the name of another potential form of experience. The concept of essence, which with Descartes functioned to bestow upon the individual the power to creatively alter and shape the world in accordance with her own desire, has come full circle and turned into its opposite: complete capitulation to the world that confronts the subject.

## Critical Theory and the Ethical Imperative: Happiness-Reason-Freedom

For Marcuse any sort of philosophical consideration that attempts to think essence as independent from the concrete material and lived reality within which the human subject is embedded is inadequate. It is for this reason that Marcuse in his early writings calls for a movement from philosophy to critical theory, which of course is nevertheless not equivalent to the indeterminate negation of philosophy. According to Marcuse the era of critical theory ushered in by Marx made philosophy "superfluous as an independent scientific discipline dealing with the structure of reality."[19] A critical theory must above all be a materialist theory, which means that it first must be concerned with human happiness, and second, must understand that such happiness can be achieved only through the radical transformation of material existence. This privileging of the concern for human happiness is the a priori of critical theory and is affirmed in some capacity by all of Marcuse's colleagues. Thus Horkheimer proclaims that for materialism, "man's striving for happiness is to be recognized as a natural fact requiring no justification."[20] Alfred Schmidt writes that "the theoretical attempt to ensure that no man in the world should suffer material or intellectual need any longer is something which does not need any metaphysical 'ultimate justification.'"[21] And Adorno will explicitly combine this a priori with the critique of bourgeois philosophy when he writes that "the smallest trace of senseless suffering in the empirical world belies all the identitarian philosophy that would talk us out of that suffering: 'While there is a beggar, there is a myth,' as Benjamin put it."[22]

For Marcuse the 11th Thesis on Feuerbach draws its force precisely from the experience of unnecessary suffering. The political imperative generated from this experience cannot be validated according to any scientific logic, thus making this imperative an ethical one.[23] Marcuse elaborates on this ethical imperative in *One-Dimensional Man*, where he maintains that all social theorizing must begin by making two value judgments. On the one hand, it is the responsibility of all theorists to make "the judgment that human life is worth living, or rather can be and ought to be made worth living. This judgment underlies all intellectual effort; it is the *a priori* of social theory, and its rejection (which is perfectly logical) rejects theory itself."[24] In other words, those theorists who deny that humanity has a fundamental claim to material happiness, defined as the satisfaction of human needs, actual and potential, immediately violate the presuppositions of theoretical endeavour. On the other hand, theorists must affirm the possibilities for the realization of the desired mode of existence; the possibilities for this realization, though, must be allowed by the given historical state.[25] For Marcuse a historical situation has come about in which the realization of reason no longer needs to be confined to the realm of pure thought: "If reason means shaping life according to men's free decisions on the basis of their knowledge, then the demand for reason henceforth means the creation of a social organization in which individuals can collectively regulate their lives in accordance with their needs."[26] Reason here is not replaced by happiness, but is rather redefined as a more all-inclusive concept that contains within itself the category of happiness. Reason is that which strives to maximize gratification. The immediate question becomes, then, what exactly constitutes human happiness and human need?

Marcuse defines happiness as nothing other than "the fulfillment of all potentialities of the individual."[27] Genuine happiness, then, requires the knowledge of a certain truth-content: individuals must be aware of their human potentialities and the means to fulfil them. Needless to say, human need and desire cannot be simply identified immediately with the form they take at the present historical juncture: "The designation of happiness as the comprehensive gratification of the individual's needs and wants is abstract and incorrect as long as it accepts needs and wants as ultimate data in their present form."[28] Marcuse here closely follows Hegel's demonstration of the negativity implicit in the concept of happiness: "Hegel's critique of eudaemonism expresses insight into the required objectivity of happiness. If happiness is no more than the immediate gratification of particular interests, then eudaemonism contains an irrational principle that keeps men within whatever forms of life are given. Human happiness should be something other than personal contentment."[29] In *One-Dimensional Man* Marcuse distinguishes, as he does in "On Hedonism" but now in much more detail, between true and false needs. False needs are those that "are superimposed upon the individual by particular social interests in his repression,"[30] needs that serve to reproduce the power of the status quo through the production of a certain type of consciousness, a consciousness that through the satisfaction of need comes to identify with the existing social state of affairs. Now, because there have been many different modes of social organization, it stands to reason that there have also been many different types of false need. False needs are thus always historical and culturally variable. It does not follow from this, however, that true needs are those permanent and universal needs that transcend all particular social formations. One notices that Marcuse does not give any examples of what a true need would look like, instead defining substantively only vital needs.[31] The reason is that the content of true needs is indeterminate and just as historically variable as that of false needs; a true need is not defined by the satisfaction of some delineable universal desire. Marcuse writes that "the question of what are true and false needs must be answered by the individuals themselves, but only in the last analysis; that is, if and when they are free to give their own answer."[32] That is, when the development of history becomes a product not of those with a vested interest in domination, but of all individuals. True needs become those needs that individuals believe to be necessary when they assume the responsibility for directing the movement of history, conscious of their own potentiality.

The connection between happiness and potentiality links the former with freedom.[33] It is no longer sufficient to merely think oneself free to actually be free: "Mankind becomes free only when the material perpetuation of life is a function of the abilities and happiness of associated individuals."[34] For Marcuse, "here reappears the old hedonistic definition which seeks happiness in the comprehensive gratification of needs and wants."[35] The establishment of such a human condition would first of all be marked by the production of an "association of free men" that "contains the explicit demand that each individual share in the social product according to his needs," a society in other words which "can inscribe on its banner, 'From each according to his abilities, to each according to his needs.'"[36] Needless to say, however, the realization of an objective reality capable of sustaining such a material perpetuation is no historical necessity. No iron law of history, whether understood as the rational unfolding of a world historical Sprit or as the progressive refinement of the social relations of production as a consequence of their conflict with the forces of production, can be depended upon. "The prevailing conditions are objectively *ambivalent*: they can offer the possibility of liberation, and that of streamlined servitude."[37] It is individuals themselves who must determine historical imperatives through their praxis, and it is precisely in this determination that individuals find their freedom:

> The Subject is free to choose: in this choice of a possible historical praxis which transcends the established praxis is the essence of human freedom. And this freedom is not a "fact," neither a transcendental nor a historical fact – it is the faculty (and activity) of man "synthesizing" (organizing) the data of experience so that they reveal their own (objective) negativity, namely, the degree to which they are the data of domination.[38]

So, to summarize the previous: happiness is that to which human life should be oriented; this happiness, though, is always a material happiness, the realization of certain variable human potentialities of gratification; reason is that which determines the direction and the structure of the activities that are to realize these potentialities; and the determination of the form of historical praxis intended to achieve happiness marks the activities as being manifestations of the exercise of freedom.

### Hegel and the Dialectic of Negativity

Marcuse's redefined concept of essence will be grounded in the previously discussed triangulation of happiness-reason-freedom. Essence will now be concerned with the realization of human potentialities within an empirical context that allows for freedom within a rationally organized society that is brought about and sustained through practice. Philosophy's emphasis must accordingly shift from the construction or discovery of reason in thought to the production of a rational social order in reality: "The philosophical ideals of a better world and of true Being are incorporated into the practical aim of struggling mankind, where they take on a human form."[39] The essence of the individual is no longer understood as that which can be made of the individual to-day, but as "the real fulfillment of everything that man desires to be when he understands himself in terms of his potentialities."[40] Marcuse redefines essence and the effort to discover it, not as any one thing but as a process. As a preliminary model for such a form of essence Marcuse returns to that philosophical place where, according to him, essence was last treated as a dialectical concept: Hegel's *Logic*. Marcuse's most sustained discussion of the *Science of Logic* occurs in *Reason and Revolution*. Marcuse here reiterates that any form of human liberation depends on some model of essence, a universal reality belonging to all individuals: "If the individual were nothing but the individual, there would be no justifiable appeal from the blind material and social forces that overpower his life, no appeal to a higher and more reasonable social ordering. If he were nothing but a member of a particular class, race, or nation, his claims could not reach beyond his particular group."[41] The relevant question, of course, is precisely what form does this essence take? Following Hegel, Marcuse affirms that essence "emerges as the process that negates all stable and delimited forms of being and negates as well the concepts of traditional logic which express these forms."[42] Essence, then, is not a positive entity or set of discernible properties whose nature can be delineated and grasped, provided one has access to the proper epistemological tools, but rather is a purely negative process of overcoming, the overcoming of the apparent forms of being, both subjective and objective and both in their empirical and their logical manifestations.

In Hegel's *Logic* the essence of objects lay in their notion, which is the logical form of the universal. The validity of an object in its immediate state is thus determined by measuring it against its notion. Marcuse reproduces Hegel's well-known account of the movement Being-Nothing-Becoming. We begin with the distinction between determinate being and being-as-such. Every thing is obviously some thing, but being as that which is common to all things is not simply some thing. But what is not some thing is nothing; pure, indeterminate being, because it is no thing, is nothing. In Hegel's words, "this pure being is the *pure abstraction*, and hence it is the *absolutely negative*, which when taken immediately, is *nothing*."[43] But to think nothing is to still to think, and to think is to think some thing. An identification of being and nothing is achieved: both being and nothing turn out to be identical to the extent that every thing includes both being and nothing. The paradox of the thing being at the same time both being and nothing will be resolved through the positing of becoming, which can hold both being and nothing to the extent that the object is seen as always being in transit: "According to Hegel, there is not a single thing in the world that does not have in it the togetherness of being and nothing. Everything *is* only in so far as, at every moment of its being, something that as yet *is not* comes into being and something that is now passes into not-being. Things *are* only in so far as they arise and pass away, or, being must be conceived as becoming."[44] This demonstrates that all forms in which the world is presented to us must be seen as being permeated with negativity: "progress from one logical category to another is stimulated by an inherent tendency in every type of being to overcome its negative conditions of existence and pass into a new mode of being where it attains its true form and content."[45]

Every being contains two elements: being-as-other and being-in-itself. Negativity is the difference between these two elements of the unity. The actual conditions of the thing, the nature of the thing as it is determined by its differential relations with other things, stand in the way of its realization of its essence. The term *determination* refers to the proper nature of a thing and *talification* to the actual state of a thing. The movement from one talification to another is generated by the conflict between the thing's present and its internal potentialities: "The process of existence is simply the contradiction between talification and potentialities; hence, to exist and to be limited are identical."[46] Thus again, being is essentially becoming: "Every site of existence has to be surpassed; it is something negative, which things, driven by their inner potentialities, desert for another state, which again reveals itself as negative, as limit."[47] In this process finitude turns into infinity as the continual overcoming of the thing's finitude is an indefinite, and hence infinite, process. The infinite is thus not a positing of an absolute Beyond in which all meaning lies, but "is precisely the inner dynamic of the finite, comprehended in its real meaning. It is nothing else but the fact that finitude 'exists only as passing beyond' itself."[48] Thus the infinite is only the finite as it is achieved in the finite through the finite's continual movement and overcoming. A thing becomes for itself when its external state becomes integrated with its genuine being. Again, this is not the achievement, though, of a positive condition of existence: "Being-for-itself is not a state but a process, for every external condition must continuously be transformed into a phase of self-realization, and each new external condition that arises must be subjected to this treatment."[49]

So, essence is thus achieved when all of a thing's determinates have been made elements of its self-realization, and consequently reintegrated into the essential movement. Marcuse will ultimately sum up what he takes to be the five key elements or moments of this process:[50] (1) essence is not a determinate state or condition: "the essence is neither something above the world, but rather the negation of all being"; (2) this negation of being is nothing, is movement beyond every determinate condition; (3) this movement is held together internally through a process of self-relation by which a subject incorporates its determinations into its self-realization; (4) this process requires a being-in-itself capable of knowing and reflecting on the movement and the determinate states that comprise it; and (5) this subject does not exist outside the process, but "is the very process itself."

Marcuse's stress on the nonidentity of appearance and essence in Hegel, and on the impossibility of the ultimate reconciliation of this nonidentity through the coming to rest of the process of becoming, puts him squarely in line with Adorno's critical appropriation of Hegel. Just as for Marcuse, so also for Adorno does the value of Hegel lie in his stress on negativity. Adorno writes that "the task of dialectical cognition is not, as its adversaries like to charge, to construe contradictions from above and to progress by resolving them – although Hegel's logic, *now and then*, proceeds in this fashion. Instead, it is up to dialectical cognition to pursue the inadequacy of thought and thing, to experience it in the thing."[51] If the negativity of the Hegelian logic is "now and then" violated by Hegel's tendency to synthesize, the preface to the *Phenomenology* preserves the purity of negation: "That Introduction bids us purely observe each concept until it starts moving, until it becomes unidentical with itself by virtue of its own meaning – in other words, of its identity. This is a commandment to analyze, not to synthesize."[52] Also for Adorno, then, the negative dialectical logic thus calls for a redefinition of the meaning of essence: "Essence can no longer be hypostatized as the pure, spiritual being-in-itself. Rather, essence passes into that which lies concealed beneath the façade of immediacy, of the supposed facts, and which makes the facts what they are."[53]

So, for Hegel essence and appearance are two intimately connected modes of being that are reciprocally related to one another by virtue of the fact that essence can become essence only through appearing. The mere empirical world is linked to truth through its harbouring of the essential in its latent form. Essence assumes a temporal form as it is realized through a gradual overcoming of the inessentially apparent.

Essence then is not eternal: it has a history, which is none other than the development of its forms of appearance.[54] The historical movement of essence, the actualization of Being through the shedding of the contingent or inessential aspects of the apparent, eliminates the bad immediacy that associates the truth of the object with those immediate characteristics the object assumes at any given time.[55] History counters reification. However, Hegel's history will ultimately turn out to be a false history. The movement of essence for Hegel takes place within the very structure of Being, independent of the actions of individuals: "It is not man who recollects essence, who grasps the world of beings which confront him, overcomes its bad immediacy and posits it anew through the knowledge of essence; rather, for Hegel all this occurs with rational Being itself. Man participates in this process only as the subject of cognition, insofar as he himself is rational being."[56] With Hegel the process remains metaphysical, the internalization of essence within Being reproducing the transcendental structure of traditional concepts of essence: "For Hegel, the totality was the totality of reason, a closed ontological system, finally identical with the rational system of history."[57] For Marcuse it is Hegel's positing of this closed system of Reason that ultimately betrays the latter's own dialectical project: "this idea of reason comprehends everything and ultimately absolves everything, because it has its place and function in the whole, and the whole is beyond good and evil, truth and falsehood."[58] It is precisely the concept of Reason that is the "undialectical element in Hegel's philosophy."[59] Essence for Hegel is a movement or process, but this movement takes place entirely within itself. As such there cannot be any genuine change, that is, any change according to the principle of freedom. Essence remains always prior to appearance, just waiting to appear. In Adorno's words, "no matter how dynamically a system may be conceived, if it is in fact to be a closed system, to tolerate nothing outside its domain, it will become a positive infinity – in other words, finite and static."[60] To the extent that it remained in the last instance finite and static, "the Hegelian system in itself was not a true becoming."[61]

As opposed to Hegel, for a materialist dialectical understanding of history, the movement from appearance to essence is dependent upon both the rational comprehension of the gap between immediate existence and fulfilled potentiality on the part of individuals and the individuals' active insertion of themselves into the historical process in an effort to stimulate the transformation from the present state to the future one. To maintain that actualization is the work of the subjects themselves, however, is not to maintain that fulfilment is constrained only by the subjects' desire. All essential determinations are historically grounded and are to be sharply distinguished from (abstract) utopia by the fact that theory is capable of demonstrating the concrete paths that lead to their realization, if not the precise form of the realization at the end of the path. A critical theory does not posit an endless horizon of possibilities; it is not engaged in the positive depiction of a future world.[62] As Marx once wrote to a friend, "The man who draws up a programme for the future is a reactionary."[63] The drawing up of such a program still belongs to the realm of traditional philosophy: it is an attempt to posit a form of existence through the utilization of the conceptual tools of pure thought, thought unencumbered by the materiality of being. The goals of critical theory can only be generated through the critical analysis of actual tendencies within the existing reality. What determines the potentiality is "the measure of control of natural and social productive forces, the level of the organization of labour, the development of needs in relation to possibilities for their fulfillment (especially the relation of what is necessary for the reproduction of 'free' needs for gratification and happiness, for the 'good and the beautiful'), the availability, as material to be appropriated, of a wealth of cultural values in all areas of life."[64]

Marcuse perhaps most forcefully separates his concept of essence from traditional models when he makes the following statement:

> The truth of this model of essence is preserved better in human misery and suffering and the struggle to overcome them than in the forms and concepts of pure thought. This truth is "indeterminate'" and remains necessarily so as long as it is measured against the idea of unconditionally certain knowledge. For it is fulfilled only through historical action, and its concretion can only result *post festum*.[65]

Marcuse's concept of essence here appears as a negative rather than an affirmative one. Essence is not a blueprint that can be set out according to an apodictic conclusion, but rather an indeterminate truth of human potentialities that have been historically denied. The process character of essence guarantees that essence cannot be deduced through reliance on some universal standard of wisdom. Essence is no longer a matter of pure theory when "orientation toward historical practice replaces orientation toward the absolute certainty and universal validity of knowledge."[66] Only in the process of historical struggle can human potentialities be understood and fulfilled, and precisely because there is no teleological scheme governing the movement of history, the ultimate reconciliation of appearance and essence in the achievement of a particular condition of existence remains an impossibility.

Essence as process always remains indeterminate to the extent that essence always depends on the possibility inherent in a given state, and the possibility inherent in a given state is always produced through the interaction of the various elements that define necessarily contingent social and historical moments. The relation of appearance to essence "originates in history and changes in history."[67] Such a conception would seem to invalidate all criticisms of it that focus on a perceived and so-called end of history. Marcuse states that materialist dialectics "understands all theory as an element of the social process of life, borne by particular historical interests. Hitherto these interests have governed theory primarily 'behind its back', unconsciously."[68] To affirm an indeterminate and developmental essence is not to eliminate history or realize totally and finally the human essence. To do so is simply to recognize that there is no affirmation of the essential that assumes an eternal form, as all of the categories that describe the given form of existence as historically variable contain their own negation. The essential recognizes that it will one day be the apparent, and it is this recognition that defines it as the essential.

## Essence and the Dialectic of Labour

Marcuse states that the starting point of every authentic form of dialectical analysis is the recognition of the difference between immediate reality and potentiality: "every particular existent is essentially different from what it could be if its potentialities were realized."[69] For Marcuse, though, this process of realization is never terminated precisely because every potentiality is historically determined, and there exists no final end point to history. Essence then cannot be the achievement of a state, but just the very movement of overcoming itself. To recognize our essential nature is to recognize our ability to transcend the given; the human feature that allows us to transcend the given, to imagine alternate forms of material existence, is creativity. Creativity is the distinctive characteristic of human life, for it is through creativity that human life transcends its immediate determinations through the projection of alternate or not yet existent modes of being-in-the-world. For Marcuse the individual's means of realizing her essence, the primary way in which she expresses her intrinsic creativity, is through participation in processes of (nonalienated) labour, which Marcuse describes as "the free and full realization of the whole man in his historical world."[70] Although Marcuse's emphasis on the significance of labour to human existence was manifest in prior works, it achieves its first systematic elaboration in the essay "On the Philosophical Foundation of the Concept of Labour in Economics."

The starting point for Marcuse is the recognition that labour is not merely an economic category but "an ontological concept of human existence as such."[71] According to Marcuse the last philosopher within the Western tradition to seriously reflect on the meaning of labour was, once again, Hegel. Marcuse notes that for Hegel labour was no mere activity, but rather a fundamental event of human beingness, a doing in which the being-for-itself of consciousness was made objectively permanent. For Hegel no single activity was capable of comprehending the totality of human existence: "every activity always concerns only partial regions of this totality and only takes place in partial regions of the world."[72] Labour, though, is no mere activity; it "is that in which every single activity is founded and to which they again return: a *doing*."[73] Labour is no other than the process of self-objectification which is initiated when the individual begins to creatively act in the world. In Andrew Feenberg's words, "work takes on an extended sense in Hegel and refers eventually not merely to the making of artefacts but to all forms of objectification, including the creation of institutions and culture. The structure of productive activity in the narrow sense becomes the model for historical creation in general."[74] Labour is thus the general form of creativity, the faculty that generates the movement from existent to potentiality. It is precisely this element of Hegel's understanding of labour that is celebrated by Marx. Hegel's great achievement, Marx says, lay in his recognition of the transformative as the essential, in his discovery of the "dialectic of negativity as the moving and generating principle."[75] He "conceives the self-genesis of man as a process, conceives objectification as loss of the object, as alienation and as transcendence of this alienation; ... he thus grasps the essence of *labour* and comprehends objective man – true because real man – as the outcome of man's *own labour*."[76] But Hegel's account is still incomplete inasmuch as it grasps the human essence only as abstract self-consciousness: "The only labour which Hegel knows and recognizes is *abstractly mental* labour."[77] Hegel "has only found the *abstract, logical speculative* expression for the movement of history; and this historical process is not yet the *real* history of man."[78] Nevertheless, he still conceives of labour as humanity's creative act of self-conception, as humanity's essence in the process of proving itself.

So, for Marcuse as for Hegel, one becomes a being-for-self through the doing of labour, through a form of creative self-objectification by which one makes oneself permanent in the objective world. It should be noted at this point, though, that this self-objectification cannot be interpreted in terms of the mere transfer of the subjective content of a stable and self-identical subject. This latter form of self-objectification would be that which characterizes the process of labour as it is inter-preted, for example, by Locke. The individual's right to property for Locke is derived from the fact that the creation of property is marked by the injection of human subjectivity into an otherwise empty thing. The transfer of human subjectivity into the object extends the indi-vidual's natural rights to life, liberty, and health – naturally embod-ied in human subjectivity – to the laboured-upon thing. Thus Locke writes that "whatsoever then he removes out of the state that nature hath provided, and left it in, he hath mixed his *labour* with, and joined it to something that is his own, and thereby makes it his property."[79] What is objectified here is the static content of the ontologically intact liberal individual, whose nature is defined prior to the process of self-objectification. Locke here makes a real advance in thinking about la-bour, but he is still constrained by his methodological individualism. Objectification for Marcuse is an expression not of the content of the subject, a content expressed through the bearing of certain permanent and universal rights, but is rather a manifestation of a certain capac-ity within the subject, the capacity for free creation. What the subject sees in the object are not those fixed properties that define her as a hu-man being, but rather an expression of her transformative capacity to overcome empirical existence. Marcuse's dynamic understanding of essence allows him to recognize, unlike Locke, that the very process of self-objectification in labour acts back upon human existence and alters the latter's structure. To labour is to continually work upon and con-sciously alter not only the world but one's essence as well. The subject, in other words, does not remain identical to itself after having initi-ated the process that allows for the manifestation of its essence. It is through labour that creative agency is not only expressed but produced anew, for example through the development and refinement of rational and physical faculties and the dynamic interaction of one's subjectiv-ity with others' subjectivities. Locke's nondialectical analysis is able to comprehend labour only in terms of transfer, not in terms of creation. For Marcuse the essence of labour lies not simply in self-expression but in the creative overcoming of subjective and objective reality.

Defined in such a way, we can recognize the error of those who attempt to speak of labour only in terms of direction, goal, or outcome: "labour here is not determined through the kind of its objects, nor through its goal, content, result, etc., but through what happens to the very human existence in labour."[80] In particular we see the error of those bourgeois political economists and vulgar Marxists who want to define labour in terms of economic activity, in terms of the mere production and reproduction of the goods needed to perpetuate material life:

> economic theory's limiting of itself to economic labour already presupposes a very specific concept of labour expressing a very specific *way* of practicing economics that contains a very specific conception of the essence and meaning of economic being in the totality of human existence – hence the apparent obviousness of the economic concept of labour is already highly prejudiced by certain presuppositions.[81]

For Marcuse production and reproduction within the process of labour have a very different meaning; specifically, they are processes of mediation. Production and reproduction refer to "the active process of human existence as a whole: appropriation, overcoming, transforming and further developing all of human existence in all of its vital spheres."[82] They thus transcend the determinations and categories that mark the analysis of abstract universal labour.

Needless to say, the failure to adequately comprehend the differentiation between Marcuse's understanding of comprehensive self-realizing labour and mere economic labour has often led to confusion. We hear, for example, from Martin Jay, that "unlike Marx, or at least the mature Marx, Marcuse believes labour can be abolished."[83] It should go without saying that Marcuse never advocated, at any point in his life, the abolition of labour. When Marcuse, or Marx for that matter, speak of the "abolition of labour," they refer of course to the abolition of the isolation of one form of labour from all others and the establishment of this form as labour's sole reality; all that is abolished is alienated labour, the tyranny of abstract universal labour. The abolition of all labour is a practical impossibility, inasmuch as labour is conceptualized as the means to the realization of the human essence, and human essence is conceptualized as transformative self-creation that is incapable of exhausting itself. Marcuse can thus write that "once the problem of alienated labour is solved there will be many others which remain. The creative and imaginative faculties of man will never be redundant."[84] Or, as Marcuse puts it even more emphatically, "the 'abolition of labour' does not seem to be the problem of the future, but rather how to avoid the abolition of labor."[85] What needs to be abolished is not labour as such, but rather labour as it presents itself in its nonrational forms. And although we should already be able to determine this from the previous discussion, Marcuse makes it explicit for us when he tells us that labour will be rational to the extent that it is oriented toward the realization of the freedom and happiness of associated individuals.[86]

Self-creation is the central want of all human existence: "All individual wants are ultimately grounded in this primordial and constant want that existence has, i.e., its full self-creation in duration and constancy."[87] It is in this sense that human want can never be satisfied, for what human existence wants is not $x$ amount of material objects or $y$ amount of freedom, but rather a "never to be 'satisfied' want of human existence itself."[88] There is no final end state, no ultimate reconciliation to be achieved: human existence is a constant state of becoming. The ontological condition of human life is one of a continual process of self-creation. Those who ignore this fundamental fact and take the production of goods to be the essential content of labour miss the point entirely. As a process that is endowed with the capacity to negate the objective or subjective given at any particular moment, the essential work of labour is transcendence:

> The essential factual content of labour is not grounded in the scarcity of goods, nor in a discontinuity between the world of disposable human goods and human needs, but, on the contrary, in an essential excess of human existence beyond every possible situation in which it finds itself and the world. Being human is always *more* than its present existence. It goes beyond every possible situation and precisely because of this there is always an ineliminable discrepancy between the two: a discrepancy that demands constant labour for its overcoming, even though human existence can never rest in possession of itself and its world.[89]

That which defines labour is not the world of objects produced through work, but rather its process character. The continuous task of labour is the creation of a future world through an overcoming and transformation of the past. Because the content of this future world can never be fixed once and for all, labour is forever an indeterminate historical practice, persistently altering the nature of both the objective world and the subject. There will never be a time when labour is unnecessary: "Man must never cease to be an artist, to criticize and negate his present self and society and to project by means of his creative imagination alternative 'images' of existence. He can never cease to imagine for he can never cease to change."[90]

This point needs to be especially stressed, especially given those interpretations of Marcuse that focus on his alleged emphasis on pacification and reconciliation. We can once again return to Jay. According to him there are two competing strains in Marcuse's thought: "first, the stress on radical action, on the deed, on self-creation as the only mode of authentic being; and second, the unity of opposites, the true harmony of pacified existence, the end of conflict and contradiction."[91] This latter dimension of Marcuse's thought, as his essay on "The Philosophical Foundation of the Concept of Labour in Economics" reveals, and as this work will attempt to demonstrate throughout, is for the most part fiction. As the earlier passages make clear, Marcuse does not posit "a utopia of identity in which all contradictions are overcome."[92] In *One-Dimensional Man* it is suggested that the expression "pacification of existence" is meant to function more or less equivalently to Marx's concept of nonalienated labour.[93] The "pacification of existence" does not refer to a terminal point in historical time when the activity of the species – the overcoming of the gap between immediate reality and fulfilled potentiality – would in some way cease through the achievement of a harmonious positive essence. On the contrary, "'pacification of existence' means the development of man's struggle with man and with nature, under conditions where the competing needs, desires, and aspirations are no longer organized by vested interests in domination and scarcity – an organization which perpetuates the destructive forms of struggle."[94] What is crucial to note here is that it is not struggle itself that is overcome, but rather struggle manifested as a form of domination. This is a crucial distinction, one that will be mapped with greater detail in the next chapter's discussion of the difference between basic and surplus repression. Here we can initially note, though, that the former expresses, to use Asher Horowitz's language, "not perfect peace, but peaceful imperfection supplanting warlike imperfection."[95] The achievement of pacification is inseparable from the actualization of autonomy, which cannot be realized independently of mediation and contradiction.[96] To the extent that it is considered in terms of autonomy, pacification must always remain activity, must always remain becoming, with this activity or becoming appearing specifically as a form of imaginative play. Just as the concept of nonalienated labour refers to the in some sense agonistic play of human forces and capacities, so too does the pacification of existence: "the 'end' of technology would be 'deplaced' toward a free play of faculties – in the literal sense of playing with the fair capabilities of man and nature: pacification of existence."[97] The pacification of existence thus takes place "within the framework of institutions which offer a greater chance for the free development of human needs and faculties."[98] The discrepancy between appearance and essence is not overcome. Rather, it would just be that here individuals would have the capacity to experiment with potentiality, to freely determine through critical analysis and action how to overcome the gap between states of existence. A pacified existence is always an active existence to the extent that it is marked by the free play of faculties and potentialities in nonalienated processes of labour. To freely participate in processes of labour is to objectively posit alternative images of existence beyond the present reality. It is through activity in processes of labour, then, that the individual gains a place within the permanent becoming of the historical world and participates in the realization of the human essence as overcoming. Human action in its essential form is a perpetual and inexhaustible process of self-creation and self-making.

Although the early essay "On the Philosophical Foundation of the Concept of Labour in Economics" probably contains Marcuse's most detailed articulation of the nature of the relation between labour and essence, it nevertheless contains within itself an important limit that Marcuse in his later writings on labour would seek to supersede. The essay is heavily influenced by Marx's well-known passage in the third volume of *Capital* regarding the relationship between the realms of freedom and necessity. Here Marx defines activity within the realm of necessity as that aiming at the satisfaction of human needs and the reproduction of human life. Human freedom *is* achievable within this realm: "Freedom, in this sphere, can consist only in this, that socialized man, the associated producers, govern the human metabolism with nature in a rational way, bringing it under their collective control instead of being dominated by it as a blind power; accomplishing it with the least expenditure of energy and in conditions most worthy and appropriate for their human nature."[99] Nevertheless, Marx quickly adds that "this always remains a realm of necessity. The *true* realm of freedom, the development of human powers as an end-in-itself, begins beyond it, though it can flourish with this realm of necessity as its basis."[100] If for Marx the realm of necessity contains all those activities that subjects have to do in order to physically survive as human beings, then it would seem as though the realm of necessity would include most productive labour, in the narrow sense. However, under nonalienated conditions of labour, the latter would be sufficiently transformed such that it would become gratifying in itself. In Alfred Schmidt's words, "the surviving, humanized realm of necessity can just as well become a sphere of man's realization as the realm of freedom which depends on it."[101] Thus, even though individuals would be compelled to undertake certain activities in the name of the satisfaction of need, because of the alteration in the structure of the necessary activities, the labour would now be seen as being intrinsically gratifying, and hence production the individual might potentially be willing to undertake irrespective of the compulsion of need. Nevertheless, despite the element of gratification inherent in such social production, and despite that individuals may very well desire to perform such activities for their own sake, the fact remains that the activities are undertaken in the service of ends external to themselves.

For Marcuse, at this stage of his thinking, labour cannot be seen as functioning as a genuine end-in-itself to the extent that it is directed toward something not yet in existence. He thus will draw a sharp distinction between labour and play. Objectification has a completely different meaning with respect to play activity than it does with respect to labour. Most importantly, although play may certainly involve objects, the subject, in the process of playing, is not compelled to conform herself to these objects. The player follows only her own will in playing; one does as one pleases when one plays, as the nature of the activity is not dictated by the object. In Marcuse's words, "play *abolishes* this 'objective' content and lawfulness and puts in place another lawfulness, created by man himself, to which the player freely adheres on his own will."[102] Play thus opens up a *new* dimension of freedom – again, as for Marx, this does not mean that labour/necessity does not potentially contain *a* dimension of freedom – unavailable in labour. Just as for the later Marx necessity is the foundation for freedom, so for Marcuse play is in a sense later than labor, to the extent that it is in a certain way a respite from the latter: "labor is necessarily and eternally 'earlier' than play: it is the starting point, foundation, and principle of play insofar as play is precisely a breaking off *from* labor and a recuperation *for* labor."[103]

For Marcuse, then, labour always contains a form of burden, to the extent that in labouring one is always distanced from one's self-being and oriented toward something else, an external being, the object.[104] This orientation toward this something else is what militates against labour establishing itself as truly an end-in-itself, an activity undertaken for its own sake. It is this distinction between the realm of freedom and the realm of necessity, which achieves one form of expression in the distinction between labour and play, this understanding of freedom as existing in some sense outside of and beyond necessity, which Marcuse would slowly begin to call into question, and eventually reject. It is precisely this rejection that allows for the possibility of thinking of all spheres of human existence as potentially functioning as media for the expression of the human essence. Just as Marcuse will eventually interpret even socially necessary labour as a form of play, it will be suggested that so too will politics eventually be able to be seen as an intrinsically gratifying and self-affirming activity that nevertheless also looks toward an externality: not the production of use-values, but rather of new institutional forms. One of the most important transitional points in this theoretical movement occurs in Marcuse's most important philosophical work, *Eros and Civilization*, which will now need to be discussed in some detail.

## 2 The Dialectic of Instinctual Liberation: Essence and Nonrepressive Sublimation

In the prior chapter I attempted to demonstrate that Marcuse's critical appropriation of Hegel is made for the sake of the affirmation of a non-identitarian model of essence. It is particularly important to recognize this given the fact that those criticisms of Marcuse that focus on his supposed positive tendencies especially emphasize his philosophical debt to Hegel. Clearly, though, Marcuse does not affirm terminal reconciliation in the way that Hegel does. Now, just as readers often take Marcuse's appropriation of Hegel to be evidence of the identitarian elements in the former's thought, so too do they also point to Marcuse's appropriation of Freud, which is criticized for being grounded in a crude biological determinism that points toward an ultimate reconciliation of psychic conflict. As I will show in this chapter, however, this reading is equally inadequate. Just as Marcuse wants to extract from Hegel a certain critical content, but without accepting the latter's stress on harmony and reconciliation, so too is this the case with respect to his use of Freud. In the case of *Eros and Civilization*, the turn to Freud is intended to assist in overcoming the latent Promethean elements in Marx's thought, to inject Marxian thinking with a more explicit concern with sensuous gratification.[1] Marx's understanding of human life-activity, despite being conceptualized as sensuous human activity, the return of the human being to her human sense organs, is ultimately seen as not being sensuous enough. In Asher Horowitz's words, for Marcuse, "Marx is not realistic enough, for one thing, in his abstraction of even nonalienated labour from the fundamentality of the libidinal and erotic relation of the subject to its sensuous reality in all of its dimensions. Production in accordance with the laws of beauty does not go nearly far enough in making sensuous activity sensuous."[2] For

Marcuse, Freud is of interest, then, to the extent that he calls attention to the libidinal and erotic elements that saturate the subject and her relations. Such an understanding of subjectivity is absolutely essential if Marcuse's concept of essence is to be affirmed.[3] The turn to Freud, though, can in no way be interpreted as being in some sense also a turn away from Marx. The fact that Marx is nowhere mentioned by name in the text is often presented as evidence by careless readers that Marcuse has in some meaningful way abandoned his prior Marxism.[4] What this chapter will attempt to demonstrate is that this appropriation of Freudian instinct theory in fact contains a theoretical reproduction of Marcuse's affirmation of the concept of essence as outlined in the previous chapter. Most importantly, it will be demonstrated that Marcuse's most substantial theoretical innovation in *Eros and Civilization* is the rethinking of nonalienated labour – the active form for the realization of the human essence – in Freudian terms as nonrepressive sublimation.[5] What Marcuse's reading of Freud thus once again reveals, as does his reading of Hegel, is his commitment to a negative ontology that stresses nothing other than the human capacity for the radical creation of self and world.

### The Problem of Repression: Individual and Social, Basic and Surplus

Marcuse's *Eros and Civilization* is framed as an immanent critique of the concept of repression. According to Freud, all civilization is marked by repression, defined merely as "turning something away, and keeping it at a distance from consciousness."[6] To say that instinctual desire is turned away is another way of saying that it is forgotten. The problem of repression is thus fundamentally a problem of memory. Freud maintains that the total libidinal gratification of humanity's instinctual demands is incompatible with the requirements of civilization. The individual must sacrifice a significant portion of her direct instinctual satisfaction for a more assured pleasure: the reality principle comes to modify the pleasure principle. Happiness, understood as the satisfaction of libidinal impulse, must be subordinated to the activity that allows for the reproduction of civilization: work. Because of the need to work, what makes us happy must be forsaken and forgotten. It is in this sense that the assemblage of worldly objects that constitutes culture is to be considered as the historical accumulation of instinctual renunciations. The balance of the instinctual structure is altered by sublimation through the latter's redirection and neutralization of libidinal energy. Every sublimation necessarily implies a forced desexualization, or repression, of the instinct, resulting in unhappiness. What Marcuse wants to do in his immanent critique is demonstrate that the idea of (as we shall see, surplus) repression as necessary for civilization is challenged by Freud's own theory: "Freud's theoretical conception itself seems to refute his consistent denial of the historical possibility of a non-repressive civilization."[7] This refutation can be seen in Freud's late metapsychology, which post-Freudian psychoanalysts have almost completely ignored.

For Marcuse the fundamental problem of contemporary psychoanalysts, especially those he will term the neo-Freudian revisionists, is their tendency to conceptually separate social and psychological modes of repression. Such separation is no longer legitimate to the extent that psychological categories have become political ones: "private disorder reflects more directly than before the disorder of the whole, and the cure of personal disorder depends more directly than before on the cure of the general disorder."[8] The human organism's originary instinctual objective is the satisfaction of its primary desire. The renunciation of this project of satisfaction marks the origin of civilization. For the sake of the security of the organism the reality principle comes to modify the pleasure principle; immediate gratification is given up for the sake of delayed and assured gratification, as the former is seen to be impossible and destructive. The individual becomes concerned no longer only with herself and her own desire, but also realizes that she is secure only in society. Thus the demands of society come to shape the structure of her desire. Here, then, is where we can see the link between social and psychological modes of repression: "The reality principle materializes in a system of institutions. And the individual, growing up within such a system, learns the requirements of the reality principle as those of law and order, and transmits them to the next generation."[9] Indeed, it is precisely the recognition of this dialectical intertwining of psychological repression and social domination that constitutes one of Freud's most important insights: "Behind all the differences among the historical forms of society, Freud saw the basic inhumanity common to all of them, and the repressive controls which perpetuate, in the instinctual structure, the domination of man by man."[10]

Freud's metapsychology will at least recognize that psychological repression is achieved through the outward expression of the social power of institutions. The problem, though, is that for Freud specific forms of empirical reality are generalized to reality as such. Freud is right to point out that specific institutions and structures act on the individual, but the social world within which these institutions and structures are embedded is no mere abstraction, but rather is in every instance a concrete historical world. This historical dimension of social life is irrelevant to Freud in that he affirms scarcity as a natural fact of any human life, making all social formations inherently repressive as such. The external world is seen as being too barren to satisfy human needs on an adequate level without organized instinctual restraint. The key means to restrain instinctual desire is work, "more or less painful arrangements and undertakings for the procurement of the means for satisfying needs."[11] The instincts have to be repressed because they strive after pleasure, and work, necessary for any civilization, involves accepting pain. Marcuse ultimately wants to challenge this conception by showing that, on the one hand, scarcity is not a natural but a social fact, and on the other hand, that work only appears as painful to the extent that it is a mechanism to enforce this social organization of scarcity.

Marcuse attempts to undo Freud's assumptions regarding scarcity through the redeployment of certain key psychoanalytic concepts according to a new logic of repression. Specifically, Marcuse distinguishes between basic and surplus repression. Surplus repression is defined as "the restrictions necessitated by social domination. This is distinguished from (basic) repression: the 'modifications' of the instincts necessary for the perpetuation of the human race in civilization."[12] Domination is defined as practice "exercised by a particular group or individual in order to sustain and enhance itself in a privileged position."[13] Under conditions of surplus repression the social institutions that serve the specific interests of domination produce controls over and above what is actually necessary to guarantee human association. History's various reality principles, including our own, the performance principle,[14] are products of specific historical forms of domination, and thus take on unique forms. What they all share, however, is the concern with the production of those external controls whose exercise constitutes surplus repression. The external institutions that enforce surplus repression "are added to the basic (phylogenetic) restrictions of the instincts which mark the development of man from the human animal to the *animal sapiens*."[15] When Marcuse thus speaks of the abolition of repression he is clearly referring only to the abolition of this surplus repression. He is perfectly aware that the reproduction of human civilization depends on basic repression. In Gad Horowitz's words, "Repression, in the sense of human self control and sublimation, in the sense of displacement of desire into the symbolic, cultural, superorganic realm, do not occur in the first instance because a particular social system requires them, but because civilization as such requires them."[16]

Needless to say, though, the relation between basic and surplus repression is itself historical and dialectical. The degree of necessary repression is a variable quantity dependent upon the maturity of a given historical social formation. It depends specifically on "the extent of the achieved rational mastery of nature and of society."[17] When civilizational development reaches a certain nodal point, quantity becomes quality, basic repression becomes surplus:

> The same and even a reduced scope of instinctual regimentation would constitute a higher degree of repression at a mature stage of civilization, when the need for renunciation and toil is greatly reduced by material and intellectual progress – when civilization could actually afford a considerable release of instinctual energy expended for domination and toil. Scope and intensity of instinctual repression obtain their full significance only in relation to the historically possible extent of freedom.[18]

According to Marcuse, what constitutes repression under the performance principle, when evaluated in light of current states of "material and intellectual" knowledge, can only be seen to be surplus, repression beyond that required to guarantee the individual a so-called good human life within her present historical environment.

It is Marcuse's contention that, despite Freud's failure to explicitly elaborate it, there is contained within orthodox psychoanalytic theory certain hints that may assist us in developing a concept of repression that includes both basic and surplus dimensions. Although Marcuse does not mention it in particular, perhaps the most explicit hint Freud provides us is to be found in his essay on "'Civilized' Sexual Morality and Modern Nervous Illness," which seemingly develops a preliminary theory of surplus repression.[19] Freud maintains that if we trace the development of the sexual instinct, we can conceptually distinguish between three different stages of civilization:

> a first one, in which the sexual instinct may be freely exercised without regard to the aims of reproduction; a second, in which all of the sexual instinct is suppressed except what serves the aims of reproduction; and a third, in which only *legitimate* reproduction is allowed as a sexual aim. This third stage is reflected in our present-day 'civilized' sexual morality.[20]

While the first historical mode corresponds to the instinctual stage of autoeroticism and the attempt to narcissistically derive pleasure from multiple erotogenic zones of the body, the second corresponds to the stage of object-love and the subordination of the erotogenic zones to the genitals in the service of reproduction – sexuality made socially useful. The third stage, however, which Freud criticizes as being characterized by unnecessary instinctual renunciation, is defined by what Freud calls "civilized" sexual morality or legitimate reproduction, reproduction between individuals bonded by marriage in a monogamous relationship. It would appear, therefore, that the shift to this third stage of civilization is marked for Freud himself by the development of a form of surplus repression, a type of instinctual renunciation that goes beyond what is necessary to preserve collective cultural life.

Although Freud here seemingly constructs a theory of surplus repression, it must be nevertheless distinguished from Marcuse's theory in a fundamental way: that concerning the nature of the experience of basic repression, and this experience's relation to the surplus component of repression. To Freud, *any* type of repression must be experienced as unhappiness. The only benefit of successful psychoanalytic treatment is the elimination of *unnecessary* suffering – the normalization of suffering: "Normal suffering represents the success of adaptation: the repressed desires are truly renounced, which means that the individual is free of neurotic anxiety, but having given up the claim to happiness is therefore barren of joys."[21] It is in this sense that Freud states that the goal of psychoanalysis cannot be considered the absolute reconciliation of psychic conflict and the achievement of a happy state of existence. On the contrary, "analysis transforms neurotic suffering into everyday misery."[22] For Freud, basic repression itself imposes such a burden on the individual as to always be experienced as pain and misery; surplus repression merely intensifies this general and universal suffering.

We have already seen how for Marcuse the categories of basic and surplus repression are not absolute ones. Depending on certain historical factors, for example a given society's general level of technical or productive expertise, what was once properly considered a basic repression in the past may in a present or future historical epoch be considered a surplus repression. A basic repression, furthermore, is experienced by individuals differently depending on the specific combination of social forces and relations prevalent at any historical juncture. What is important to grasp is that Marcuse wants not to treat basic and surplus repression as absolute and static categories whose content remains invariable throughout the flux of history. These concepts must be treated dialectically, not just in terms of their internal movements but with respect to their relations with each other as well. Horowitz points out that basic and surplus repression are not mutually exclusive spheres, but exist in a dialectical relationship in which they are constantly interacting with and interpenetrating each other.[23] Because of such interpenetration, any attempt to alter the nature of one –for example in the attempt to eliminate surplus repression – must alter the other in some meaningful way:

> The *pressure* of basic repression – the meaning, the quality, of our experience of alienation from mere nature – is a function of the pressure of surplus repression. The two "tensions" – that which is inseparable from human existence and that which is the result of "a particular historical contingency" – interpenetrate; they do not simply co-exist as in watertight compartments. If the latter is eliminated, the former must in some way be radically transformed – it must become other than what it is.[24]

Marcuse wants to show that by eliminating surplus repression, basic repression is overcome, overcome not in the sense of being eliminated, but in the sense that it is experienced by individuals not as simple pain and suffering but as the means to a more lasting and assured gratification. While basic repression remains, its function has been radically altered: "basic repressions essential for civilization will no longer be externally imposed in the service of unfreedom, but internally and voluntarily imposed so as to sustain the rational 'order of gratification.'"[25]

## The Affirmation of Sensuousness: Primary Narcissism and Nonrepressive Sublimation

It is crucial to note here the manner in which Marcuse again dialectically juxtaposes the concepts of reason and gratification. We have already seen in the previous chapter how for Marcuse these two categories must not be thought of as necessarily mutually exclusive. The concept of reason – or Logos – is central to Marcuse's thought, a centrality that for him accords with the centrality of reason to philosophy and with his effort to realize the historical commitment of philosophy in the context of critical theory and practice. His immanent critique of the concept of essence and his affirmation of an indeterminate notion of essence are both part of his deliberate engagement in a historical struggle to achieve a rational form of existence. In thus affirming reason, however,

Marcuse carefully distinguishes his understanding of its meaning from what he suggests has been a betrayal of reason within Western philosophical and theological traditions: "Whatever the implications of the original Greek conception of Logos as the essence of being, since the canonization of the Aristotelian logic, the term merges with the idea of ordering, classifying, mastering reason."[26] The latter form is what Marcuse calls the Logos of domination. Here Marcuse is clearly at one with the immanent critique of reason developed in *Dialectic of Enlightenment*. More clearly than Horkheimer and Adorno, however, Marcuse enthusiastically celebrates reason in the form of the Logos of gratification. Here, "the traditional ontology is contested: against the conception of being in terms of Logos rises the conception of being in a-logical terms: will and joy. This countertrend strives to formulate its own Logos: the logic of gratification."[27] The identification of joy and will here refers us to Marcuse's understanding of the creative attempt to realize nonteleological potentialities, to institute news modes of being and doing, as an intrinsically gratifying activity: "Here reappears the old hedonistic definition which seeks happiness in the comprehensive gratification of needs and wants."[28] Indeed, with the Logos of gratification, "reason and happiness converge," as reasonable is that which "sustains the order of gratification," that which "comprehends and organizes necessity in terms of protecting and enriching the life instincts."[29] In order to determine the nature of these life instincts, Marcuse returns to Freud's account of the structure of infantile sexuality.

Marcuse claims that although certain elements of eighteenth-century aesthetic theory, particularly as manifested in the work of Kant and Schiller, go some way toward developing a richer understanding of reason via the identification of sensuousness and aesthetic representation, they do not go far enough in thinking a mode of practical activity in the world capable of affirming such a sensuous reason. Such an effort must begin with Freud's concept of infantile sexuality. To Marcuse the fact that infantile sexuality is inherently imaginative reveals the degree to which the human being is that which is ontologically oriented toward creation. Almost twenty years before *Eros and Civilization* Marcuse would identify phantasy as that mental capacity capable of bridging in thought the gap between present and what is perceived to be rational existence, and hence the foundational faculty of autonomy: "Owing to its unique capacity to 'intuit' an object though the latter be not present and to create something new out of given material of cognition, imagination denotes a considerable degree of independence from the given, of freedom amid a world of unfreedom. In surpassing what is present, it can anticipate the future."[30] Marcuse points out that for Freud phantasy, or imagination, is the only mental faculty which, after the socialization of the individual, maintains a degree of freedom from the reality principle. The introduction of the reality principle necessitates an alteration in the psychic structure of the mind: "The mental process formerly unified in the pleasure ego is now split: its main stream is channelled into the domain of the reality principle and brought into line with its requirements. Thus conditioned, this part of the mind obtains the monopoly of interpreting, manipulating, and altering reality – of governing remembrance and oblivion, even of defining what reality is and how it should be used and altered."[31] The other part of the mental process, imagination, remains free from the reality principle but is forced to pay for this freedom with a newfound ineffectuality; it becomes "powerless, inconsequential, unrealistic."[32] Prior to individuation, though, the imaginative orientation is revealed in the infant's polymorphous perversity: its attempt to take itself as its own object for the sake of the gratification of all parts of the body. Under the performance principle the human body must be desexualized "in order to make the organism into a subject-object of socially useful performances."[33] If the body no longer needs to be used in this way, however, and we have seen already that according to Marcuse it does not, its resexualization becomes a real possibility. The resexualization of the organism would first of all be marked by the overturning of genital primacy and the return to polymorphous perversity, the pleasure associated with the play of all aspects of the body: "the body in its entirety would become an object of cathexis, a thing to be enjoyed – an instrument of pleasure."[34] Imagination is the faculty that allows for the play of the body that characterizes infantile sexuality to take on new forms and modes of being, that which makes possible the active and creative structure of polymorphous perversity. Marcuse's interest in affirming this creative structure is revealed in his statement that, with desexualization, "Eros is no longer the life instinct governing the whole organism and striving to become the *formative principle* for a human and natural environment."[35]

Phantasy is not simply a romantic longing for a denied past, but is above all oriented toward the future: "in its refusal to accept as final the limitations imposed upon freedom and happiness by the reality principle, in its refusal to forget what *can be*, lies the critical function of phantasy."[36] The performance principle relegates the demands of phantasy to the unrealistic and unrealizable sphere of utopia; however, "if the construction of a non-repressive instinctual development is oriented, not on the subhistorical past, but on the historical present and mature civilization, the very notion of utopia loses its meaning. The negation of the performance principle emerges not against but *with* the progress of conscious rationality."[37] What Marcuse is concerned with in *Eros and Civilization* is thinking about the possibility of what Freud considered impossible: the institution of a rational form of existence, the construction of a certain reality principle, which does not necessitate the desexualization of the body and the marginalization of imagination, or in other words, a form of society in which the capacity for the creation of new modes of being is a generally recognized possibility. It is claimed that the key to such thinking lay in certain hints Freud left regarding the relation between narcissism and sublimation.

According to Marcuse, Freud's discovery of primary narcissism, of a "primal condition in which object-libido and ego-libido cannot be distinguished,"[38] suggests the possibility of a fundamentally other mode of being with and relating to the world than those permitted by the performance principle. In the former's words, "narcissism may contain the germ of a different reality principle: the libidinal cathexis of the ego (one's own body) may become the source and reservoir for a new libidinal cathexis of the objective world – transforming this world into a new mode of being."[39] Crucially, though, this new mode of being is, as we shall see, not thought of in terms of a regression to a predifferentiated unitary state in which the distinction between subject and object is overcome. The image of Narcissus, the mythic representation of primary narcissism, is inseparable from the image of Orpheus, the mythic representation of nonrepressive sublimation, "the poet as *liberator* and *creator*."[40] The reappropriation of the concept of primary narcissism is made for the sake of the affirmation of the principle of creativity, the recuperation at a higher level of the former suggesting the possibility of a generalization of the latter, the possibility of a nonantagonistic social production that always strives to overcome subjective and objective actualities, which always attempts to break closure and institute the new.

Marcuse is especially interested in Freud's late theory of sublimation as it is presented in *The Ego and the Id*, in particular Freud's question as to "whether all sublimation does not take place through the mediation of the ego, which begins by changing sexual object-libido into narcissistic libido and then, perhaps, goes on to give it another aim."[41] According to Marcuse this "hypothesis all but revolutionizes the idea of sublimation: it hints at a non-repressive sublimation which results from an extension rather than from a constraining of libido."[42] As Marcuse's critique of repressive desublimation makes clear, however, such an extension would not take the form of a spontaneous and immediate discharge of sexual energy, as some of his critics often allege. Marcuse is quick to point out that this transformation of the quality of sexuality would not lead to the production of "a society of sex maniacs" – which is equivalent "to no society" at all – precisely because it is a qualitative transformation and not a simple release of sexual energy: "It is a spread rather than explosion of libido – a spread over private and social relations which bridges the gap maintained between them by a repressive reality principle. This transformation of the libido would be the result of a societal transformation that released the free play of individual needs and faculties."[43] The release of the transformed instinctual energy thus presupposes a movement beyond the performance principle, whose institutions are only capable of facilitating energetic discharge in the form of repressive desublimation. Marcuse observes that "it has often been noted that advanced industrial society operates with a greater degree of sexual freedom – 'operates' in the sense that the latter becomes a market value and a factor of social mores. Without ceasing to be an instrument of labour, the body is allowed to exhibit its sexual features in the everyday work world and in work relations."[44] Repressive desublimation involves an extension of the boundaries of liberty with regard to sexual behaviour – the widespread integration of sex into the economy and culture – and the isolation of this behaviour from the broader erotic potentialities of human life.

Contrary to sublimation, a process referring to the desexualization of an originally highly libidinous instinct, a shift in the aim and object of an instinct in such a way so as to allow for the diversion of sexual energy to an end that, postsublimation, is no longer sexually but rather socially useful, desublimation refers to the direct and unmediated satisfaction of sexual instinct. Desublimation is repressive at the psychological level to the extent that it is intended to function as a defence mechanism against the expression of other components of sexuality. Although desublimation in advanced industrial society is characterized by the release of sexual energy, this release is ultimately restrictive in that the potential range of gratification has been drastically reduced in scope. Eros has been reduced to sexuality, or, sexuality in the expansive sense has been concentrated exclusively in one particular drive or mode of expression: genital activity. In order to be made fit to function within a highly rationalized work process, the body of the human organism has undergone a decisive reduction: the body as whole is no longer considered a potential object of pleasure, and consequently sexuality is no longer considered a threat to the smooth functioning of the society. To allow for the full expression of Eros would require a transformation in the material structure of the social formation. To the extent that sexuality has been reduced to genital sexuality, however, its direct expression does not in any way challenge the rationality of the work process: the body can function as an object within the process while at the same time gratifying its limited sexual desires. The medium for the expression of the partial sex drive is thus the mechanized work world: "Sex is integrated into work and public relations and is thus made more susceptible to (controlled) satisfaction. Technical progress and more comfortable living permit the systematic inclusion of libidinal components into the realm of commodity production and exchange."[45] The mechanization that characterizes existence within advanced industrial society has absorbed libido such that the latter is capable of expressing itself only within the machine process. The media in which the individual can potentially experience pleasure has been reduced to just one medium: pleasure can now be perceived only within the technical universe. "The effect is a localization and contraction of libido, the reduction of erotic to sexual experience and satisfaction."[46]

Desublimation, then, is repressive at the social level to the extent that the liberation of sexuality proceeds through "socially constructed forms."[47] The world is no longer essentially hostile to the demands of the individual because these demands are so limited, and hence grantable within the established universe. The immediate granting of direct pleasure is only permitted to the extent that advanced industrial society has succeeding in making the individual's interests identical with its own: "it is desublimation practiced from a 'position of strength' on the part of society, which can afford to grant more than before because its interests have become the innermost drives of its citizens, and because the joys which it grants promote social cohesion and contentment."[48] The individual is formed in such a way that her desires and goals reproduce those of the society, thus making reliance on force and terror – whether internal or external – for the preservation of order superfluous. Compliance is voluntary as there exists a prestructured identity between the individual and the social formation. The psychic structure of the individual undergoes a decisive reduction: because of the perception of this identity, the need for a superego to restrict the action of the individual becomes unnecessary. With no superego there is no guilt. Consciousness is perpetually happy: "loss of conscience due to the satisfactory liberties granted by an unfree society makes for a *happy consciousness* which facilitates acceptance of the misdeeds of this society."[49] Because there is no longer any tension between the individual and her environment, because consciousness is perpetually contented, there is no longer any need for a critical disposition. The individual is incapable of mounting any challenge to the existing structure of the given.

Under such conditions

> the libido continues to bear the mark of suppression and manifests itself in the hideous forms so well known in the history of civilization; in the sadistic and masochistic orgies of desperate masses, of "society elites," of starved bands of mercenaries, of prison and concentration camp guards. Such release of sexuality provides a periodically necessary outlet for unbearable frustration; it strengthens rather than weakens the roots of instinctual constraint; consequently, it has been used time and again as a prop for suppressive regimes.[50]

The resexualization of the body in the affirmation of polymorphous perversity, the recuperation of the structure of infantile sexuality at a higher and more mature level,[51] is what characterizes what Marcuse now specifically calls the "transformation of sexuality into Eros,"[52] the "quantitative and qualitative aggrandizement of sexuality."[53] This transformation would require a correlative transformation in the concept of sublimation, for Eros would necessarily be sublimated differently than would mere sexuality. Freud's concept of sublimation "refers to the fate of sexuality under a repressive reality principle. Thus sublimation means a change in the aim and object of the instinct 'with regard to which our social values come into the picture.'"[54] Above all, it means the surplus repressive desexualization of the instinct such that instinctual energy may be channelled into socially useful tasks. Marcuse points out, though, that there exist other forms of activity, approximating sublimation, which nevertheless are able to preserve in their expression their libidinous quality. He mentions, for example, aim-inhibited sexual impulses, such as the relations between parent and child or friend and friend, which retain their sexual aims but which are internally restricted from giving them a direct expression.[55] For Marcuse "such concepts come close to recognizing the possibility of non-repressive sublimation. The rest is left to speculation."[56]

For Marcuse it is of the utmost importance to realize that repressive sublimation occurs after early childhood: the repressive modification of the pleasure principle has thus already been achieved; it takes place before the actualization of specific processes of sublimation. Repressive sublimation, therefore,

> operates on a preconditioned instinctual structure, which includes the functional and temporal restraints of sexuality, its channelling into mono- gamic reproduction, and the desexualization of most of the body. Sub- limation works with the thus preconditioned libido and its possessive, exploitative, aggressive force. The repressive "modification" of the plea- sure principle precedes the actual sublimation, and the latter carries over into the socially useful activities.[57]

If libidinal energy, though, is not susceptible to this originary modifi- cation, the possibility of the sublimation of a highly sexual instinctual content becomes a real possibility. Such a nonrepressive sublimation would be "sublimation without desexualization," as energy would not be deflected from its aim but gratified directly in its relations and activities. Here it is worth pointing out again, though, the distinction Marcuse draws between basic and surplus modes of repression, a dis- tinction that clearly has relevance to the concept of sublimation. Just as when Marcuse speaks of a nonrepressive civilization, he is in actual fact referring to a non–surplus repressive civilization, so too when he speaks of nonrepressive sublimation is he in actual fact referring to non– surplus repressive sublimation.[58] From a strictly Freudian standpoint, of course, the notion of a sublimation without repression is a concep- tual impossibility. Sublimation always involves a displacement, a mov- ing away of drive energy. In Gad Horowitz's words, "Man is the animal that neutralizes drive energy, i.e. transforms it from id energy into ego energy. All concern for the other and all cultural activity (indeed all *human* sexual activity) are based on sublimation in the sense that they depend on drive energy which has been diverted from its original aim (total and immediate bodily gratification)."[59] All sublimation must con- tain a basic repressive element to the extent that "it is based on repres- sions which are essential for the construction of an integrated ego able to test and master reality, successfully to defend itself against desires which must be renounced no matter what the social conditions, to con- struct permanent and affectionate object relations, and advance infan- tile to mature gratifications."[60]

Such basic repression would be self-imposed by the organism for the sake of the reproduction of the conditions necessary for the achievement of happiness. Marcuse suggests that there is even a mechanism internal to the instinct that acts as a restraint delaying satisfaction – a delay, however, that does not reduce fulfilment, but enhances it as part of a Logos of gratification. Such delays are not externally imposed by a repressive reality principle but introduced by Eros itself "because they have inherent libidinal value."[61] As Marcuse indicates, Freud himself seemed to have believed that the unregulated release of sexual energy would never be capable of achieving a satisfactory gratification, and that an internal restrictive mechanism existed that delayed such release: "It is very easy to show that the value the mind sets on erotic needs instantly sinks as soon as satisfaction becomes readily obtainable. Some obstacle is necessary to swell the tide of the libido to its height."[62] The instinct must contain some device by which it can inhibit sexuality, this inhibition serving to enhance gratification. It is thus that Marcuse conceptualizes the transformation of sexuality into Eros through a form of self-sublimation in which basic repression is internally imposed by the willing organism. Under such conditions "basic repressions essential for civilization will no longer be externally imposed in the service of unfreedom, but internally and voluntarily imposed so as to sustain the rational 'order of gratification.'"[63] Pleasure here becomes linked to autonomy: "Pleasure contains an element of self-determination," Marcuse says, "which is the token of human triumph over blind necessity."[64] He goes on to quote Horkheimer and Adorno: "Nature does not feature enjoyment as such; natural pleasure does not go beyond the appeasement of need. All pleasure is social – in unsublimated no less than sublimated emotions."[65] Following Hegel, enjoyment is thus conceived of as a rising above immediate impulse through the transcendence of the direct and immediate satiation of desire. As Marcuse puts it in *One-Dimensional Man*, "All joy and happiness derive from the ability to transcend nature – a transcendence in which the mastery of nature is itself subordinated to liberation and pacification of existence."[66]

To affirm that nonrepressive sublimation is self-sublimation, furthermore, is not to affirm that it is a form of instinctual release expressed through the action of the autonomous individual isolated from her fellows. Marcuse states that "even if sublimation does not proceed *against* the instincts but as their affirmation, it must be a supra-individual process on common ground. As an isolated individual phenomenon, the reactivation of narcissistic libido is not culture building but neurotic."[67]

Here Marcuse follows quite closely Géza Róheim, who points out that the difference between a neurosis and a sublimation lay in the latter's social aspect: "In a sublimation something new is created – a house, or a community, or a tool – and it is created *in a group or for the use of a group*."[68] Marcuse thus emphasizes that "libido can take the road of self-sublimation only as a *social* phenomenon: as an unrepressed force, it can promote the formation of culture only under conditions which relate associated individuals to each other in the cultivation of the environment for their developing needs and faculties."[69] In light of a social nonrepressive sublimation, Freud's formulation regarding the nature of Eros as a fundamental striving to organize living substances into increasingly expansive unities – "the drive toward ever larger unities belongs to the biological-organic nature of Eros itself"[70] – takes on a new meaning, as the resexualization of the body, the transformation of sexuality into Eros, at the same time creates more complex associations of people.[71] Hence, "the culture-building power of Eros *is* non-repressive sublimation: sexuality is neither deflected from nor blocked in its objective; rather, in attaining its objective, it transcends it to others, searching for fuller gratification."[72]

## Nonrepressive Sublimation and Nonalienated Labour

For Marcuse the self-sublimation of sexuality, marked by the basic repressive internal restriction of the expression of libidinal energy, "implies that sexuality can, under specific conditions, create highly civilized human relations without being subjected to the repressive organization which the established civilization has imposed upon the instinct."[73] This latter surplus repression primarily takes the form of the neutralization of the creative and active nature of the human being, which manifests itself, for example, in the modes of being of infantile sexuality. For Marcuse, then, any form of concrete social liberation must affirm this becoming-structure of the human being. In an emancipated society "existence would still be activity," the latter becoming "display – the free manifestation of potentialities."[74] The goal is thus not the construction of a perfect harmony that permanently fixes the nature of subject and object, but rather the construction of an objective world that is no longer a barrier to subjective development, to movement, becoming, and activity. The subject thus remains always in process, never becoming static or self-identical. New social institutions must be capable of facilitating the becoming-structure, or essence, of the individual. The model of the subject as one in need of continual over-coming thus reproduces itself. Marcuse is explicit on this point: "The erotic aim of sustaining the entire body as subject-object of pleasure calls for the *continual refinement of the organism*, the intensification of its receptivity, the growth of its sensuousness."[75] This refinement is pur-sued through the participation of the organism in various "projects of realization: the abolition of toil, the ameliorization of the environment, the conquest of disease and decay, the creation of luxury."[76] These ac-tivities are forms of *work* that both alter the nature of the organism and combine organisms into new and more complex unities: "There is sublimation and, consequently, culture; but this sublimation proceeds in a system of expanding and enduring work relations."[77] The trans-formed sexuality, Eros, expressed within new non–surplus repressive institutions, allows for a richer and more inclusive expression of libido, manifesting itself in a far more expansive context, "*including the order of work*."[78] Marcuse is clear that under conditions of nonalienated labour "sublimation would not cease but instead, as erotic energy, surge up in new forces of cultural creation" that would take the form of the "free play of human faculties and forces." [79]

Hence, labour is here seen as potentially being an activity capable of facilitating the expression of energy of a highly libidinous quality. This expression would be for the sake of the gratification of the individual, which is once again associated with the free play of the potentialities of the subject. It is far too simplistic to simply think of work as being necessarily painful activity driven by desexualized impulses. Marcuse points out, for one, that work can in fact be highly pleasurable: "To be sure, there is a mode of work which offers a high degree of libidinal sat-isfaction, which is pleasurable in its execution."[80] It is true, though, that the vast majority of work under the performance principle, and under all prior reality principles, are and were forms of toil characterized by unpleasure: "The work that created and enlarged the material basis of civilization was chiefly labour, alienated labour, painful and miserable – and still is. The performance of such work hardly gratifies *individual* needs and inclinations."[81] For Marcuse work can be transformed such that it does not contradict the pleasure principle; this is not just a reor-ganization of the distribution of the objects of work, but rather a trans-formation of the very nature of work itself, such that it allows the body to express its libidinal and erotic dimensions: "If pleasure is indeed in the act of working and not extraneous to it, such pleasure must be de-rived from the acting organs of the body and the body itself, activating the erotogenic zones or eroticizing the body as a whole; in other words, it must be libidinal pleasure."[82] It was Freud's failure to distinguish between alienated and nonalienated modes of labour that prevented him from realizing that in modern society work could express libidinal pleasure, despite his concession that certain types of work are capable of "displacing a large amount of libidinal components, whether narcissistic, aggressive, even erotic."[83] According to Marcuse, originally all labour was of necessity essentially libidinal:

> The *work* that has contributed so essentially to the development of man from animal is *originally libidinous*. Freud states expressly that sexual as well as sublimated love is 'connected to communal labour.' Man begins working because he finds pleasure in work, not only after work, pleasure in the play of his faculties and the fulfillment of his life needs, not as a means of life but as life itself. Man begins the cultivation of nature and of himself, cooperation, in order to secure and perpetuate the gaining of pleasure.[84]

If this is indeed the case, then the transformation of the organism into an instrument of alienated labour is not the necessary psychic condition of humankind. Freud, however, was unwilling to follow such observations to their most radical conclusions. He ultimately affirms the psychological impossibility of the institution of communism and the creation of a social order in which individuals can find a high level of instinctual fulfilment at the same time that they can physically reproduce their lives in a so-called civilized manner.[85] Civilization required alienated labour in order to reproduce itself; instinctual energy thus had to be altered prior to sublimation in order to allow the body to be transformed into an instrument of work, into a "subject-object of socially useful labour."[86] For Marcuse, of course, such repression is not carried out to preserve the existence of the species, but rather to preserve domination, and is hence unnecessary. The abolition of domination and the construction of a new basic repressive reality principle, capable of simultaneously affirming the pleasure principle, would necessarily involve the reorganization of the form of work: "the elimination of surplus-repression would *per se* tend to eliminate, not labour, but the organization of the human existence into an instrument of labour. If this is true, the emergence of a non-repressive reality principle would alter rather than destroy the social organization of labour: the liberation of Eros could create new and durable work relations."[87]

We will recall that in "On the Philosophical Foundation of the Concept of Labour in Economics" Marcuse followed quite closely Marx's lead in maintaining the permanent nonequivalency between work and play. In the *Grundrisse* Marx states that labour can potentially function as "self-realization, objectification of the subject, hence real freedom."[88] The fact that all labour up to the present has historically been *"external forced labour"*[89] does not mean that in the future it cannot be self-realization, cannot be a means to freedom and happiness. Nevertheless, Marx still takes to task Fourier, for even under nonalienated conditions labour cannot be interpreted simply as "mere fun, mere amusement."[90] Even free labour – "attractive work, the individual's self-realization" – will still be "the most damned seriousness, and hence it "cannot become play as Fourier would like."[91] In *Eros and Civilization*, however, Marcuse calls for a reassertion of the dignity of Fourier on the grounds of the latter's anticipation of the potential reconceptualization of labour as play.[92] In *An Essay on Liberation* he even goes so far as to call for a movement from Marx to Fourier. Fourier "did not shrink back in fear, as Marx still did, from speaking of a possible society in which work becomes play, a society in which even socially necessary labour can be organized in harmony with the liberated, genuine needs of man."[93] Marcuse now maintains that if labour becomes the free play of human faculties, then external incentives to work become unnecessary. People would work as a consequence of their perception of the intrinsic enjoyment achieved through participation in social production. This in fact could be considered a world "in which work becomes play."[94]

According to Marcuse, within the psychoanalytic tradition the individual who has contributed the most to theorizing the assimilation of work and play, the reconceptualization of labour as the "free play of human faculties," is Barbara Lantos.[95] Lantos notes that what marks a specific activity as work or play is not its content but its purpose. Whereas play looks to itself as an end and seeks gratification through its own activity, work looks to ends outside itself, specifically those concerned with self-preservation. In Lantos's words, "The fundamental feature of play is, that it is gratifying in itself, without serving any other purpose than that of instinctual gratification,"[96] whereas "to work is the active effort of the ego, enriched during the period of learning, to get from the outside world whatever is needed for self-preservation."[97] This latter purposeful extraction from the outside world is said to require the neutralization of libidinal energy if it is to be successful. Nevertheless, it still operates with the same energy as play, however modified: "In childhood, the energies of these instinctual forces were transferred on to highly skilful ego-activities and used in play and learning, building up – for use in later adult life – the ego that is to meet the demands of civilization. The same libidinal and aggressive forces are *now* used in dealing with or controlling the environment, to extract from it the complicated objects needed in the service of complicated self-preservation."[98]

Thus in all work activities "it is the derivatives of the original instinctual drives which are operating."[99] What Marcuse would like to show, however, is just that self-preservation is not so complicated, that scarcity is socially produced, and that hence a reeroticization of work is possible. External surplus repressive forces produce within us a superego that generates an urge to work. "It is not the object or the skill of the activity which makes the difference between work and play, but the participation of the superego, which changes play-activities into work-activities."[100] If the superego force is lessened, though, work can assume play characteristics. In Marcuse's words, "a transformation in the instinctual structure (such as that from the pregenital to the genital stage) would entail a change in the instinctual value of the human activity *regardless of its content*. For example, if work were accompanied by a reactivation of pregenital polymorphous eroticism, it would tend to become more gratifying in itself without losing its *work* content."[101] The preservation of its work content would ensure that the activity would still be oriented toward the production of objects, would still be objectification. Just because an activity is of intrinsic value and therefore gratifying does not mean that it necessarily excludes all extrinsic considerations, and vice versa. We can see that this is the case, for example, in animal activity: "Food will be captured or collected by the animal in a way which is essentially a form of playing. The component instincts, enjoyment of movement and cruelty, sometimes with the addition of the collecting impulse, are sufficient for the mastery of this task. The activity of finding food is pleasurable in itself."[102] So, for Marcuse now, as opposed to in "On the Philosophical Foundation of the Concept of Labour in Economics," what defines play is no longer the lack of objectification in the exercise of the activity, but rather just the fact that the activity is seen as being intrinsically gratifying, a process the subject would be willing to initiate for its own sake, irrespective of the demands of necessity.

Although in *Eros and Civilization* Marcuse still speaks of the perpetuation of some minimum quantity of alienated labour even after the transformation of work into play,[103] and the continuing existence of the realm of freedom – now inclusive, though of socially necessary labour – outside of the realm of necessity, he soon realizes that the coalescence of work and play logically implies the coalescence of necessity and freedom. Hence, in *An Essay on Liberation*, he states, "Marx rejects the idea that work can ever become play. Alienation would be reduced with the progressive reduction of the working day, but the latter would remain a day of unfreedom, rational but not free. However, the development of the productive forces beyond their capitalist organization suggests the possibility of freedom *within* the realm of necessity."[104] Marx's ideal of socialism was not radical or utopian enough:

> He underrated the level which the productivity of labour under the capitalist system itself could attain and the possibilities suggested by the attainment of this level. The technical achievements of capitalism would make possible a socialist development which would surpass the Marxian distinction between socially necessary labour and creative work, between alienated labour and non-alienated work, between the realm of necessity and the realm of freedom.[105]

Marcuse, in the middle to late 1960s, now influenced by the social and cultural climate of the time, will appear at his most utopian. For him, though, this utopian optimism is in actual fact expressive of what has become, through the development of a certain level of economic and technological ability, the end of utopia. Given the current technical possibilities, Marcuse maintains that we can only speak of utopia with respect to social projects that explicitly contradict the established physical and scientific laws of nature.[106] Concrete utopia has become a real possibility: "Industrial civilization has reached the stage where most of what could formerly be called Utopian now has a '*topos*' among the real possibilities and capabilities of this civilization."[107] The most important manifestation of this realization or end of utopia is the emergence of the real potential for the coalescence of freedom and necessity: "I believe that one of the new possibilities, which gives an indication of the qualitative difference between the free and unfree society, is that of letting the realm of freedom appear within the realm of necessity – in labour and not only beyond labour."[108]

Interestingly enough, Marcuse maintains that the most advanced vision of the potential convergence of freedom and necessity is to be found in the same book in which the permanent nonequivalency of labour and play is affirmed, specifically, in the passage on automation in the *Grundrisse*. For Marx the natural tendency of capital is to increasingly take the form of fixed capital, and of fixed capital to increasingly take the form of the machine, an autonomous mechanical apparatus whose power is generated through its own movements. However, "while machinery is the most appropriate form of the use value of fixed capital, it does not at all follow that therefore subsumption under the social relation of capital is the most appropriate and ultimate social relation of production for the application of machinery."[109] Under the capital relation, living labour becomes "a mere living accessory of this machinery."[110] Machinery is used by capital not in order to produce an increase in the quantity of free time for the worker, or an increase in human independence and creativity in labour: "Through this process, the amount of labour necessary for the production of a given object is indeed reduced to a minimum, but only in order to realize a maximum of labour in the maximum number of such objects."[111] Nevertheless, capital does through the development of the machine system, "quite unintentionally," reduce the quantum of energy required to produce an object to a minimum, and "this will redound to the benefit of emancipated labour, and is the condition of its emancipation."[112] Needless to say, though, machinery cannot emancipate labour if it is taken over and used in the future society in the same way as it is in the present one. The revolutionary dimensions of automated technology will not explicitly become visible until the specifically capitalist technological apparatus is overcome. Technology is not neutral; the nature of the individual's relation to the assembly line is not qualitatively altered simply as a consequence of a reorganization of the nature of the social relations of production. Rather, the activity itself must be transformed. The individual's concrete relations with the forces of production, the way in which she appropriates the technological apparatus, must be remade. Technology, in other words, must be reshaped such that it can supplement creative work.

It is this latter dimension of Marx's account of automation that Marcuse would like to seize upon. Marcuse sees in Marx's account not simply automation's potential to increase the quantity of human time expendable in the realm of freedom, but the foundation of a qualitatively new relation between human and machine: "This concept envisages conditions of full automation, where the immediate producer is indeed 'dissociated' from the material process of production and becomes a free 'Subject' in the sense that he can play with, experiment with the technical material, with the possibilities of the machine and of the things produced and transformed by the machines."[113] Automation, therefore, is not beneficial simply to the extent that it reduces the quantum of labour necessarily invested in the productive process, thus potentially freeing up time for the pursuit of human ends in the separate realm of freedom, but rather to the extent that it actually transforms the very nature of work: "The work process itself, the socially necessary work, becomes, in its rationality, subject to the free play of the mind, of imagination, the free play with the pleasurable possibilities of things and nature."[114] Thus the technological rationality "also contains an element of playfulness which is constrained and distorted by the repressive usage of technology: playing with (the possibilities of) things, with their combination, order, form, and so forth."[115] In playing with the technological apparatus, in experimenting with its form and structure, the individual expresses and develops her imaginative and creative powers. This is Marcuse's most advanced position on labour as a means to the actualization of the human essence, on the discovery, creation, and realization of the potentialities of subject and object.

It is crucial to note at this stage to what degree Marcuse's position on labour and essence here surpasses the account provided by traditional Marxism. The most systematic critique of traditional Marxism's understanding of the meaning of labour is produced by Moishe Postone. Postone argues that Marx's concept of labour refers to a historically specific, as opposed to a transhistorical, mode of human doing: "the notion that labour constitutes the social world and is the source of all wealth does not refer to society in general, but to capitalist, or modern, society alone."[116] For Marx the historical specificity of capitalist labour demonstrates the degree to which capitalist social production is shaped by capitalist social relations. In particular, capitalist production uses the form of labour that is specifically structured according to the logic of value. Traditional Marxism errs in uncritically focusing on the role of capitalist productive development in the creation of the conditions necessary for the institution of socialism. Socialism is conceptualized not in terms of the overcoming of the mode of social production, but rather simply in terms of the reorientation of the administrative form of the identical productive apparatus. Hence, for traditional Marxism the central contradiction is between the forces of production and the relations of production, as opposed to between the value form of production and the potential for the actualization of a new mode of labour, based on the increasing accumulation of real wealth. Labour as it appears in the capitalist social formation is transformed from the object to the standpoint of criticism: "Whereas the form of labour (hence of production) is the object of Marx's critique, an unexamined 'labour' is, for traditional Marxism, the transhistorical source of wealth and the basis of social constitution. The result is not a *critique of political economy* but a *critical political economy*, that is, a critique solely of the mode of distribution."[117] The emancipation of the human being is thus thought of in terms of the affirmation, as opposed to the abolition, of the capitalist productive worker.

Significantly, Postone believes that the members of the Frankfurt School, although operating on a higher level of sophistication than most other Marxists, nevertheless repeat the errors of traditional Marxism, with this repetition ultimately accounting for their much-noted political pessimism.[118] Horkheimer, who it is claimed thinks of labour abstractly in terms of the mastery of nature, is taken to be typical in this respect. Postone argues that in Horkheimer's early work, represented especially well in "Traditional and Critical Theory,"[119] "the idea of a rational social organization adequate to all its members – a community of free persons – is a possibility immanent to human labour."[120] Emancipation is ultimately seen as being rooted in the conscious and rational realization of free labour's constitution of the world of objects. Horkheimer's pessimistic turn, however, is seen as the result of his increasing realization that the supposedly transhistorical concept of labour is not a legitimate means to the actualization of human freedom. This realization, though, does not lead him to historically specify the concept, but simply to reinterpret it in terms of social domination: "He claims that the nature of social domination has changed and increasingly has become a function of technocratic or instrumental reason, which he grounds in 'labour.' Production has become the source of unfreedom."[121] In both instances, though, whether considered in terms of freedom or unfreedom, the form of labour is ultimately seen as universal and transhistorical.

Regardless of the efficacy of Postone's critique of Horkheimer, what I have suggested in the previous two chapters is that Marcuse's theoretical treatment of labour cannot be comprehended in these terms, according to the logic of traditional Marxism. Marcuse quite clearly critiques the historically specific mode of capitalist social production in the name of an alternate form of labour that is able to facilitate or give an expression to what he takes to be the creative and aesthetic energies of the human being. Indeed, Marcuse's formulations on this subject are very close to how Postone imagines an alternate form of emancipated production at the end of *Time, Labour, and Social Domination*: "a situation of historical freedom would also allow for a consciously regulated process of interaction with nature that should not be understood in terms of the romanticized 'harmony' that expresses the subjection of humanity to the blind forces of nature, or the 'freedom' that entails the blind subjugation of nature."[122] Rather, socialism implies the emergence of a new mode of production that "would allow for new modes of individual labour and activity that are richer and more satisfying."[123] Such modes would "enrich rather than impoverish individuals," as here "people might begin to control what they create rather than being controlled by it."[124] As I will argue in the next chapter, if there is a limit to Marcuse's understanding of socialism, it lies not in any ahistorical understanding of the nature of labour, but rather in a one-dimensional and identitarian understanding of the nature of politics. It is thus to the specifically political question that I will now turn.

# 3 The Problem of Politics

In the previous two chapters I demonstrated the degree to which Marcuse considers labour to be a potential medium for the expression of a specifically negative and nonidentitarian model of essence. As was mentioned in the introduction to this text, however, such a consideration does not go far enough from the standpoint of Marcuse's understanding of the nature of socialism. The latter is considered not simply in terms of a reorientation of the mode of distribution, nor a revolution in the mode of production, but rather the actualization of the impulse for radical creation in all human spheres, including the political one. We know that for Marcuse it is no longer theoretically justified to forcibly separate determinations regarding essence from concrete facts of empirical existence. Essence only realizes itself in history, and it is defined precisely in the historical fluctuations of its forms: "We are no longer dealing with an abstract human essence, which remains equally valid at every stage of concrete history, but with an essence which can be defined in *history* and *only* in history."[1] But the very fact that facticity has perverted essence, that the individual is blocked from expressing her essence through participation in processes of historical becoming, produces an imperative to alter facticity. Theory, which is concerned with the delineation of the negative structure of essence and the critique of the forms of facticity that bar this essence's actualization, thus intrinsically implies the question of politics. Politics assumes a central importance: "we shouldn't talk ourselves into thinking we can ignore politics today or put politics on ice until we're in the mood again or happen to find time for a political discussion."[2] It is typical that Marcuse would, for example, write to Horkheimer, in clear reference to Adorno, to say that "I'm just not one for leaving 'messages in a bottle'. What we have to say is not just for some mythical future."[3] For Marcuse essence and appearance thus relate to each other in the conflict between a society's present state and a society's actual material possibilities, politics functioning as a form of practice oriented toward overcoming this surplus discrepancy through the reinstitutionalization of society.

I have argued throughout the present work, however, that Marcuse is no prophet of identity. Successful political intervention does not result in the production of a closed and harmonious totality in which all human contradictions are once and for all reconciled. Marcuse is quite explicit on this point. In the future society "there may still be the sick, the insane, and the criminal,"[4] but more importantly, even beyond this there will exist inevitable discord between so-called normal or pacified individuals: "The institutions of socialist society, even in their most democratic form, could never resolve all the conflicts between the universal and the particular, between human beings and nature, between individual and individual."[5] Marcuse notes that any society, no matter how justly organized, will be characterized by social conflict. Marcuse's theoretical endeavours are just aimed at thinking a form of society in which such conflicts can be resolved without the use of terror, oppression, and cruelty.[6] The idea of a world without pain and without conflict is "not only an impossible but also an unbearable thought!"[7] The relevant question is how are these pains and conflicts to be negotiated without recourse to the institutions and techniques of surplus repression? Here, then, is the special relevance of the question of politics. Politics is not just about the stimulation of the transition from a surplus repressive to a basic repressive social formation. To the extent that social conflicts will continue to be perpetuated in any society, politics assumes a perpetual place in the life and reproduction of the human species. The political, in other words, is an always-relevant and always-necessary sphere of human existence. Marcuse maintains that socialism, although conceived of as a totality, is nevertheless a "qualitatively different *totality*" to the extent that it encompasses all spheres of human life, not only economic ones, but moral and aesthetic ones as well.[8] Social liberation thus involves the "*totality* of human existence,"[9] the liberation of the individual as, for example, an economic being, a moral being, and an aesthetic being. And now we may add, a political being. In the context of the present discussion, the realization of the total individual would be the actualization of essence in all of the spheres or worlds that in their collective mediation constitute human existence. The relevant question with respect to politics is therefore, what form of concrete political activity would be capable of affirming the indeterminate and negative model of essence as process that Marcuse develops? What would a creative and intrinsically gratifying form of political activity look like, and does Marcuse take any steps toward thinking it? Just as Marcuse would attempt to refine Marx's theory of essence, so too will he attempt to root his political theory in the Marxian problematic. In doing so, however, he intensifies what remains one of the fundamental ambiguities in Marx's thought, the potential tension between the latter's account of subjectivity and his account of politics. In this chapter I will explore this contradiction as it manifests itself in the work of Marx, certain key representatives of Western Marxism, and finally Marcuse himself.

## Marx's Political Ambiguity

It is often pointed out that Marx wrote relatively little on the nature of political life. This is not to say that Marx does not recognize that qualitative social transformation depends necessarily on political intervention, but rather to say that Marx appears to be inconsistent with respect to the recognition of the potential for politics to serve as an appropriate field for the manifestation of essence, or in other words, a permanent sphere of human life-activity. Marx's political philosophy is perhaps the most underdeveloped dimension of his critical theory. While it is no doubt true that there are indications that Marx did consider political action as a potential medium for the expression of essence, it is also true that at times Marx seems to consider politics as simply a means to an end, the means to the realization of a socialized humanity, to true communism as a positive form of existence. The Marxian political theory contains each possibility: it can be read as affirming either a negative and nonidentitarian form of political practice, or a positive and instrumental type of antipolitics. It appears as though, at least upon an initial reading, that it is this latter possibility that Marcuse realizes in his own work.

Initially, in a set of articles written for the *Rheinische Zeitung* strongly under the influence of Hegel, Marx would understand the political state as functioning as the potential embodiment of human freedom, of course being cognizant of the fact that the actually existing state in no way lives up to this potential. Marx would more and more come to see, however, that the actions of the state were in fact consequences of external pressures, and not the result of the exercise of the collective will of the occupiers of state institutions. Marx's first attempt to consider the nature of these external pressures is undertaken in his *Critique of Hegel's Philosophy of Right*. Here Marx notes that although Hegel is correct to perceive a general contradiction between civil society and the state, he is wrong to suppose that these two moments could be potentially reconciled through the mediation of a set of political institutions. The state now is seen as being always subordinate to private property, affirming the private interest over the general one. Nevertheless, although the political state is inadequate as an objective structure capable of affirming essence, this is not the case for all modes of political organization in themselves. Specifically, Marx affirms true democracy as the one genuine form of political constitution capable of realizing human nature. It is only in the true democracy that the individual herself is the creator and shaper of political life, the democratic polity being a concrete objectification of human essence, an affirmation of species-being. In the true democracy "the constitution not only in itself, according to essence, but according to existence and actuality is returned to its real ground, actual man, the actual people, and established as its own work. The constitution appears as what is the free product of men."[10] Whereas Hegel begins from the objective fact of the state and consequently transforms the people into a derivative subjective product of it, true democracy begins with the people and understands the state as an objectified product of their action. The realization of true democracy depends on the abolition of the state and its replacement with a set of democratic institutions capable of facilitating free public participation in the political sphere. It is thus that "in true democracy the *political state disappears*."[11]

One of the most significant attempts to detail the significance of the identification of the truth of politics with true democracy's abolition of the political state is undertaken by Miguel Abensour in his *Democracy against the State: Marx and the Machiavellian Moment*. According to Abensour there are four characteristics defining true democracy. First, the establishment of true democracy is considered by Marx to be the realization of the essence of the political as the struggle on the part of the people for liberty.[12] Indeed, when Marx claims that democracy is the riddle of all constitutions solved, he is pointing out that to the extent that the structures of all political regimes are objective reflections of the existence of the *demos* as the society's determining force, in true democracy this latter determination is finally made explicit. Second, the process by which the *demos* objectifies itself in the political constitution takes the form of a reduction: "once the objectification is brought back

to the instituting subject and this recognition has occurred, it is necessary to *reduce* this objectification to what it is – a mere moment of a more
global process – and to determine quite exactly the limits of the objectification in order better to control the theoretical and practical energy
dispensed in the political realm."[13] Significantly, the reduction reveals
the process of objectification to be a dynamic expression of the creative
essence of the species-being. The universality of the species-being,
the existence of the being as the creative social being, is realized only
through the participation of the being in the political element, in political objectification. Indeed, all other sites of human existence are, relative to the political site, "inessential links that keep man at a distance
from man."[14] In fact, the people's achievement of a consciousness of political objectification as a manifestation of their own self-activity serves
as a ground for an extension whereby this self-activity can "launch into
all spheres of existence. Thus the objectification of the *demos* wins out
in all domains where it is meant to manifest itself, in the multiplicity
of its being."[15] Third, political objectification is never terminal, democratic temporality extending creation indeterminately through time.
The "aim of a self-constitution of the people, of an objectification of
human dealings in a political mode that would never deteriorate into
political alienation culminates in a conception of the democratic self-
institution of society following the model of a self-institution of an ongoing self-determination."[16] And last, true democracy must be seen as
being radically distinct from all other state forms to the extent that it
signifies the abolition, certainly not of the political, but of the political
state as an organizing form.[17] In the final instance the process by which
essence is politically objectified can be broken down into three interre-
lated moments: reduction, the reducing of the political form to its being
as the objective product of the creative energy of the *demos*; blocking,
the prevention of this form from hardening into an organizing form
that once and for all fixes human reality; and extension, the extending
of the creative activity to multiple spheres of human life-activity. Thus
"the 1843 Critique seems like it can be read as the implementation, in
the political field, of an ontology in which being is thought of as action
or, to express this better by privileging the verbal form, as *acting*."[18]

According to Abensour, however, there exists a fundamental ambiguity in Marx, to the extent that the latter's increasing concern with
the issue of the exploitation of labour is seen to tend toward the displacement of the so-called Machiavellian moment in his critical theory. Nevertheless, "what surfaced in the 1843 Critique in the name of

'true democracy' did not totally disappear, but persisted as a hidden and latent dimension of Marx's writings, ready to resurge, susceptible to awaken by the shock of the event."[19] The most notable such resurgence occurs in Marx's interpretation of the Paris Commune in *The Civil War in France*.[20] Here Marx interprets the Commune as an example of a potential positive form of political being existing beyond class rule, a democratic polity that allows for mass civic participation in affairs regarding public life. Such participation is achieved, for example, through the replacement of the standing army with a citizen's militia, the decentralization of the executive and legislative bodies into a system of wards composed of elected councillors who are responsible and revocable, the elimination of high offices, the elimination of the church apparatus, and the democratization of the judiciary.[21] The Commune represented the desired dismantling of the state, but in such a way so as to preserve public power, which was now to be exercised through the participation of citizens in institutions of democracy. Here Marx even links economic freedom to political freedom in a reciprocal relation in which each is dependent upon the other for its realization: "It was essentially a working-class government, the product of the struggle of the producing against the appropriating class, the political form at last discovered under which to work out the economic emancipation of labour."[22] It is in light of this reappearance of the problematic of 1843 that Abensour asks, "If [Marx] leaves this [Machiavellian] moment behind when he turns toward production in order to think through his monadology, does he not return to it when, in the Constitution of the Paris Commune, he revives the figure of democracy?"[23]

These two texts at least, *Critique of Hegel's* Philosophy of Right and *The Civil War in France*, seem to posit a model of democratic existence that could at the very least serve as the germ for the thinking of a negative and nonidentitarian politics of becoming. As mentioned, however, the Marxian political theory is marked by a certain problematic ambiguity. Readers of Marx sometimes point out the radical democratic elements of the latter's thought. Notable in this respect is Hal Draper, who sees in Marx an unwavering commitment to a democratic and specifically self-emancipatory political project. For Draper "Marx was the first socialist figure to come to an acceptance of the socialist idea *through* the battle for the consistent extension of democratic control from below."[24] Now, although this is one of the possibilities given in the Marxian political theory, Draper himself, in certain of his readings of Marx, reveals the other possibility, the possibility that opens onto an antipolitics affirming both instrumentalism and managerialism. With respect to the former, in *The 'Dictatorship of the Proletariat' from Marx to Lenin* Draper criticizes the tendency of certain late nineteenth-century socialists to associate the dictatorship of the proletariat with a specific governmental form, the unitary rule of the revolutionary party. Such an association transforms the concept of the dictatorship of the proletariat into the dictatorship of the party, even though for both Marx and Engels the former "meant nothing more and nothing less that 'rule of the proletariat' – the 'conquest of political power' by the working class, the establishment of a workers' state in the immediate postrevolutionary activity."[25]

However, it is precisely the unhinging of the concept from any substantive, which is not to say organizing, form, which opens up the possibility of a strictly instrumental interpretation of the concept. As Draper writes, "If 'dictatorship of the proletariat' referred strictly to the class content of a *state*, the governmental form might vary widely, without affecting this class content."[26] Indeed, it is no doubt the case that Marx's theorizations of the potential political form of the transitional governmental body varied widely across an axis marked on one end by a decentralized ward system of workers' councils, and on the other by a centralized state apparatus. We have already seen a manifestation of the former in *The Civil War in France*. The latter can be seen in, for example, Marx's and Engel's "Address of the Central Committee to the Communist League." Here, the party is seen as the necessary form of worker organization, the independence of workers requiring the elimination of decentralized local organization, easily corrupted by petty bourgeois elements, and the concentration of worker power into a central authority.[27] According to Marx, revolutionaries "must not allow themselves to be misguided by the democratic talk of freedom for the communities, of self-government, etc."[28] Indeed, "it must under no circumstances be permitted that every village, every town and every province should put a new obstacle in the path of revolutionary activity, which can proceed with full force only from the centre."[29] Precisely because successful revolutionary activity can proceed only from the centre, "it is the task of the really revolutionary party to carry through the strictest centralization."[30]

A critique of the instrumental dimension latent in Marx's thought was already launched in the latter's own day, it forming a part of the well-known social anarchist critique of Marxian political theory.[31] What is of the utmost significance in the present context, though, is that the existence of this dimension will be noted, noncritically, by Marcuse himself. Marcuse writes, "To Marx and Engels, precisely because the transition from capitalism to socialism was the historical function of the proletariat as a revolutionary class, the specific political *forms* of this transition appeared as variables which could not be fixed and established by theory."[32] The revolutionary method was not justified as · a consequence of its ability to function as a means to political objectification, but rather fluctuated greatly as a consequence of the indeterminacy of the historical field: "the ways and means for accomplishing its tasks were to be derived from the then prevailing political and economic situation."[33]

The nonconsideration of the political as a possible sphere for the manifestation of essence not only leads to the degradation of politics to the status of mere means, but also potentially eliminates it as a human mode of being after the realization of the desired end. We can again return to Draper, who will make a point of noting that "class dynamics is the foundation of *all* of Marx's politics."[34] But if class is defined in terms of a relation to the control over a surplus of production, and if the actualization of socialism is considered in terms of the abolition of exploitation, then the question that presents itself is this: is not politics itself eliminated in this movement? Although Marx and Engels do not believe that the political state functions exclusively as an ideological apparatus advancing the economic interests of the bourgeoisie, they do seem to believe that it is an embodiment of the multiple manifestations of class struggle. If the conflicts within and over the political state can nevertheless determine the conditions of historical development through the mis- and redirection of economic tendencies, the overcoming of the essential productive contradictions of society makes the state superfluous as a social institution. Engels will define the state as "a product of society at a certain stage of development; it is the admission that this society has become entangled in an insoluble contradiction with itself, that it is cleft into irreconcilable antagonisms which it is powerless to dispel."[35] The state is precisely the mechanism through which these class conflicts are expressed and moderated. The tendency, though by no means an inevitability, is for the economically dominant class to, through the mediation of the state, become also the politically dominant one, thus acquiring a "new means of holding down and exploiting the oppressed class."[36] The state, then, is not an eternal institution; its existence depends upon the presence of irreconcilable class division within a social formation. If the division of classes in a society is no longer a necessity, then neither is the state: "The society that will organize production on the basis of a free and equal association of the producers will put the whole machinery of state where it will then belong: into the Museum of Antiquities, by the side of the spinning wheel and the bronze axe."[37]

What is significant, though, is that Marx and Engels do not seem to distinguish between the political state as a particular form of public power and public power in general. They seem, in other words, to equate politics with the political state. After the end of class domination "(1) no governmental functions any longer exist."[38] But it is also clear that no public functions are to exist either; hence, "(2) the distribution of general functions takes on a *business character* and involves no domination."[39] Once class domination is eradicated there is no need for political interference in the realm of the social: "the government of persons is replaced by the administration of things, and by the conduct of processes of production."[40] Cornelius Castoriadis notes that such a revolutionary "transformation of social institutions … is hard to distinguish, ultimately, from the idea of the total suppression of all institutions."[41] Under such conditions "public functions will lose their political character and be transformed into the simple administrative functions of watching over the true interests of society."[42] Because political power is primarily just the ability of one class to oppress another, "the class identity between the subject and object of the state now tends to transform coercion into rational administration."[43] This image of the overcoming of the need for an institutionalized public sphere through the affirmation of a vast technoadministrative system has certainly been criticized enough by readers of Marx. Thus Jean Cohen, for example, writes that

> the image of a collectively planned, fully socialized society, instituted by the class representatives of the socialized productive forces, freed from the tyranny of private property, liberated from the fetishes of commodity and capital, in which the rationality of production no longer confronts the irrational barriers of capitalist valorization and in which the fully transparent organization of social and material life processes replaces their mystification, is simply a rationalist myth combined with a technocratic utopia.[44]

What is made much less explicit, however, is the relation of Marx's affirmation of the desirability of the administration of things to his understanding of essence. Thus, for Cohen the positing of the administration of things is a consequence of Marx's one-sided concern with distributive justice. It is quite obvious, though, that much more is involved in Marx's ontology of labour than the mere satisfaction of the needs of having. Marx is concerned with the affirmation of a specific mode of being that is characterized by free and spontaneous creation. For Marx, though, this creation is, *most of the time*, to be realized only in the sphere of material production. As Adorno writes, "The revolution desired by [Engels] and Marx was one of economic conditions in society as a whole, in the basic stratum of its self-preservation; it was not revolution as a change in society's political form, in the rules of the game of dominion."[45] Hence the ambiguity in Marx's political theory, and the potential for locating in it an antipolitical double-form: on the one hand, one can understand his politics as instrumental activity existing only within a means-end continuum;  on the other hand, one can see in his desire for the abolition of alienated labour, the actualization of the potential for creative expression in the production of use-values, the desire to overcome politics and public life. Marx often appears ignorant of the fact that even after the institution of true communism there will still be the need for public or political action. Not all conflict can be traced back to the productive process, as we already saw Marcuse note. Social conflicts will always continue to persist, over not only the typical Marxian concerns of what to produce, how to produce, how to distribute, and so on, but also over the meaning of normative understandings of the nature of need, the good, the right, and others. Indeed, adequate solutions to the former set of problems necessarily require consideration of the latter. What is more, these conflicts will not only express themselves in the relations between individuals and social groups in the present, but also over time. Precisely because the essential attribute of human subjectivity is creativity, the species is continually producing new values and norms. The function of politics is to work out and negotiate conflicts over these values and norms, and for this an administrative apparatus is wholly unsuitable. It is not at all clear, though, that a form of politics cannot be thought that performs this negotiation at the same time that it allows for the expression of essence. Indeed, such a possibility is on occasion recognized by Marx himself, even if not by his most notable followers.

## The Limits of Western Marxism

It must be stressed that the previous reading is only one *possibility* given by a certain *ambiguity* in Marx's thought. It was precisely this possibility, however, which was realized in various traditions of Marxism throughout the twentieth century, the theory and practice of Leninism being only the most well-known (and exaggerated) example.[46] In this section I would like to look in particular, however, at how certain of these relevant dynamics play themselves out in the thought of the most outstanding representatives of the first generation of Western Marxism: Karl Korsch and Georg Lukács. Such an analysis will be especially relevant given Marcuse's acknowledged philosophical debt to Western Marxism, in particular what Marcuse takes to be its rejection of mechanistic logics of development, its emphasis on subjectivity and mediation, and its stress on the relation between theory and practice. As Kellner notes, Marcuse believed that the Hegelian-Marxism of Korsch and Lukács represented the most theoretically advanced strain of Marxism, and thus most influenced his own reading of Marx's work. Kellner recounts in particular how Marcuse stated that "he believed that Korsch and Lukács represented the 'most authentic' current of Marxism."[47] I will begin, then, by outlining what Marcuse took to be the specific theoretical virtues of each of these theorists, before noting their ultimate failure to adequately theorize the nature of politics.

As Marcuse makes clear in his review of *Marxism and Philosophy*, Korsch's great contribution to Marxist thought was to treat the question of philosophy's specific location within revolutionary theory as a "genuine problem."[48] Korsch criticized the theorists of the Second International to the degree that they operated under the assumption "that Marxism as a theory and practice was in essence totally unalterable and involved no specific position on any philosophical questions whatever."[49] On the contrary, we must reject those understandings of Marxism that are framed in terms of "some abstract canon of 'pure and unfalsified' theory," seeing it instead in an *"historical, materialist, and dialectical perspective."*[50] The theoretical recognition of the contradiction between the forces and relations of production provides only the material precondition for revolutionary practice, which cannot be seen as stimulated simply by certain quasi-natural laws of historical development. Revolutionary change, rather, can only be achieved through "subjective, human-sensuous, practico-critical" activity.[51] Needless to say, Marcuse was highly impressed with Korsch's emphasis on the sensuous structure of human subjectivity and this subjectivity's receptiveness to philosophical contents, and with Korsch's recognition of the potential for philosophy to critically analyse the state of empirical reality and dialectically stimulate active modes that might sublate this reality. Nevertheless, Marcuse locates a certain tension in Korsch's work between the latter's stress on a philosophically informed praxis and a latent positivism that can be seen to permeate his thought. In Marcuse's own words, "Korsch's Marxism had a very strong positivistic content. And my friends in the Frankfurt School were against this positivistic content."[52] Where, however, does this content lie, and how does it relate to our specific question about the nature of politics?

Although it is true that Korsch criticizes Marxists who "believe that the question of 'scientific' method is solved once and for all in the empirical methods of the natural sciences and the corresponding positive-historical method of the social sciences," it is also true that these methods are seen as simply manifestations of the specifically bourgeois scientific method.[53] The materialist dialectic is not a bourgeois science because it "can only be applied *concretely* in the practice of the proletarian revolution and in a theory which is an immanent real component of this revolutionary practice."[54] Nevertheless, once it acquires its properly dialectical form, socialist practice can be transformed into a "strict 'science,'"[55] a strict science that is able to arrive at "*the real developmental laws* of the existing capitalist society."[56] The Marxian philosophy thus "includes from the point of view of the *object* an empirical investigation, 'conducted with the precision of natural science,' of all its relations and development."[57] This belief in the fundamentally scientific nature of Marxist theory, to the degree that theory is dialectically engaged with Marxist practice, will have significant consequences for Korsch's specifically political thought. As we will now see, although Marxism is not an abstract science in that it engages with the dialectical social totality as opposed to with isolated and autonomous spheres of knowledge, it nevertheless espouses a "scientific politics – a politics which describes causal connections."[58] To the degree to which Korsch considers politics to be attached to the question of historical causality, even if such a causality is not rooted in a necessary logic of development, it assumes the form of a technical activity. In his words, "the revolutionary proletariat cannot, in its practical fight, dispense with the distinction between *true* and *false* scientific propositions ... just as the *technician* in constructing an engine must have exact knowledge of at least some physical laws, so must the *proletariat* possess a sufficiently true knowledge in economic, political and other objective matters in order to carry the revolutionary class struggle to a successful consummation."[59] In the final instance, a Marxist politics is seen to be based upon "empirically verifiable knowledge, marked by 'all the precision of natural science.'"[60]

Korsch's reduction of political consideration to the application of technical principles grounded in empirical scientific observation is quite obviously antithetical to any sort of politics of creation. Indeed, given the former reduction, it is not surprising to find out that for Korsch politics contains no inherent value in itself worth preserving after its actualization of its scientific end, but is rather oriented toward its own indeterminate abolition. This may initially seem strange in light of Korsch's well-known engagement with the council tradition. While it is true that Korsch often speaks of the councils as potential media for the expression of worker autonomy, in the final instance their true value lay not in their political form, but rather in their merely social content. The system of councils is considered by him to be one element of a process of development, this process' specifically political manifestation, which actually aims at the elimination of the political, which is seemingly necessarily identified with state rule. According to Korsch, for example, Marx erred in stressing the *formal differences which distinguished the Paris Commune from parliamentarism and other surpassed forms of the bourgeois state constitution.*[61] For Korsch there is no political form that does not take the character of class rule, the council or communal form being no exception. Hence, "The essential *final goal* of proletarian class struggle is not any one *state*, however 'democratic,' communal,' or even 'council-like,' but is rather the stateless Communist *society* whose comprehensive *form* is not any longer some kind of political power but is *'that association in which the free development of every person is the condition for the free development of all' ('Communist Manifesto').*[62] The revolutionary goal is thus the production of a certain society, a society that is predicated on the end of the political. Although it is true that Korsch criticizes the bourgeois dialectic for terminating in "the great all-embracing synthesis" that is the liberal state,[63] he still considers the Marxian dialectic in terms of termination, this termination now just being represented in the dissolution of opposites that is realized in the production "of the classless Communist society."[64] His is thus still a positive dialectic, one realized, however, not in the actualization of a certain determinate political form, but rather in the overcoming of the very need for politics.

As with Korsch, Marcuse was highly appreciative of certain of the philosophical contributions made by Lukács to the theory and practice of Marxism, going so far as to write that the lack of recognition of such contributions constituted a "long-standing and gross injustice."[65] As Andrew Feenberg notes, the influence of Lukács on Marcuse can largely be found in the latter's account of technological rationality as a form of one-dimensionality: "In Marcuse's work the concept of 'technological' rationality takes over the functions of the earlier concept of reification as objective social appearance determining the very paradigm of rationality in the culture of capitalism. A straight path leads from Lukács' theory of reification to Marcuse's theory of 'one-dimensional' society."[66] Indeed, it can be speculated that it was Lukács's sensitivity to the modes of dehumanization resulting from the increasing quantification of social life that accompanies reification that led him to adopt, relative to Korsch, a much more critical understanding of the function of a universal science to any project of emancipation. Although Lukács still refers to historical materialism as a scientific method, unlike for Korsch this method is historically contextualized and nonuniversal. In the former's words, "the substantive truths of historical materialism are of the same type as were the truths of classical economics in Marx's view: they are truths within a particular social order and system of production."[67] Lukács's critique of universal science, furthermore, is accompanied by a constant emphasis on the historical emergence of new modes and forms of being, which is only a possibility to the degree that there does not exist an objective structure of the world whose component parts can be isolated, arranged, and mapped in a systematic way. Throughout *History and Class Consciousness* Lukács thus emphasizes the human potential for creation, birth, genesis, and so on. Historical materialism, for example, "proceeds from the assumption that the development of society constantly produces *new* phenomena, i.e. new in a qualitative sense."[68] The human being is thus apparently theorized in terms of its creative subjectivity: "Man must be able to comprehend the present as a becoming. He can do this by seeing in it the tendencies out of whose dialectical opposition he can *make* the future. Only when he does this will the present be a process of becoming, that belongs to *him*."[69] Although it may appear that Lukács is on the threshold of thinking the possibility of a politics of radical creation, he ultimately, like Hegel before him, situates human becoming within a quasi-theological logic that structures in advance historical time.

In the final instance Lukács's is not a true, or a radical, becoming, to the extent to which the appearance of the new can be logically traced back to identifiable forces within the existent: "The truth of becoming is the future that is to be created but has not yet been born ... it is the new that resides in the tendencies that (with our conscious aid) will be realized."[70] Even more explicitly, "the dialectics of history is objectively impelled."[71] Such dialectics need simply be actively recognized; the consciousness of the proletariat as the identical subject-object of history reveals the consciousness of the historical process as a self-contained totality: "The totality of history is itself a real historical power – even though one that has not hitherto become conscious and has therefore gone unrecognized."[72] The historical is thus theorized as a potentially transparent object, while the actualization of such transparency, furthermore, is identified as the "ultimate goal."[73] To comprehend this ultimate goal "is to recognize the direction taken (unconsciously) by events and tendencies towards the totality. It is to know the direction that determines concretely the correct course of action at any given moment – in terms of the interest of the total process, viz. the emancipation of the proletariat."[74] Indeed, it is precisely Lukács's understanding of class consciousness and its relation to objective history that Marcuse takes to be the major flaw in the former's dialectic: "this notion is (as the conception of class consciousness has been on the whole) a violation of the dimension of historicity, a fixation 'outside' of what happens from whence an artificially abstract connection with history must be produced."[75]

If Lukács's concept of class consciousness, though, does not allow him to theorize a philosophy of history genuinely open to creation and contingency, neither does it allow him to theorize a democratic politics. The proletariat is the class that is able to penetrate the core of society, able to comprehend this society's nature as a social whole. Such comprehension "lies in the ability to look beyond the divisive symptoms of the economic process to the unity of the total social system underlying it."[76] This ability, though, is not actualizable given the immediate psychological disposition of the proletariat. Lukács appropriates Marx's distinction between the class in itself and the class for itself, proclaiming that "class struggle must be raised from the level of economic necessity to the level of conscious aim and effective class consciousness."[77] It is precisely this gap between immediate and true consciousness that justifies the existence of the vanguard party, for the idea of "an 'organic,' *purely proletarian* revolution is an illusion."[78] Lukács elaborates most clearly on this illusion of a spontaneously generated proletarian subjectivity in his book on Lenin: "it would be a mechanistic application of Marxism, and therefore a totally unhistorical illusion, to conclude that a correct proletarian class-consciousness – adequate to the proletariat's leading role – can gradually develop on its own."[79] The Party, to the extent that its function is to impute proper historical understanding to the proletarian masses, comes to be seen as the objectification of the unconscious will of the proletariat, the *"bearer of the class consciousness of the proletariat and the conscience of its historical vocation."*[80] Thus not only is Lukács's understanding of political creation a false creation, to the extent that all emergences can be logically traced back to prior moments within the historical totality, but what is more, the subject of this creation is not the people themselves, who lack the ability to develop the specific consciousness required for informed action, but rather a vanguard of intellectual elites considered to be the objective manifestation of a unified collective will.

To conclude, both Korsch and Lukács are to be congratulated to the degree that they at least attempted to overturn the dominant socialist paradigm's marginalization of the political via the latter's subordination to the independent movement of objective economic laws. They both understood socialism as something that had to be produced via subjective political intervention. I have argued, though, that such political intervention cannot, for various reasons, be properly considered performative. It is not, in other words, able to affirm the nonidentitarian ethic that structures the Marcusean concept of essence. In the final instance both Korsch and Lukács, although to varying degrees and in varying modes, reproduce the Marxian political deficiency.

## Marcuse's Reproduction of the Marxian Antipolitics

Given the political deficits of Korsch and Lukács, Marcuse would, if he were to construct a nonidentitarian account of political action, make a serious contribution to the philosophy of Marxism. Upon first reading, however, it appears as though Marcuse for the most part replicates Marx's thinking on the nature of the political. The contradiction between essence and politics in Marcuse, though, will appear even more exaggerated to the extent that Marcuse much more than Marx recognizes the extent to which the perpetuation of social conflict is a historical necessity. There are, however, certain key distinctions to be made. Marcuse, for example, will challenge Marx's understanding of the nature of the revolutionary subject. In *Counter-revolution and Revolt* he notes that more segments of the population are becoming directly involved in processes of capitalist valorization through being separated from the means of production and compelled to sell their labour-power, including, for example, the "formerly independent" middle classes, service sector, and intelligentsia.[81] The extended scope of exploitation requires capitalism to increasingly attempt to organize society as a whole, primarily through the transformation of the entire individual into an instrument for the production of surplus value: "Capital now produces, for the majority of the population in the metropoles, not so much material privation as steered satisfaction of material needs, while making the entire human being – intelligence and senses – into an object of administration, agreed to produce and reproduce not only the goals but also the values and promises of the system."[82] The commodity-form is thus said to have reached its highest stage of generalization. Although there is the appearance of a hierarchy of position within the process of production that produces semblances of class tension, for example between high-tech technicians and low-wage manufacturing workers and between organized labour and a "subproletariat" of national and racialized minorities, these conflicts are only apparent to the extent that increasingly all individuals are coming to share a common objective position. All individuals are exploited to the extent that they all contribute to the reproduction of capital: "The extension of exploitation to a larger part of the population, accompanied by a higher standard of living, is the reality behind the façade of the *consumer society*; this reality is the unifying force which integrates, behind the back of individuals, the widely different and conflicting classes of the underlying population."[83] If the working class is to be considered the potentially revolutionary subject, it must be a greatly enlarged working class, one "which no longer corresponds directly to the Marxian proletariat."[84] In the final instance the classical Marxist concept of class needs to be revised for several reasons, such as the fact that the majority of the working class is no longer engaged in material production; the fact that large sectors of the working class are involved in unproductive labour; the fact that the quantity of white-collar workers, individuals who are separate from the means of production but who are nevertheless wage-labourers, has expanded; and the fact that class consciousness has fractured along multiple lines.[85] What all of these facts point to is the need for a new definition of the working class: "The structural changes in capitalism are accompanied by changes in the classes and in their situations. There is nothing more inadmissable and more dangerous for a Marxist than to employ a reified concept of the working class."[86] Although Marcuse himself is not willing to explicitly provide a new definition, he might very well agree with Guy Debord, for whom the proletariat is constituted by all those who have lost control of their lives.[87] Indeed, such a definition would seem particularly apt given Marcuse's understanding of essence as creative and autonomous action.

If the proletariat is not quite so narrowly conceived for Marcuse as it is for Marx, the fundamental question of the proletariat remains: that is, how are its members to come to an awareness of their objective situation, their noncontrol over their lives, their inability to act? For Marcuse the distinction between true and false consciousness is still meaningful.[88] All activism depends on theory to the extent that social transformation presupposes a necessary change in the nature of consciousness. The primary liberation is the liberation of the consciousness of individuals from what has been made of it in the present society. As for Lukács, though, this liberation cannot be spontaneous, for spontaneity would here only represent and express the logic of the status quo.[89] Education thus assumes a vitally important role: "Self-liberation is self-education but as such it *pre*supposes education by others."[90] There is an inevitable gap between the educators and those to be educated in a society characterized by unequal access to knowledge of reality, and hence "those who are educated have a commitment to use their knowledge to help men and women realize and enjoy their truly human capabilities."[91] For Marcuse education is impossible without leadership, whose function is to transform spontaneous protest into conscious and organized action. The educators who will shape consciousness in order to effect this movement constitute for Marcuse the new revolutionary subject.

Marcuse defines the revolutionary subject as "that class or group which, by virtue of its function and position in society, is in vital need and is capable of risking what they have and what they can get within the established system in order to replace this system – a radical change which would indeed involve destruction, abolition of the existing system."[92] Although Marcuse concedes that any social revolution is impossible without the participation of the working class, he argues that in the advanced capitalist countries the vast majority of the working class lacks the "vital need" for revolution. He here, again like Lukács, plays on the Marxian distinction between the class in itself and the class for itself. Although the working class is in itself the revolutionary subject, so long as it is the class that functions as the human base of the material process of production, it is not for itself revolutionary. To the extent that the majority of individuals who compose this class have been thoroughly integrated into the one-dimensional society, "they do not have the political and class consciousness which remains a decisive force in the revolutionary process."[93] The vital need for changes comes, according to Marcuse, from a drastically narrower group, specifically, "those groups whose consciousness and needs are not yet integrated into the system of domination, and who, by virtue of this fact, are capable and willing to develop a radical consciousness."[94] These groups are thus the de facto revolutionary subjects, for only they are "free for the radical transvaluation of values."[95] Throughout his life Marcuse would identify a number of potential revolutionary subjects, for example, critical academics, the student intelligentsia, racialized groups, and more. Although the groups identified as being potentially able to function as the revolutionary subject may have varied, the fundamental principle was always the same. Joan Alway notes that "as much as Marcuse objects to a dogmatic and fetishistic identification of the working class with the revolutionary subject, he himself never fully severs this connection."[96] Marcuse never abandoned the search for the revolutionary subject, looking for it in "non-integrated outsiders or minorities, students and intellectuals, a 'new sensibility,' 'catalyst groups,' and in Rudolf Bahro's concept of 'surplus consciousness.'"[97] The fact that Marcuse was constantly searching for the agents of revolutionary change demonstrates the extent to which he was still caught up in the Leninist paradigm. Indeed, the latent Leninism in Marcuse's position was even explicitly noted by Marcuse himself, when he suggested that capitalism's integration of the proletariat was a confirmation of the theory and practice of Lenin: "The development has confirmed the correctness of the Leninist conception of the vanguard party as the subject of the revolution."[98] What has changed since Lenin's time is just the nature of this revolutionary subject.

Probably Marcuse's most detailed elaboration on the nature of the revolutionary subject and its privileged position is to be found in his reflections on the work of Rudolf Bahro. Marcuse calls Bahro's *The Alternative in Eastern Europe* "the most important contribution to Marxist theory and practice to appear in several decades."[99] The importance of this contribution is largely to be found in the fact that Bahro does not simply cling dogmatically to historically outdated Marxist concepts – like class, for example – but develops concepts in accordance with the concretely shifting realities of late capitalism. In particular, Bahro advances past the belief in the objective necessity of the laws of Marxist political economy to a subjective understanding of consciousness "as a potential material force for radical change," thus regrasping a certain essential content from idealism.[100] The transformed nature of class is of central importance to the generation of this material consciousness. Marcuse notes that in *The Theories of Surplus Value* Marx himself predicts that the growing productivity of labour will be accompanied by an increase in the forms of tertiary nonmaterial production: "They form an ever more essential base of capitalist reproduction in the realization and, we can add today, in the creation of surplus value."[101] According to Marcuse, as a consequence of this increasing intellectualization of labour, combined with the increasing mechanization of labour in the sphere of material production, there develops in advanced capitalism a greatly expanded quantity of general human capacities and abilities. These capacities and abilities, though, cannot be fully developed within a capitalist mode of production since such an actualization would contradict the need for permanent alienated labour. They are thus channelled into unnecessary work, "unnecessary in that it is not required for the construction and preservation of a better society, but is necessitated only by the requirements of capitalist production."[102] As a consequence of these conditions there develops a form of consciousness that becomes increasingly aware of the meaninglessness of the ever less productive organization of labour; this form is what Bahro calls "surplus consciousness."[103]

Surplus consciousness "designates a quality of the mental energy expressed in the actual behaviour of men and women under the impact of late capitalism. This energy is 'surplus' over and above the energy spent daily in the alienated performances required by the established production relations."[104] It is specifically "the growing quantity of free psychological energy which is no longer tied up in necessary labour and hierarchical knowledge."[105] To the extent that surplus consciousness is a consciousness of the meaninglessness of the surplus repressive organization of labour, it is a consciousness "of frustration, humiliation, and waste."[106] Prior to the diversion of labour into unnecessary and nonmaterial tasks and performances, the individual could at least achieve a partial satisfaction through the recognition that her labour was productive, a recognition, however dim as a consequence of the fact of alienated labour, that she in some way contributed to society's reproduction. Increasingly, though, individuals perceive the futility and pointlessness of their work. Their being denied an even alienated material production produces within them an inarticulate demand for the satisfaction of the needs of self-determination. Although the production of the demand for autonomy is most definitely an emancipatory interest, however, surplus consciousness contains also certain compensatory interests. These mainly take the form of demands for the material satisfaction of desire, and although these are still manifestations of the psychological desire for happiness and gratification, they are compensatory to the extent that they can be theoretically satisfied within the context of the present society.[107] For Marcuse these two types of interest coexist within surplus consciousness in a contradictory unity of opposites. If the partiality of the compensatory interests is to be recognized and the emancipatory interests are to be made fully articulate, then one must presuppose the activity of a revolutionary subject.

The dependant population's inarticulate sense of surplus consciousness becomes a concrete awareness in the knowledge of certain "catalyst groups," for example the student movement, the women's liberation movement, scientists, and more. According to Marcuse, any time the majority of the working class are integrated into the system of one-dimensionality, politics must take on an elitist form in which an intellectual vanguard stand in for those who are not capable of fully perceiving their interest. Specifically, a revolutionary consciousness "would have to emerge among those social classes which assume an increasingly vital role in the process of production, namely, the cadres of technical and scientific intelligentsia, who in turn would activate the consciousness of the traditional working classes."[108] The intelligentsia will in particular assume a fundamental role within the intellectual vanguard for two reasons. First, "more than ever before, knowledge is power."[109] Specifically, knowledge of those tendencies that are necessary for the reproduction of the social formation gives those who have this knowledge additional information regarding how the social formation could be changed. Second, "for the intelligentsia, the realization of their compensatory interests is no longer a matter of daily concern."[110] The overcoming of the need to struggle for physical existence frees up energies that can be redirected to nonmaterial interests and concerns. The privilege of higher education, for example, allows intellectuals in their very work activity access to information regarding new possibilities of existence. The articulation of new social values always precedes structural changes in class relations and productive organization, this fact confirming the potentially central role of the intelligentsia in stimulating social change.[111] Overall, "the privilege of education, the result of the separation between intellectual and manual labour, isolates the intelligentsia from the masses. However, this has also given it the opportunity to think freely, to learn, to understand the facts in their social context, and – to transmit this knowledge."[112] This transmission of knowledge, though, does not take the form of any mode of education that could be justly called a critical democratic pedagogy.

Perhaps not surprisingly given what has been said thus far, Bahro will end up advocating the perpetuation of the hierarchical state (although he refers to it as the state as antistate), reorganized such as to maximize the authority of the vanguard catalyst groups who are to educate the masses:

> He envisages a democratically constituted and controlled hierarchy from the base to the top. At the summit, this hierarchy becomes a dual power: the communist party and a "league of communists." The latter would be independent of the party, recruited from those members of the intelligentsia in all strata of society whose consciousness is most advanced. This league is the brain of the whole: a democratic elite, with a decisive voice in the discussion of plans, education, the redistribution of work, etc.[113]

Marcuse explicitly retreats from his earlier position in *Eros and Civilization* regarding the obsolescence of the idea of the educational dictatorship,[114] maintaining now that we must learn from both Plato and Rousseau: from Plato we must take the recognition of the necessity of the educational dictatorship of those who are as a consequence of their nature and education capable of perceiving the truth, and from Rousseau we must take the recognition that individuals themselves have been so integrated into bourgeois society that they lack the capacity to spontaneously and rationally will the general. The recuperation of emancipatory interest cannot be achieved by dependent subaltern consciousness, but only by an exalted minority, which must force all others to be free.[115]

## Administration as Domination and Liberation

It would be difficult for Marcuse to justify his recourse to such a politics if the latter were not considered by him only within an instrumental framework. Indeed, in a short essay titled "Ethics and Revolution" Marcuse makes explicit the connection between instrumentality and vanguardism, maintaining the necessity of both to revolutionary politics. Here politics is considered as historical action determined by rational calculation, justified to the extent that the desired ends outweigh the repressive means. Indeed, the fundamental ethical problem of revolution is taken to be the means-end relation. The increasing potential to separate means from ends is here, in the sphere of politics, considered to be the very marker of rationality: "The possibilities and contents of freedom today are coming more and more under the control of men: they are becoming increasingly calculable. And with this advance in effective control and calculability, the inhuman distinction between violence and violence, sacrifice and sacrifice becomes increasingly rational."[116] In particular, the more computable historical action has become, the more justified is vanguardism: "It seems to me characteristic that, the more calculable and controllable the technical apparatus of modern industrial society becomes, the more does the chance of human progress depend upon the intellectual and moral qualities of the leaders, and on their willingness and ability to educate the controlled population and to make it recognize the possibility, nay, the necessity of pacification and humanization."[117] This passage is significant not only to the extent that Marcuse quite clearly demonstrates his political instrumentalism, but also to the extent that he tacitly concedes that political determinations, determinations regarding the content and direction of historical action, become all the more historically effective the greater they are determinable by a "technical apparatus." Marcuse not only reproduces the first element of Marx's antipolitical thought – his thinking of politics within a means-end continuum – but also his second – his advocacy of the administration of things as a replacement for political negotiation.

Marcuse's advocacy of political managerialism is especially curious given his production of one of the twentieth century's most acute critiques of administrative authority, most famously expressed in *One-Dimensional Man*. Even here, however, Marcuse is quick to qualify his criticism of technoadministrative authority: "To be sure, a mature and free industrial society would continue to depend on a division of labour which involves inequality of functions. Such inequality is necessitated by genuine social needs, technical requirements, and the physical and mental differences among the individuals."[118] On its own, this appears as a relatively innocuous and banal claim; few would suppose that in a non–surplus repressive society individuals would be rendered so identical as to be able to generate a universal exchangeability of function. Marcuse, though, will go on to maintain that deliberations regarding social function and other collective life-considerations are best determined through the exercise of a technical apparatus. Marcuse agrees with Marx on the permanent need for functional-administrative authority: "There is a kind of authority which is inseparably linked with all 'organization,' a kind of subordination, based on functional-rational assumptions, to genuine management and performance – labour discipline. Such functional authority is necessary in every social organization as a condition of production; it will play an important role in a future society."[119] This authority will be exercised through the administration of things, which is differentiated from bureaucracy, one of its apparent forms: "The term 'bureaucracy' covers (as does the term 'administration') very different and even conflicting realities: the bureaucracy of domination and exploitation is quite another than that of the 'administration of things,' planfully directed toward the development and satisfaction of vital individual needs. In the advanced industrial societies, the administration of things still proceeds under the bureaucracy of domination."[120] There is no evidence, though, that Marcuse distinguishes the content of the administration of things from that of bureaucracy – the organizational schematic is simply transferred over into the future society and is distinguished from its predecessor only to the extent that it is not exercised in the service of domination. The structure of the activity, the nature of the administrative techniques, remains the same. Marcuse can thus write that "capitalism, no matter how mathematized and 'scientific,' remains the mathematized, technological *domination* of men; and socialism, no matter how scientific and technological, is the construction or demolition of domination."[121]

For Marcuse any new social order will have to rely on a high degree of technical authority carried over from the surplus repressive society: "The historical heritage of the performance principle is administration, not of men, but of things: mature civilization depends for its functioning on a multitude of coordinated arrangements. These arrangements in turn must carry recognized and recognizable authority."[122] Following Engels' line in "On Authority,"[123] Marcuse distinguishes between rational authority and domination: "Hierarchical relationships are not unfree *per se*; civilization relies to a great extent on rational authority, based on knowledge and necessity, and aiming at the protection and preservation of life. Such is the authority of the engineer, of the traffic policeman, of the airplane pilot in flight. Once again, the distinction between repression and surplus-repression must be recalled."[124] Although Marcuse is certainly right to call attention to the meaningfulness of this distinction, he greatly exaggerates the extent to which basic repression in a free society must be understood as administration. Authority must not be reduced to the mechanical enforcement of administratively derived laws and decrees. The need for political negotiation will always be a fact of human life, to determine, for example, the nature of the authority's power, which is not static but dependent on a whole host of historical and social variables. In the case of the police officer, then, there will remain always the need for a constant interaction and dialogue between the institutions of the police apparatus and, for example, various civic groups and local communities, which will reshape and redesign the meaning, content, and form of the authority. An administrative apparatus can take the place of such political debate only where potential political subjects are seen as being conscious of their fundamental identity of interest, that is, when the existence of a privileged historical actor or revolutionary subject is presupposed. The discarding of the assumption of this privilege will necessarily render politics an essentiality to the extent that the former will free up as politically relevant a multiplicity of diverse agents with diverse interests. Under such conditions authority cannot be considered as simply administration, "a multitude of coordinated arrangements." In short, formulations such as these seem to sharply contradict Marcuse's recognition of the inevitability of social division and difference, even in an emancipated society. Marcuse here seems unable to think the potential for constructing a form of institutionalization which is able to mediate such division without the use of instruments of domination. He thus ends up positing the possibility of reducing all human subjects to an identical generic content, thus rendering them fit objects of control by something like an administration of things.

Marcuse is unfortunately not the only Marxist thinker to fetishize technical administration. Jeremy Shapiro will identify the latter as a perpetually reoccurring element of socialist thought. Bourgeois political theory negated the classical concern, originating with the Greeks, with judgment in politics through its positing of a system of technical institutions capable of discerning justice independently of the actions of individuals. This bourgeois tendency, perhaps as a consequence of the articulation of modern socialist theory in a historical era characterized by the preoccupation with scientism, has carried over into socialist political thinking: "Socialism is supposed to replace an existing, technically imperfect system (the anarchy of socialized production) with a technically perfect system (socialism), and the political theory for effecting the change is itself often regarded as a technical doctrine, containing its criteria of application and accordingly not requiring individual experience and decision."[125] The individual is in this way divested of the capacity for spontaneous action, at least in the sphere of the political, and consequently also of judgment and ethical responsibility.

If we are to accept Marcuse's suggestion that the actualization of socialism implies the liberation of the human being in all those human worlds within which she acts, that is, the realization of essence in the plurality of her activities, then the practice of politics itself must be understood as being potentially able to function as an intrinsically gratifying activity that allows individuals to express those capacities and faculties that look toward the overcoming of the permanent discrepancy between potentiality and actuality, that look toward the overcoming of subjective and objective reality. Marcuse's acceptance of the double-form of Marx's antipolitical thought – his affirmation of an instrumental vanguardism and a political functionalism – would thus seem to contradict in a fundamental way, to the extent that he recognizes the permanence of social conflict, his revolutionary project. Marcuse does not provide us with a political theory capable of affirming or corresponding to his theory of subjectivity. Richard Bernstein would seem to criticize Marcuse along similar line when he critiques the latter for not sketching, however tentatively, the nature of those political or social institutions that would realize the desired convergence of reason and happiness: "If we are to take seriously (or even playfully) the suggestion that the qualitative difference between 'socialist society as a free society and the existing society' is to be found in the 'aesthetic-erotic dimension' then we must not only comprehend what we are talking about, but ask ourselves what type of social institutions in a 'post-industrial' world can embody such a 'rationality of gratification.'"[126] The problem is how to realize potentiality in a plural world. In Bernstein's words, "What always seems to be missing in Marcuse is not 'Man' or 'human potentialities,' but *men* – or better, human beings in their plurality who only *achieve* their humanity in and through each other."[127] Bernstein will ultimately see the solution to this problem in a Habermasian approach, and thus stresses the necessity of a dialogical and communicative understanding of practical rationality influenced by pragmatism. It is difficult to see, though, how the advocacy of a form of specifically liberal institutionalization, which Habermas's affirmation of communicative rationality necessarily demands, could ultimately be reconciled with Marcuse's revolutionary Marxism. Bernstein himself, however, seems to allude to another of Marcuse's contemporaries who is potentially capable of assisting us in thinking through the central contradiction. When he refers to the distinction between a thought looking toward "Man" and a thought looking toward "men," it is difficult not to recall another of the preeminent twentieth-century theorists of revolution – Hannah Arendt. Although Arendt's utter hostility to the tradition of revolutionary Marxism may immediately suggest the reproduction of an essential noncorrespondence with Marcuse, an investigation of her political thought will in fact reveal that she comes extremely close to affirming the type of creative nonidentitarian politics that Marcuse's theory of essence demands. The next chapter will thus attempt just such an investigation.

# 4 Hannah Arendt's Theory of Public Freedom

Like Marcuse, Arendt was wary about deploying terms such as ontology and essence in theoretical discussions. She was always adamant, for example, that her political theory could not be traced back to some foundational affirmation of the basic principles of human nature. In *The Human Condition* she maintains that it is impossible to posit a human nature if for no other reason than the simple fact that human existence is always conditioned, that whatever enters the human world is assimilated into the human condition and acts back upon the human being, altering the latter's basic structure.[1] At the same time, though, the fact that we are not conditioned absolutely means that human nature can neither be discerned through an analysis of those objects that condition us.[2] The objects of Arendt's critique here, however, are clearly those ahistorical models of human nature that Marcuse attempted to discredit in "The Concept of Essence." The deciphering of human nature is considered by Arendt an impossibility only to the extent that the human condition is constantly in flux, to the extent that it is impossible for the subjects and objects of the historical world to assume a static and transhistorical constitution. We have already seen with respect to Marcuse, though, that ontology cannot be reduced to those theoretical practices that attempt to analytically abstract from diverse social and historical conditions sets of identifiable properties or contents that are understood as being valid regardless of the spatial or temporal variations of the human environments considered. If Arendt clearly recognizes the inadequacy of such positive ontologies, she just as clearly will end up affirming a negative ontology that attempts to come to grips with the historical instability of the human condition. This negative ontology will be rooted in an understanding of the basic human fact of natality, the recognition that what all human beings potentially share is the capacity to initiate beginnings, to interrupt causal chains through the creation of the radically new. Just as for Marcuse, then, the human essence has no positive content. What is taken to be the content of human nature is thoroughly historical, shaped by the social and political institutions of the human community. In this chapter I will attempt to trace the philosophical assumptions structuring Arendt's account of human natality, certain uniquely political manifestations of the human capacity to begin, and that mode of institutionalization that Arendt considers to be most appropriate for political creation in the period of late modernity: the council system. The ultimate suggestion will be that Arendt's political ontology can be read as affirming the negative model of essence posited by Marcuse, giving the latter a specifically civic mode of expression.

### Performativity and Essence: The Need for Radical Creation

Arendt's political ontology rests first of all on the recognition of the multiplicity – or what Marcuse might call the nonidentity – of appearance that characterizes life on earth. We are born into a world of many things that present themselves to us in the form of appearances, and that we appropriate in a plurality of sensuous ways. To appear means to appear for something, and it is in this appearing for something that is found the basic fact of the world: "Nothing, that is, insofar as it appears, exists in the singular; everything that is is meant to be perceived by somebody. Not Man but men inhabit this planet. Plurality is the law of the earth."[3] Beings are meant to appear, but they appear to others as beings who are themselves appearances. It is for this reason that spectators are never mere subjects; every subject, as an appearance, is also an object: "Living beings, men and animals, are not just in the world, they are *of the world*, and this precisely because they are subjects and objects – perceiving and being perceived – at the same time."[4] The world in this way functions as a type of stage upon which beings appear or show themselves to observing spectators. Following the biozoological work of Adolf Portmann, Arendt affirms an innate impulse present in all living organisms toward self-display: "*whatever can see wants to be seen, whatever can hear calls out to be heard, whatever can touch presents itself to be touched*. It is indeed as though everything that is alive … has an *urge to appear*, to fit itself into the world of appearances by displaying and showing, not its 'inner self' but itself as an individual."[5] This organic or biological urge to self-display achieves its highest form of expression in the human species, which is claimed to be unique to the extent that its members share not only the capacity to display themselves, but also the desire to appear in a particular way and the ability to actively attempt to do so. Self-presentation is thus differentiated from self-display "by the active and conscious choice of the image shown; self-display has no choice but to show whatever properties a living being possesses."[6] What make possible the capacity for self-presentation, the active attempt to formulate a specific appearance, are speech and action.

In *The Human Condition* Arendt distinguishes between otherness, which marks the relations between all inorganic beings, and distinctness, which marks the relations between all organic beings.[7] Human beings in their relations, though, will move beyond even distinctness to the extent that they possess the capacity for self-preservation as well as the capacity for self-display, to the extent that they are able to distinguish themselves from one another through speech and action: "In man, otherness, which he shares with everything that is, and distinctness, which he shares with everything alive, becomes uniqueness, and human plurality is the paradoxical plurality of unique beings."[8] Human plurality is a paradoxical plurality to the extent that in their utter uniqueness human beings reveal themselves to be the same, not necessarily with respect to the possession of certain properties, but with respect to a certain ontological capacity to express uniqueness: "Plurality is the condition of human action because we are all the same, that is, human, in such a way that nobody is ever the same as anyone else who ever lived, lives, or will live."[9] In order to distinguish ourselves, to manifest our uniqueness, we must appear in the world, and this appearing in the world always rests on initiative. According to Arendt, a life in which an individual no longer initiates speech and action for the purposes of appearance and hence differentiation is no longer a properly human life.[10] But what exactly does it mean to initiate? For Arendt to initiate is above all to begin something, "to set something in motion."[11]

To initiate is not only to bring into existence something that had not an existence before, but to bring into existence something whose present existence cannot be traced back to any prior determinations that constitute moments of a causal sequence, culminating in the logical appearance of the new thing. To initiate is thus not just to create the new but to create the radically new: "It is in the nature of beginning that something new is started which cannot be expected from whatever may have happened before. This character of startling unexpectedness is inherent in all beginnings and in all origins."[12] It is precisely because the radically new in this way springs up from what appears to be nothing at all that it seems miraculous. Evaluated in the context of the perceived processes that predictably govern the movement of human life, all beginnings appear as miracles, which are defined as just "interruptions of some natural series of events, of some automatic process, in whose context they constitute the wholly unexpected."[13] What is obscured by the fact that in the surplus repressive society individuals are so consistently blocked from acting is the fact that so-called miraculousness is in fact the essence of all human action. It is the function "of all action, as distinguished from mere behaviour, to interrupt what otherwise would have proceeded automatically and therefore predictably."[14] When considered without an understanding that the human being's essence is that of an actor and beginner, such actions seem as miraculous as those events of physical history that contributed to the creation of the human species itself: "whenever something new occurs, it bursts into the context of predictable processes as something unexpected, unpredictable, and ultimately causally inexplicable – just like a miracle. In other words every new beginning is by nature a miracle when seen from the standpoint of the processes it necessarily interrupts."[15] What distinguishes, though, "the 'infinite' improbabilities on which the reality of our earthly life rests and the miraculous character inherent in those events which establish historical reality is that, in the realm of human affairs, we know the author of the 'miracles'. It is men who perform them – men who because they have received the twofold gift of freedom and action can establish a reality of their own."[16]

The production of the miraculous, the initiation of the radically new, is valued by Arendt not as a consequence of a singular consideration of the specific objects brought into existence, but rather because of the intrinsic nature of the activity itself. The nature of action is to "break through the commonly accepted and reach into the extraordinary, where whatever is true in common and everyday life no longer applies because everything that exists is unique and *sui generis*."[17] It is because of this that action can only be judged according to the standard of greatness. The greatness of human action lies not specifically in the action's motivation or end, but rather in the very performance of the deed.[18] Action for Arendt is essentially performative; the highest good is to act, to confirm one's uniqueness via the calling forth of the new. Although it would be Machiavelli who would develop the most systematic account of the performative dimensions of human political action through his explication of the nature of *virtù*,[19] Arendt sees the origins of performativity in Aristotle's understanding of *praxis* as a form of *energeia*.[20]

Dana Villa points out that the importance of Aristotle's *praxis-poiesis* distinction for Arendt lay in the fact that "it reminds us that action and plurality have intrinsic value; that *freedom resides in the self-containedness of action*. It is only by deploying the distinction between *praxis* and *poiesis* in its original, rigorous, and hierarchical form that action's unique capacity to create meaning and to express plurality can be brought to light and the 'gap' between public and private, the free and the unfree, can be revealed once again."[21] Villa notes, though, that Aristotle will ultimately reduce *praxis* to *poiesis* to the extent that action is in the last instance seen as a means to the development of a virtuous character and the realization or achievement of happiness. Aristotle will universalize instrumentalism to the extent that all phenomena are understood to exist in a causal continuum with a clear *telos*: "The result is a context in which the only thing that deserves to be called self-sufficient is the final product or goal (*eudaimonia*, the just *polis*). It is no exaggeration to state that, within the Aristotelian framework, *praxis* is ultimately subsumed by *poiesis*."[22] Arendt's theory of action will represent a radical affirmation of human freedom and performativity to the extent that it attempts to overcome all teleological frameworks, Aristotle's included.

Arendt's emphasis on the performative dimension of action leads her to recharacterize the latter in aesthetic terms, as an art, not of making, but of performing. Indeed, Arendt points to the theatre as the most political of all aesthetic forms, as through it the political realm of human beings is transposed into art, into an intrinsically desirable creative expression:

> The specific revelatory quality of action and speech, the implicit manifestation of the agent and speaker, is so indissolubly tied to the living flux of acting and speaking that it can be represented and "reified" only through a kind of repetition, the imitation or *mimesis*, which according to Aristotle prevails in all arts but is actually appropriate only to the *drama*, whose very name (from the Greek verb *dran*, 'to act') indicates that playmaking actually is an imitation of acting.[23]

Arendt's aestheticization of human action has often been criticized for necessarily implying a degradation of the normative dimensions of action, for excluding all ethical, religious, instrumental, economic, and rational considerations.[24] Arendt's position, though, was never to deny the existence of extrinsic or instrumental values that enter considerations regarding the initiation of action. What she did deny was that political considerations could be revealed in their essence to be reducible to the language and logic of means and ends, if for no other reason that for "as long as we believe that we deal with ends and means in the political realm, we shall not be able to prevent anybody's using all means to pursue recognized ends."[25] James T. Knauer, in an early account of the strategic and normative elements of Arendt's thought, suggests that if the latter emphasizes expressivity and performativity in her account of action, it is precisely because these qualities have been completely left out of almost all accounts of the nature of action in the history of political philosophy. "What she did was to choose language, focus, and emphasis as part of an effort to act against history. Why should she emphasize the instrumental aspect of politics when her aim was to overcome its instrumentalization and trivialization? Why should she elaborate the strategic aspects of politics when her goal was to recommend politics as an activity transcending the mere struggle for power?"[26] Building upon her tripartite structural division of the *vita activa*, Douglas Torgerson extracts from Arendt a three-dimensional model of politics, with each level corresponding to one of the moments of the active life. Corresponding to labour is functional politics, which "deals with the operations of a socio-economic system, especially in its interchange with non-human nature."[27] Corresponding to work is constitutive politics, which "deals with constructing or changing a civilization as a cultural artifice, from the shape of its institutions to the identities of its inhabitants and the character of their discourse."[28] Functional and constitutive modes of political activity represent the instrumental side of politics, whereas a performative politics, which corresponds to action, is seen as essentially noninstrumental. Performative politics, though, are not isolated from these other two instrumental dimensions: "Arendt's performative politics clearly presuppose functional and constitutive outcomes. In functional terms, there clearly must be some provision for human needs. In constitutive terms, performance depends on a human artifice, a cultural space of institutions and identities that allows for political action."[29] The relevant question is whether a specific form of politics can be seen as being not only functional or constitutive but performative as well? In the case of Marcuse's politics the answer would seem to be no, and this noninclusion must necessarily degrade the activity into a nonpolitical form. Again in Torgerson's words, without a celebration of the intrinsic value of politics, neither functional nor constitutive political activity has any apparent rationale for continuing once its ends have been achieved. Functional politics might well be replaced by a technocratic management of advanced industrial society. A constitutive politics intent on social transformation might well be eclipsed by the coordinated direction of a cohesive social movement. In neither case would any need be left for what Arendt takes to be the essence of politics: there would be no need for debate.[30]

For Arendt genuine freedom lies in the ability to bring into existence something that did not exist prior, "not even as an object of cognition or imagination, and which therefore, strictly speaking, could not be known."[31] What Arendt desires to show is just that free action is not *determined absolutely* by either motive or goal. Needless to say, this does not mean "that motives and aims are not important factors in every single act, but they are its determining factors, and action is free to the extent that it is able to transcend them."[32] For Arendt ends are not identical with goals. Political actions must preserve goals, which "are never anything more than the guidelines and directives by which we orient ourselves and which, as such, are never cast in stone, but whose concrete realizations are constantly changing because we are dealing with other people who also have goals."[33] Politics disappears precisely where goals are thought of as ends, "which are as firmly defined as the model on which any physical object is produced and like it determine the choice of means and justify or even sanctify them."[34] Nothing is more hostile to performativity and action than this transmutation of goals into ends. Indeed, Arendt writes that

> democratic society as a living reality is threatened at the very moment that democracy becomes a "cause," because then actions are likely to be judged and opinions evaluated in terms of ultimate ends and not on their inherent merits. The democratic way of life can be threatened only by people who see everything as a means to an end, i.e., in some necessary chain of motives and consequences, and who are prone to judge actions "objectively," independent of the conscious motives of the doer, or to deduce certain consequences from opinions of which the holder is unaware.[35]

Both goals and ends are different than meaning, which is intrinsic to the activity itself and which does not survive the completion of the latter.[36] And finally, the last element of every political action is the principle for which it is undertaken or launched: "Principles do no operate from within the self as motives do ... but inspire, as it were, from without; and they are much to general to prescribe particular goals, although every particular aim can be judged in the light of its principle once the act has been started."[37] Following Montesquieu, Arendt lists as examples of principles the love of honour, glory, and equality.[38] Freedom appears when people act in accordance with a principle, when they act in the effort to realize a principle, creating something new in the effort to actualize it. For Arendt the capacity for action, to bring about something radically new, is an ontological condition embedded in every human being by nothing other than the fact of their being born into the world. Something radically new can be brought forward only because each person is a unique being, because each birth brings into the world someone completely new: "The miracle of freedom is inherent in this ability to make a beginning, which itself is inherent in the fact that every human being, simply by being born into a world that was there before him and will be there after him, is itself a beginning."[39] Human natality is initially revealed through the consideration of the physical birth of the new human being, through which the power to begin arises. Arendt traces this insight into the significance of birth for the exercise of freedom to Augustine: "In the birth of each man this initial beginning is reaffirmed, because in each instance something new comes into an already existing world which will continue to exist after each individual's death. Because he *is* a beginning, man can begin; to be human and to be free are one and the same. God created man in order to introduce into the world the faculty of beginning: freedom."[40] Clearly, though, other forms of biological life also partake in the physical process of birth. Again, what distinguishes these births from human births is that the latter produce beings with the capacity for not just self-display but self-presentation. Human birth represents the production of a radical newness to the extent that it brings into existence beings with the capacity to distinguish themselves from one another through speech.

> If the creation of man coincides with the creation of a beginning in the universe (and what else does this mean but the creation of freedom?), then the birth of individual men, being new beginnings, re-affirms the *original* character of man in such a way that origin can never become entirely a thing of the past; the very fact of the memorable continuity of these beginnings in the sequence of generations guarantees a history which can never end because it is the history of beings whose essence is beginning.[41]

Just as it was for Marcuse, then, the human being is thus that being whose essence it is to begin or create.

Despite sharing the general capacity to initiate activities that upset automatic processes, all individuals are radically unique to the extent that they possess speech: "if action as beginning corresponds to the fact of birth, if it is the actualization of the human condition of natality, then speech corresponds to the fact of distinctness and is the actualization of the human condition of plurality, that is, of living as a distinct and unique being among equals."[42] Only a unique subject can initiate unique actions, and the subject reveals it uniqueness through the production of individualized significations. "In acting and speaking, men show who they are, reveal actively their appearance in the human world."[43] Such revelation, though, does not take the form of the presentation of fixed identifiable markers that outline the complete structure of the subject. The subject does not reveal herself as a "what," but as a "who," and to be a "who" is to be no more than a being with the ontological potential to initiate beginnings. Action is not the expression of an identical and previously constituted self that exists before the initiation of speech. The revelation of such a self would be no more than the revelation of a "what." The self considered as a "who" constitutes itself through its action, for "prior to or apart from action, this self has no identity; it is fragmented, discontinuous, indistinct, and most certainly uninteresting."[44] In transcending its "what" character in the creation of itself through the production of unique significations the subject reveals itself to be one in a constant state of becoming. Indeed, it is precisely for this reason that for Arendt we can only really know someone after he or she is dead, for it is only here that the subject ceases its movement and presents itself as an object capable of being grasped in its completeness.[45]

## The Subject of Radical Creation: Politics and the We

The potential for the production of radical beginnings is dependent not only on the existence of an incomplete and plural self, but also on this incomplete and plural self's intersubjective relations with other human subjects. Because the uniqueness of the subject is revealed in the subject's self-presentation in the world of appearance, and because appearance always demands spectators, revelation always "implies an at least potential recognition and acknowledgement."[46] The theatricality of action is once again invoked: "The theater is the political act par excellence; only there is the political sphere of human life transposed into art. By the same token, it is the only art whose sole subject is man in his relationship to others."[47] The political realm is that in which freedom is actualized, in which individuals can display their virtuosity through acting: "performing artists – dancers, play-actors, musicians, and the like – need an audience to show their virtuosity, just as acting men need the presence of others before whom they can appear; both need a publicly organized space for their 'work,' and both depend upon others for the performance itself."[48] In no way, however, can this performative recognition be reduced to a process of thematization, precisely because of the indeterminate nature of the significations produced by the subject through speech. Again, the subject does not have the capacity for complete self-presentation. If we as subjects are incapable of presenting the totality of ourselves, others are incapable of grasping us as totalities through the consideration of that which we present to them. Speech aims not at the presentation of a "what"-content, but rather at the revelation of a "who"-capacity. The actor has to be disclosed as the one who is attached to the act, for unless the agent is revealed as being behind the act, the action loses its specificity and becomes merely instrumental. Here human togetherness, the necessary precondition for mutual acknowledgment through signification, is not recognized, and speech is degraded to "mere talk."[49] If subjects do not recognize the "whoness" of the one behind the act, the sense of uniqueness that characterizes human beingness is lost, as is the potential for the production of beginnings that arises as a consequence of the interpenetration of the wills of "whos" in their relations.

The significations produced by unique subjects represent opinion. The trajectory of group action is determined by the exchange of opinion between unique "whos" who have constituted themselves into a group for the purposes of political creation. This exchange receives perhaps its first articulation in the notion of Homeric impartiality, which further demonstrates the extent to which the greatness of the deed is self-contained within itself, as opposed to within a particular determinable end. For Homer it did not matter whether the great deed was performed by his ancestors or by his ancestor's enemies; the deed was great because it aspired to immortality as a consequence of its own logic. "Impartiality, and with it all true historiography, came into existence when Homer decided to sing the deeds of the Trojans no less than those of the Achaeans, and to praise the glory of Hector no less than the greatness of Achilles."[50] For Arendt this impartiality is dependent upon the Greek discovery that the world is viewed from a multiplicity of different perspectives: "In a sheer inexhaustible flow of arguments, as the Sophists presented them to the citizenry of Athens, the Greek learned to exchange his own viewpoint, his own "opinion"' ... with those of his fellow citizens. Greeks learned to *understand* – not to understand one another as individual persons, but to look upon the same world from one another's standpoint, to see the same in very different and frequently opposing aspects."[51] In recognizing the multiplicity of opinion through the representation of the perspectives of others, individuals manage to practically take account of the fact of the plurality of appearance and produce a ground for the construction of a system of political judgment.

Determinations regarding human action are thus marked above all by the reciprocal exchange of opinions between nonidentical equals. Exchange takes this form as a consequence of the fact of human appearance: "If it is true that a thing *is* real within both the historical-political and sensate world only if it can show itself and be perceived from all its sides, then there must always be a plurality of standpoints to make reality even possible and to guarantee its continuation."[52] Whereas concepts of rational and absolute truth present themselves as modes of knowing appropriate to individuals considered in the singular, opinion presupposes the existence of plural individuals relating to one another as equals. Indeed, all claims of absolute truth in the human sphere are attacks on the political, which necessarily depends upon the existence of opinion: "every claim in the sphere of human affairs to an absolute truth, whose validity needs no support from the side of opinion, strikes at the very roots of all politics and all governments."[53] Political thinking is representative to the extent that the subject must attempt to represent in her mind the opinions or standpoints of those to whom she relates: "The more people's standpoints I have present in my mind while I am pondering a given issue, and the better I can imagine how I would feel and think if I were in their place, the stronger will be my capacity for representative thinking and the more valid my final conclusions, my opinion."[54] Political thinking is thus above all discursive: it aims at negotiating the multiplicity of opinion for the sake of the generation of trajectories of political action, the latter being possible only through the exercise of power, which "corresponds to the human ability not just to act but to act in concert."[55]

Political action is that which affects change in the world, and yet change in the world can only occur when individuals are willing and able to act together in concert: "What makes man a political being is his faculty of action; it enables him to get together with his peers, to act in concert, and to reach out for goals and enterprises that would never enter his mind, let alone the desires of his heart, had he not been given this gift – the gift to embark on something new."[56] Individuals must above all constitute themselves as a *We* through their organization into a political body that aims at the production of new modes of being and that is marked by the mutual negotiation of interest or opinion regarding a topic, for "every topic has as many sides and can appear in as many perspectives as there are people to discuss it."[57] Such negotiation is practiced in the public sphere, that space common to all in which citizens may present themselves to others, the space that allows for the expression of the multiplicity of opinion regarding the topic of discussion. Hence, "being able to persuade and influence others, which was how the citizens of the polis interacted politically, presumed a kind of freedom that was not irrevocably bound, either mentally or physically, to one's own standpoint or point of view."[58] The space of appearance necessary for political negotiation is produced wherever and whenever individuals come together to speak and act with one another, and dissolves and disappears only when power is degraded, when individuals disperse.[59] Indeed, the only requirement for the production of power is the togetherness of people in a public space of appearance: "What keeps people together after the fleeting moment of action has passed (what we today call 'organization') and what, at the same time, they keep alive through remaining together is power. And whoever, for whatever reasons, isolated himself and does not partake in such being together, forfeits power and becomes impotent, no matter how great his strength and how valid his reasons."[60]

Although actors may come together in order to solve a particular problem that they all seek to overcome, this coming together is always marked by a certain form of conflict, to the extent that all the subjects who organize to articulate the political task lack an absolute identity of mind. Articulating a specific interest thus does not mean effacing difference, but in Lisa Jane Disch's words, "coming to understand how different we may be apart from our concern with the specific matter at hand."[61] Arendt writes that "politics deals with the coexistence and association of *different* men. Men organize themselves politically according to certain essential commonalities found within or abstracted from an absolute chaos of differences."[62] In presenting to others one's own opinions, which are never fixed but the product of a subject in flux, and representing to oneself others' opinions, which are never fixed as a consequence of the preceding, as well as the fact that the specific combination of subjects related to is always variable, one contributes to the construction of a fundamentally new We. The We is the community formed for the purposes of political creation, but precisely because every member of the political community is nonidentical, both with respect to her own being and the being of her fellows, the specific constitution of the We is never given. The We thus assumes a variety of forms to the extent that the constitution of each We is the coming together of an always unique body of always unique subjects. The We, created for the purpose of initiating beginnings, is thus in every instance itself a radical beginning; it is a beginning brought about for the purpose of making beginnings. In coming together to exchange opinions political actors form a new beginning, a never-before-seen We. This specific constellation of people cannot be traced back to prior constellations or organizations. As a new constellation, the individuals who constitute the We act in an entirely new way, to the extent that the interpenetration of willed significations produce entirely new political permutations.

We must note, however, that when we speak of the will in this context, we quite clearly are not referring to it as it is generally thought of in the philosophical tradition, as essentially antipolitical. A freedom of the will conceptualized in terms of the isolation of the willing subject from her peers obviously has no political relevance. Political freedom can only be exercised in political communities, "where the many who live together have their intercourse both in word and in deed regulated by a great number of *rapports*."[63] Political freedom, in other words, is a freedom conscious of the fundamental fact of human plurality. Arendt's most detailed critique of the antipolitical nature of the will occurs in the essay "What Is Freedom?" Here, "freedom as related to politics is not a phenomenon of the will."[64] For Arendt political freedom is the exact opposite of what the philosophical tradition knows as inner freedom, "the inward space into which men may escape from external coercion and *feel* free."[65] Arendt reproduces an element of Marcuse's critique of the concept of essence when she notes that this latter type of freedom presupposes for its realization a human withdrawal and retreat from the world, being in fact stimulated by the actual feeling of political unfreedom in the external world, and thus functioning as a form of compensation.[66] The philosophical tradition will almost universally understand freedom as being potentially manifest only where and when individuals leave the world, freedom thus being seen as beginning where politics ends. Genuine freedom for Arendt, of course, is not dependent on an escape from the world or from politics, but precisely on the world and politics, for "without a politically guaranteed public realm, freedom lacks the worldly space to make its appearance."[67] It is only when this guaranteed space disappears that individuals, in the attempt to salvage some semblance of freedom, will dissociate the world from the mind, locating freedom exclusively in the latter. As Arendt would state in her lecture on Lessing, "When men are deprived of the public space – which is constituted by acting together and then fills of its own accord with the events and stories that develop into history – they retreat into their freedom of thought."[68]

For Arendt the Christian and the modern traditions of thought participate in this reduction of freedom through their association of the latter with the exercise of the free will. The will that Arendt is referring to here is the conscious organ of the self-aware author, the faculty that is exercised in utter solitude and that requires the subject's isolation from those temptations of the world that may potentially tempt and corrupt it. Here, willing is associated exclusively with the I-will for myself, with willing in the context of self-intercourse: "Will, will-power, and will-to-power are for us almost identical notions; the seat of power is to us the faculty of the will as known and experienced by man in his intercourse with himself."[69] This will clearly can never achieve power, which is always the result of acting in concert. As such, it is always an I-will-and-cannot, which is to say, the I-will is always subordinate to the self: "However far the will-to-power may reach out, and even if somebody possessed by it begins to conquer the whole world, the I-will can never get rid of the self; it always remains bound to it and, indeed, under its bondage."[70] The distinction between free will and political freedom is rooted in the difference between the I-will and the We-can. Something of this distinction is to be found in Montesquieu, who separates political freedom from philosophical freedom on the basis of his observation of the fact that political freedom "consists in being able to do what one ought to will."[71] Here, then, is the foundation for the thinking of a political will, of an I-will that implies a We-can, or rather, a We-can that is dependent upon a plurality of I-wills. Arendt notes that "for Montesquieu as for the ancients it was obvious that an agent could no longer be called free when he lacked the capacity to do – whereby it is irrelevant whether this failure is caused by exterior or interior circumstance."[72] If an individual is to do, she must act with her peers. This action, though, involves not the renunciation of the notion of the will, but rather the substitution of the theological and philosophical sovereign will with the political will. The political will is the will that is engaged in the agonistic conflict with other wills for the sake of the determination of trajectories of human action.

In any case, it is precisely because action takes place in public with others, whose wills can be neither determined nor discerned as a consequence of their instability and becoming-structure, that action is inherently unpredictable: "by linking men of action together, each relationship established by action ends up in a web of ties and relationships in which it triggers new links, changes the constellation of existing relationships, and thus always reaches out ever further, setting much more into interconnected motion than the man who initiates action ever could have foreseen."[73] All actors exist in a preexisting web of human relationships, and "it is because of this already existing web of human relationships, with it innumerable, conflicting wills and intentions, that action almost never achieves its purpose."[74] Arendt writes that

> human action, projected into a web of relationships where many and opposing ends are pursued, almost never fulfills its original intention; no act can ever be recognized by its author as his own with the same happy certainty with which a piece of work of any kind can be recognized by its maker. Whoever begins to act must know that he has started something whose end he can never foretell, if only because his own deed has already changed everything and made it even more unpredictable.[75]

The disclosure of the identity of the actor through speech and the birth of new beginnings through action initiates an unprecedented process that emerges as the unique life story of the new or reborn individual, a story that necessarily affects and is affected by the stories of all other individuals with whom the actor comes into contact. In this sense actors cannot be understood to function as perfectly autonomous authors or producers, but can at best be isolated and identified as agents who initiate specific actions, which nevertheless are carried out within a plural context.[76] Because action always depends upon others, every actor is at the same time a sufferer: "to do and to suffer are like opposite sides of the same coin, and the story that an act starts is composed of its consequent deeds and sufferings."[77] The chain reaction of events produced by every action is what constitutes the latter's boundlessness and marks its unpredictability. Action cannot be premapped, for every act "always establishes relationships and therefore has an inherent tendency to force open all limitations and cut across boundaries."[78] The consequence of action's unpredictability is this: because the outcomes of the act cannot be predetermined, it is impossible to conceptualize an image of the specific organization of reality that will constitute the end of the act, and because there exists no conception of an end, their logically can exist no conception of a means – in the purely instrumental sense – for the actors know not where they mean to end. One is free with respect to means only when one is convinced that one knows what one is doing, but the end of history can never be known, and if one cannot know the end of history, one is not justified in interpreting history within a means-end continuum.[79]

Action thus produces unpredictable results. The coming into existence of such productions, however, cannot be reversed, and hence the second element constituting the indeterminacy of action: its irreversibility. The remedy for these two elements lies in the human being's unique capacity for forgiveness and promise: "The two faculties belong together in so far as one of them, forgiving, serves to undo the deeds of the past, whose 'sins' hang like Damocles' sword over every new generation; and the other, binding oneself through promises, serves to set up in the ocean of uncertainty, which the future is by definition, islands of security without which not even continuity, let alone durability of any kind, would be possible in the relationships between men."[80] The continuation of action is only possible if individuals can be forgiven for that which they did unknowingly. Arendt states, "We've all been taught to say: Lord forgive them, for they know not what they do. That is true of all action. Quite simply and concretely true, because one *cannot* know."[81] Promise, meanwhile, is the faculty that keeps individuals together for the sake of acting in concert, and it is in fact only here that the idea of sovereignty achieves "a certain limited reality."[82] Sovereignty here lies in the individual's limited escape from the unpredictability of the future, an escape guaranteed precisely through the individual's communion with her peers. It is thus radically distinct from sovereignty as it is traditionally understood in the philosophical tradition, an understanding that must be completely rejected if action is to be affirmed.

According to Arendt, the philosophic affirmation of sovereignty, like that of the will, and the affirmation of the integrity of the unitary subject upon which both depend, is in fact a mechanism to overcome or escape the human condition of plurality, and the element of unpredictability that arises as a consequence of it: "If it were true that sovereignty and freedom are the same, then indeed no man could be free, because sovereignty, the ideal of uncompromising self-sufficiency and mastership, is contradictory to the very condition of plurality. No man can be sovereign because not one man, but men inhabit the earth."[83] To the extent that human plurality can never be entirely overcome, sovereignty remains an illusion. It is precisely as a consequence of this illusory character, however, that the maintenance of the concept has historically depended upon the exercise of techniques of violence.[84] There is a double danger existing in philosophy's identification of sovereignty and freedom, in philosophy's positing of "the ideal of a free will, independent from others and eventually prevailing against them."[85] Such an identification "leads either to a denial of human freedom – namely, if it is realized that whatever men may be, they are never sovereign – or to the insight that the freedom of one man, or a group, or a body politic can be purchased only at the price of the freedom, i.e. the sovereignty, of all others."[86] The problem with sovereignty is that for the power that is generated between individuals, it substitutes the power of one individual or a group of individuals over all others. Power *over* can only be affirmed to the extent that plurality has been eliminated through the denial of the political in-*between* space that makes action in concert possible. The elimination of plurality would result in "not so much sovereign domination of one's self as arbitrary domination of all others, or, as in Stoicism, the exchange of the real world for an imaginary one where these others would simply not exist."[87] Hence Arendt's claims that "if men wish to be free, it is precisely sovereignty they must renounce," and that "perhaps the greatest American innovation in politics as such was the consistent abolition of sovereignty within the body politics of the republic, the insight that in the realm of human affairs sovereignty and tyranny are the same."[88]

## Agonism, Democracy, and Political Objectification

The ideal form of political interaction, then, is not one that is able to give an expression to the sovereign will, but rather is that which is able to maximize the conflictual interaction between nonidentical significations for the sake of the determination of action oriented toward changing the world. It is hence a type of agonism rooted in the expression of the uniqueness of beings that is most adequate to the creation of the radically new.[89] The agonistic conflicts within the public spaces that relate individuals to one another look toward the production of events, "occurrences that interrupt routine processes and routine procedures,"[90] the historical accumulation and objectification of which constitute history. For Arendt human life is unique to the extent that, whereas all others forms of biological existence are marked by a repetitive and circular movement, its temporal trajectory is rectilinear.[91] Just as human rectilinear movement cuts across cyclical organic life, interrupting the latter's repetitive movement, so too do the acts that characterize this rectilinear movement disrupt existing human trajectories through the initiation of new flights and arcs. Hence, "history has many ends and many beginnings, each of its ends being a new beginning, each of its beginnings putting an end to what was there before."[92] These acts that interrupt already existing processes or sequences are the extraordinary, and it is precisely these events that are the subject matter of history. The task of history is to preserve the remembrance of these interruptions, which are not permanent in the way that the objects of a cycle are. The historiographical impulse can be traced to Herodotus's observation that the goal of history is the preservation of the impermanent deeds of human life.[93] Creation can be guaranteed a worldly reality only if its productions become objectified: "In order to become worldy things, that is, deeds and facts and events and patterns of thoughts or ideas, they must first be seen, heard, and remembered and then transformed, reified as it were, into things – into sayings of poetry, the written page or the printed book, into paintings or sculpture, into all sorts of records, documents, and monuments."[94] For the historian the great is that which is deserving of having its substance preserved forever through remembrance, achieved by way of a variety of forms of objectification. The events that call out to be remembered are those that interrupt history's expected trajectory. It is these that deserve glory.[95]

Arendt's celebration of the human achievement of glory has often been taken as a manifestation of the elitist and antidemocratic tendencies presumed to be inherent in her thought, glory being here associated in some sense with the isolated individual's separation of herself from the mediocrity that permeates the life of the so-called average and everyday members of the species.[96] The critique of Arendt's alleged elitism is very often tied to the perception of what is taken to be a tension in her thought between a communicative and dialogical understanding of politics and an agonistic and performative one. It is the latter politics that gives the impression of Arendt as an elitist, to the extent that the expressions of performative political acts are seen as being extraordinarily uncommon occurrences. In Seyla Benhabib's words, "agonal action is episodic and rare; only some human actions attain that quality of 'shining forth' and 'manifesting a principle' that Arendt associates with agonal action."[97] The fact that throughout history there have been so few deeds deserving of remembrance, of being recounted throughout time as a consequence of the radiance of their glory, separates these deeds from those that constitute the everyday and normal practice of politics: "Such action is rare; it transcends and in many ways transfigures everydayness and our understanding of ourselves. But the many small gestures and doings that constitute human everydayness do not usually attain such dimensions of brilliance of expression and intensity of passion."[98] It is, though, precisely this separation of the glorious and the everyday that needs to be resisted. What is missed here is the revolutionary normative dimension to Arendt's thought. Arendt is perfectly willing to concede the historical rarity of great and glorious action, writing that "politics as such has existed so rarely and in so few places that, historically speaking, only a few great epochs have known it and turned it into a reality."[99] Agonal action is in fact rare. Arendt's point, though, is just that it should not be. The recognition of the exceptionality of agonal action produces for Arendt a political imperative to reorganize human reality such that all citizens are able to express themselves performatively.[100] In the face of the episodic appearance of greatness in the world, Arendt desires not a retreat into an everyday politics that preserves equality through the denial of creative expression to all, but a qualitative reorganization of the nature of everyday politics. In Hanna Pitkin's words, "a general theory of ongoing free citizenship would have to suit people's everyday concerns, their ordinary low-profile interests and conflicts, without succumbing to triviality, apathy, or privatization. What was needed was a vision of 'normal,' ongoing, ordinary politics that was not really normal or ordinary: not in accord with the now conventional understanding of politics, nor like the now ordinary practice of politics – petty, banal, and quotidian."[101] The inability to recognize Arendt's desire to transform everyday politics, to situate agonal action within a plural public sphere that allows for general citizen participation, is often based on a misreading of the meaning of glory in Arendt. Glory most certainly does not refer to the activity of the single great individual who transcends the banality of the human masses through a Nietzschean form of separation. Leon Botstein notes that Arendt's "use of the notion of glory is ancient, not modern. Arendt uses it in the Roman and biblical sense, which endows glory with ethical rather than narrow self-serving qualities."[102] In *Eichmann in Jerusalem* Arendt writes that "the glory of the uprising in the Warsaw ghetto and the heroism of the few others who fought back lay precisely in their having refused the comparatively easy death the Nazis offered them – before the firing squad or in the gas chamber."[103] Here glory refers not to the exalted deeds of a privileged few, but to a capacity that even the most oppressed have – the refusal to become a passive object of history. In a world marked by systematic and widespread surplus repression, though, such revelation is bound to be episodic and rare. For Arendt the relevant question is how are we to construct a political order that is capable of democratically institutionalizing a form of agonistic practice that would in fact manifest greatness in the everyday?

We have already seen that political action requires for its preservation a form of objectification. Initially, this objectification took a poetical form: great deeds were preserved in the works of poets and artists. Poetical objectification is transcended with the construction of the polis, which achieves the desired generalization of the performative impulse. The function of the polis was to allow all citizens to achieve glory: "its foremost aim was to make the extraordinary an *ordinary occurrence of everyday life*."[104] The polis both allowed for the multiplication of the potential for action and provided a ground for the preservation of this action. Citizens henceforth no longer needed a Homer to immortalize their deeds, as was pointed out already by Pericles:

> The *polis* – if we trust the famous words of Pericles in the Funeral Oration – gives a guaranty that those who forced every sea and land to become the scene of their daring will not remain without witness and will need neither Homer nor anyone else who knows how to turn words to praise them; without assistance from others, those who acted will be able to establish together the everlasting remembrance of their good and bad deeds, to inspire admiration in the present and future ages.[105]

What the polis ensures is that individuals will never be lacking a space within which they will be able to appear, where they will be able to be seen and heard, and potentially achieve glory. "What Homer had done was to immortalize human deeds, and the polis could dispense with the service of 'others of his craft' because it offered each of its citizens that public-political space that it assumed would confer immortality upon his acts."[106] Hence the double function of the polis: to overcome the fleetingness of action through a mode of objective preservation, and to valorize the everyday through the expansion of the realm of performance such that all citizens are, through their very activity, capable of acting greatly. Arendt's celebration of the polis, though, is no romantic Grecophilic retreat into a long-lost and irrecoverable time. Maurizio Passerin D'Entrèves is correct to note that the polis refers not to the specific political structure of the Greek city-state, but is rather a metaphor for any public-political realm in which individuals are able to show themselves to one another in speech and deed.[107] Within the context of late modernity, that mode of political organization most amenable to the actualization of the human potential for beginning is the revolutionary council tradition, which Arendt investigates in some detail in what is probably her most neglected theoretical work, *On Revolution*.

## Arendt and Revolutionary History

Critics of *On Revolution* are often inclined to point to inconsistencies, gaps, oversights, and inaccuracies within Arendt's reading of the historical events that form the subject matter of the book, essentially taking her to be a poor historian of the revolutions she discusses. Eric Hobsbawm, for example, notes that "she does not take her revolutions as they come, but constructs herself an ideal type, defining her subject matter accordingly, excluding what does not measure up to her specifications."[108] There is an element of correctness in Hobsbawm's criticism, yet the larger truth of Arendt's reading of revolution is completely lost here to the extent that Hobsbawm obscures the specific normative dimension of Arendt's political theory. Arendt is quite clearly not concerned with the production of a historically sound record of the combination of events that mark the phenomenon under discussion – however such a record could be imagined – but rather with a thinking of the ideal mode of political action through the imaginative recollection and recombination of certain historical fragments. Here the influence of Walter Benjamin on Arendt is quite clear.[109] James Miller will go so far as to suggest that a proper reading of *On Revolution* cannot be made independently of a reading of Benjamin's "Theses on the Philosophy of History." For both Benjamin and Arendt, storytelling is not concerned with telling the story exactly as it occurred, but rather with the preservation of the memory of those major events[110] that shatter historicism. Arendt "follows Benjamin in constructing revolutionary history as an episodic set of stories needing to be remembered and told again, lest the true revolutionary spirit, with its redeeming commitment to freedom, be lost 'through the failure of thought and remembrance.'"[111] For Arendt "it is necessary to redeem from the past those moments worth preserving, to save those fragments from past treasures that are significant for us. Only by means of this *selective appropriation* can we discover the past anew, endow it with relevance and meaning for the present, and make it the source of inspiration for a future yet to come."[112] The form this selective appropriation takes mimics the activity of the pearl diver who scavenges the ruins of the oceans in search of those objects that can be brought up to the surface and salvaged for the sake of the living. It is worth quoting Arendt at some length on this point:

> And this thinking, fed by the present, works with the "thought fragments" it can wrest from the past and gather about itself. Like a pearl diver who descends to the bottom of the sea, not to excavate the bottom and bring it to light but to pry loose the rich and the strange, the pearls and the coral in the depths and to carry them to the surface, this thinking delves into the depths of the past – but not in order to resuscitate it the way it was and to contribute to the renewal of extinct ages. What guides this thinking is the conviction that although the living is subject to the ruin of time, the process of decay is at the same time a process of crystallization, that in the depth of the sea, into which sinks and is dissolved what once was alive, some things "suffer a sea-change" and survive in new crystallized forms and shapes that remain immune to the elements, as though they waited only for the pearl diver who one day will come down to them and bring them up into the world of the living – as "thought fragments," as something "rich and strange," and perhaps even as everlasting as *Urphänomene*.[113]

In *On Revolution* Arendt attempts to imaginatively reappropriate those elements of the revolutionary tradition that can, through their being combined and reorganized into specific constellations of thought, potentially contribute to a theorization of a mode of political activity conducive to the human production of beginnings.

According to Arendt, revolutions are the only political events that in their essence directly refer us to the problem of beginnings.[114] Prior to the American and French revolutions, the idea that the flow of history could be interrupted and restarted was unknown, the latter becoming recognized only at some point during revolutionary history itself. These revolutions functioned as stories, stories whose central narrative was the emergence of freedom, the idea of radical beginning thus coinciding with the emergence of the idea of freedom as the organizing

principle of action. As was alluded to previously, the concept of political freedom first became manifest with the rise of the Greek polis.
Ever since Herodotus, the polis "was understood as a form of political
organization in which citizens lived together under conditions of no-
rule, without a division between rulers and ruled."[115] The polis was
thus not a rule of some over others, but an isonomy, which assumes not
a natural equality of condition or capacity between all, but an equality
between those who are understood as existing with one another in a
specific relation as peers. Individuals are not equal by nature, or rather,
are equal only to the extent that they all share the negative capacity for
initiation, and thus require an artificial institution – the polis – to make
them equal, and thus provide a ground for the stabilization of their relations. Hence, "equality existed only in this specifically political realm,
where men met one another as citizens and not as private persons."[116]
Since one clearly needs others if one can only be free and equal among
one's peers, one requires also a public space of appearance in which
one can come together to congregate with these peers. In ancient Greece
this space was the polis, and as we have seen, the specific structure of
this congregation was what produced the potential for political natality.

For Arendt freedom is the right to positive participation in political
affairs. It is as such to be sharply distinguished from the essentially
negative right of liberty, which is nevertheless a condition of freedom.
It is considered by Arendt to be a fact "that the notion of liberty implied
in liberation can only be negative, and hence, that even the intention
of liberating is not identical with the desire for freedom."[117] Unfortunately the concept of freedom has been increasingly separated from
considerations of political action, associated instead with "the more or
less free range of non-political activities which a given body politic will
permit and guarantee to those who constitute it."[118] Needless to say,
such a separation and association constitutes a violation of the spirit of
the concept, which should be substantively concerned with "participation in public affairs, or admission to the public realm."[119] For Arendt
what the great revolutions attempted to do was return to humanity the
genuine experience of being free, which had been lost ever since the
decline of the polis. The reproduction of the experience of freedom was
at the same time the expression of the capacity to make something new.
Hence, "only where this pathos of novelty is present and where novelty
is connected with the idea of freedom are we entitled to speak of revolution."[120] What revolution looks to is not just change, but change perceived of as being the start of something new, as radical beginning. Prior

to the great eighteenth-century revolutions, there was much discourse aimed at extolling the virtue of rebellion and revolt, yet for Arendt the content of such discussion was oriented toward the advocacy of the simple exchange of the person or persons occupying a specific office or offices of rule. Although the people could decide who could not rule, they were not supposed to offer opinions as to who should, and there was certainly no concept that could describe a political change that would allow the people to become rulers themselves and start history anew. This state of affairs necessarily affected not only the motivations of the revolutionaries, but also the very language of revolution itself. Arendt notes that the term *revolution* originally belonged to astronomy, and that it is no coincidence that the original emphasis of the revolutionaries was on the human contribution to the movement of a cyclical historical process marked by degeneration and reinstallation. The word "revolution" originally meant restoration, and it was indeed restoration that the revolutionaries were originally aiming at. The American and French revolutions "were played in their initial stages by men who were firmly convinced that they would do no more than restore an old order of things that had been disturbed and violated by the despotism of absolute monarchy or the abuses of colonial government."[121] Even when it became apparent to the revolutionaries that restoration was impossible and that something new would have to be created if their desire for action was to be satisfied, the old language still crept in, as could be witnessed, for example, in Paine's tendency to refer to the American and French revolutions as counterrevolutions.[122] The political formations that sprung up as a consequence of the revolutionary activity, though, were anything but representations of old orders; rather, they were radically new institutions suggesting the possibility of a radically new mode of being-in-the-world.

The account of the nature of revolutionary activity in *On Revolution* makes overt what is only implicit in Arendt's prior account of the nature of politics ideally considered; that is, to the extent that action is understood as an end-in-itself, it is also understood as being an intrinsically gratifying and pleasurable endeavour. The emphasis on action as glory is thus supplemented by the emphasis on action as joy. According to Arendt, the content of political life is "the *joy and gratification* that arise out of being in company with our peers," out of "acting together and appearing in public," out of "inserting ourselves into the world by word and deed, thus acquiring and sustaining our personal identity and beginning something entirely new."[123] For Arendt the American political tradition, at least as it existed in its revolutionary and prerevolutionary period, had a robust concept of public happiness. The Americans knew that in order to be free one had to participate in the affairs of public life, but also that this civic participation was not a sacrificial act but a good in itself; participation in public affairs was seen to generate a unique happiness that could not be achieved elsewhere. The Americans understood "that the people went to the town assemblies, as their representatives later were to go to the famous Conventions, neither exclusively because of duty nor, and even less, to serve their own interests but most of all because they enjoyed the discussions, the deliberations, and the making of decisions."[124] In other words, the fact of political natality, of producing the radically new in the context of the political, was recognized as an intrinsically pleasurable experience affirming the becoming-structure of the human being. Needless to say, however, Arendt was quite aware of the degradation of the concept of joy after the revolution in America, as represented, for example, in the Declaration of Independence's substitution of the term *happiness* for public happiness, the former being seen as a condition of existence to be enjoyed in private life. Government would eventually come to be understood as the means to ensure the happiness of a society of individuals, which was achieved through the production of a given state of private welfare rather than through an active process capable of generating an intrinsic public happiness.[125]

Regardless, it was this initial recognition of the nature of public happiness that for Arendt characterized the better elements of the activism of the social movements of the 1960s, the student movement in particular. Arendt had an admittedly ambivalent attitude toward the student movement; she approved of many of its goals and techniques, was neutral to others, and regarded some as "dangerous nonsense."[126] For her what distinguished the global student movement as a political force, in its best moments, was "its determination to act, its joy in action, the assurance of being able to change things by one's own efforts."[127] The New Left "seems everywhere characterized by sheer courage, an astounding will to action, and by a no less astounding confidence in the possibility of change."[128] Arendt writes that "for the first time in a very long while a spontaneous political movement arose which not only did not simply carry on propaganda, but acted, *and, moreover, acted almost exclusively from moral motives*."[129] Politics was not considered by the students in simply instrumental terms as strategic activity justified by means-end calculations, but rather as a mode for the actualization of an immanent desire for creative action. What they discovered was that "acting is fun," what in the eighteenth century the Americans recognized as public happiness, the gratification that is achieved through participation in civic life.[130] Despite all of its flaws, for example its theoretical immaturity and its inability to comprehend the nature of power, the student movement is to be nevertheless commended for its perception of the nature of political joy, for its active delight in action, and for its desire to make politics gratifying and fun – precisely that which Marcuse celebrated it for, as we will see in chapter 6. The most positive political slogan to come out of the New Left was the call for "participatory democracy," which derives in fact from the council system, "the always defeated but only authentic outgrowth of every revolution since the eighteenth century."[131]

In *On Revolution* Arendt will be concerned with thinking the possibility of constructing a set of political orders capable of institutionalizing the capacity for spontaneous political creation as it was expressed, for example, in the international student movement, thus generalizing and stabilizing political natality. It is this need for institutionalization within revolutionary movements that produces perhaps the most significant tension within, and oftentimes the degradation of, the revolutionary spirit. The latter was in fact the case in the American Revolution. The problem is that of foundation. We know that for Arendt, unlike strength, which belongs to individuals, power comes into existence wherever individuals bind together into a We for the purpose of action. When individuals attempt to preserve the power created through a collective generative act, the process of foundation, "of constituting a stable worldy structure to house, as it were, their combined power of action," has begun.[132] The We are a beginning for the purpose of making beginnings, yet if they are to preserve this capacity for making beginnings they must produce a stable foundation for the principle of action that united them. They attempt to preserve the capacity for making beginnings through the act of political ordering, which is always motivated by the "love of freedom, and this both in the negative sense of liberation from oppression and in the positive sense of the establishment of Freedom as a stable, tangible reality."[133] Power thus demands foundation for its perpetuation, which is the prerequisite for the indeterminate continuation of the potential for action: "The grammar of action: that action is the only human faculty that demands a plurality of men; and the syntax of power: that power is the only human attribute which applies solely to the worldly in-between space by which men are mutually related, combine in the act of foundation by virtue of the making and the keeping of promises, which, in the realm of politics, may well be the highest human faculty."[134] According to Arendt, within the context of revolutionary history it was only in America that action prior to the revolution, specifically the formation of public civic structures, was able to generate a power capable of being preserved through promise.

The Americans recognized not only the need for foundation and its preservation, but also that this preservation could be achieved only through augmentation. In the political realm foundation, preservation, and augmentation are all closely connected, for to the extent that it is necessary to preserve foundation, this preservation depends for its actualization on augmentation.[135] The American founding fathers recognized this triangular relation in the Roman political tradition and consciously attempted to replicate it within their own historical context, in, for example, their assertion of the need for Constitutional amendment: "This notion of coincidence of foundation and preservation by virtue of augmentation – that the 'revolutionary' act of beginning something entirely new, and conservative care, which will shield this new beginning through the centuries, are interconnected – was deeply rooted in the Roman spirit and could be read from almost every page of Roman history."[136] Amendment is ultimately seen to be justified to the extent that it makes possible the reproduction of the ontological condition of human life, which is in fact its own end. According to Arendt the American revolutionaries recognized that the authority of the body politic flows from the very act of foundation itself, and not from some divine or transcendent source: "It is futile to search for an absolute to break the vicious circle in which all beginning is inevitably caught, because this 'absolute' lies in the very act of beginning itself."[137] Foundation is a beginning for the purposes of beginning, which is its own end. It is paradoxically, then, the creation of a stable foundation that allows for the perpetuation of what is ultimately the fundamental condition of human existence, the creation of the radically new or the upsetting of stability. Needless to say, only very specifically ordered institutional arrangements are capable of providing a ground able to negotiate this paradox.

The apparent tension in the revolutionary spirit is that the greatest event in the process of revolution is the act of foundation, which requires both the building and the preservation of stable structures to house action, the latter being marked by the creation of something that is always radically new. In the present political context these two moments, the concern with stability and the concern with the radically new, have become isolated and posited as opposites, in for example the opposition between conservatism and radicalism. For Arendt, if the revolutionary tradition is to be in some meaningful sense recollected, this opposition must be resolved into some sort of coherent unity of opposites: "Terminologically speaking, the effort to recapture the lost spirit of revolution must, to a certain extent, consist in the attempt at thinking together and combining meaningfully what our present vocabulary presents to us in terms of opposition and contradiction."[138] The failure of postrevolutionary thought to conceptually comprehend and remember this unity of opposites was preceded by the failure of the revolution to produce a lasting institution: specifically, the republic that was to represent the culmination of the revolution did not allow for the perpetuation of the qualities and modes that were necessary to bring it about in the first place. For example, the institutions of the American republic on the federal and state level overwhelmed the town councils at the local level, as practically speaking, only the representatives of the people were granted access to spaces of action. For this reason "the Revolution, while it had given freedom to the people, had failed to provide a space where this freedom could be exercised."[139] Because the revolutionary spirit was in clear existence throughout the colonial era in America, there was not deemed a real need to provide a set of institutions capable of preserving it after the revolution – it was assumed that it would naturally reproduce itself. Because it was assumed that the revolutionary impulse toward political creation would continue to express itself unabated regardless of the specific structure of the political medium within which it was being expressed, the recognition of the fundamental need to create institutions specifically oriented toward active citizen participation was lost; the concern became one of the need for foundation as such, the latter producing the Constitution and its new institutions, which focused not on freedom but liberty, and not on participation but representation. The stagnation of the American Revolution, then, was to a large extent a consequence of the withdrawal of theory from action after the Revolution had been achieved. All thought begins with remembrance, but remembrance is not guaranteed unless it becomes congealed in a conceptual framework that will allow it to manifest itself.

Experiences and even the stories which grow out of what men do and endure, of happenings and events, sink back into the futility inherent in the living word and deed unless they are talked about over and over again. What saves the affairs of mortal men from their inherent futility is nothing but this incessant talk about them, which in turn remains futile unless certain concepts, certain guideposts for future remembrance, and even for sheer reference, arise out of it.[140]

The loss of those institutions capable of affirming active political life generated a failure of thought to preserve the truths of the revolutionary spirit, the three principles to which the latter looks: public freedom, public happiness, and public spirit, which when forgotten are replaced with just civil liberties, private welfare, and public opinion.[141] The recuperation of the elements of the revolutionary spirit thus depends on the production of a form of institution capable of allowing for the former's continual expression. If the orders of the American republic were incapable of sustaining and expressing the revolutionary spirit, of providing a space for the perpetuation of the creative or overcoming impulse, the question of course then becomes, what form of institution is? For Arendt the answer is to be found in the revolutionary council tradition.

## The Institutionalization of the Revolutionary Impulse: The Council Tradition

When Arendt's critical appropriation of the council tradition is not ignored altogether by her commentators, it is generally explained away as being a juvenile and utopian tendency within her thought, more of an embarrassment than a theme to be grappled with. Elisabeth Young-Bruehl writes that "in the decades since Arendt's death, her appreciation of the power of promising and the potestas in populo of the council system have seldom been taken seriously by contemporary political theorists, most of whom cannot imagine a political life that is not organized primarily around electing representatives to governments which then dominate their citizens. Her appreciation of the council system is said to be the unrealistic or utopian streak in her thinking."[142] Arendt's political ontology, though, her understanding of the nature of the human essence as beginning and the political as the institutionalized sphere responsible for the actualization of beginning, is in fact incomprehensible without her account of the nature of the revolutionary council system. The understanding of political action as being oriented toward the achievement of glory, the creation of the radically new, has been gradually displaced by the rise of statism and its corresponding understanding of politics as rule, as expressed primarily in the form of the statesman who gives laws. Rulership is characterized by a relation between two sets of individuals, one of whom knows and one of whom does not, the latter simply executing the orders of the former. As I argued in the last chapter, it is such a relation that is apparently present in Marcuse's account of political education. Such a conception of politics, though, is completely antithetical to action, for the function of the statesman "was not to act but to impose permanent rules on the changing circumstances and unstable affairs of acting men."[143] The desire for the erection of an all-inclusive framework capable of assimilating acts into itself led necessarily to a bias against the new and unique: "the mere tendency to exclude everything that was not consistent developed into a great power of exclusion, which kept the tradition intact against all new, contradictory, and conflicting appearances."[144] Within the contemporary context the recuperation of the possibility for creation depends upon the abolition of rulership and the institution of a direct and participatory form of democracy that allows citizens to both freely and consciously determine the trajectories of their actions, and to subsequently act these trajectories themselves.

According to Arendt, the revolutionary moment produced both the party system and the council system, the subsequent success of the former being achieved through the destruction of the latter during the course of revolutionary history. The triumph of the party was largely accomplished as a consequence of the refinement of rulership as it was represented in the ascendancy of the nation-state, and as it was theoretically expressed in not only the emerging bourgeois political ideologies, but in radical social theory as well: "The spectacular success of the party system and the no less spectacular failure of the council system were both due to the rise of the nation-state, which elevated the one and crushed the other, whereby the leftist and revolutionary parties have shown themselves to be no less hostile to the council system than the conservative or reactionary right."[145] Arendt argues that both Marx and Lenin ultimately chose the party over the system of councils. Not only this, though, but "the councils, the only true outgrowth of the revolutions themselves as distinguished from revolutionary parties and ideologies, have been mercilessly destroyed precisely by the Communist party and by Lenin himself."[146] Both Lenin and Marx were shocked by the appearance of the council system as it arose during periods of revolutionary unrest, both in 1905 during the first Russian Revolution and in 1871 during the Paris Commune. The council system seemed to contradict most Marxist theorizing on the nature of the political, which had generally assessed the councils as potentially functioning as at most temporary organs that would dissolve after the revolution was completed. The very notion that the revolution could be completed, though, fundamentally contradicts the revolutionary spirit and the understanding of politics as performative creation. I have noted already the instrumentalism underlying the Marxist understanding of politics: revolution was considered as a mere means for the seizure of power. During the revolutions, though, established power in fact disintegrated as a consequence of the popular withdrawal of consent, and an entirely new power structure rose up. Although Marx was initially impressed by this new power structure as it appeared in the form of the Commune, according to Arendt he "soon became aware to what an extent this political form contradicted all notions of a 'dictatorship of the proletariat' by means of a socialist or communist party whose monopoly of power and violence was modeled upon the highly centralized governments of nation-states, and he concluded that the communal councils were, after all, only temporary organs of the revolution."[147] This same sequence repeats itself in Lenin, who initially praised the councils at the beginning of the 1905 and 1917 revolutions before attempting to destroy them via their forced subordination to the control of the centralized party apparatus.[148] In the case of both Marx and Lenin, "put before the alternative of either adjusting their thoughts and deeds to the new and the unexpected or going to the extreme of tyranny and suppression, they hardly hesitated in their decision for the latter."[149]

Despite the centrality of the antagonism between the councils and the party within revolutionary history, for Arendt it is the activity that is generated out of the former that stimulates the revolution in the first place. Revolutions are not made by the professional revolutionists who lead the revolutionary parties: "The part of the professional revolutionists usually consists in not making a revolution but in rising to power after it has broken out, and their great advantage in this power struggle lies less in their theories and mental or organizational preparation than in the simple fact that their names are the only ones which are publicly known."[150] Although the professional revolutionists have never instigated a revolution, once the latter is triggered, they come to play a major role. Parties are always institutions designed to grant a parliamentary faction the popular support of a people, but they themselves do not produce a medium for the actualization of these people as actors. Indeed, when parties do support or advocate public participation, it is always a sign of their decay and ill-health: "If parties become militant and step actively into the domain of political action, they violate their own principle as well as their function in parliamentary government, that is, they become subversive, and this regardless of their doctrines and ideologies."[151] The parties' hostility to action is not only produced as a consequence of the implied division of individuals into leaders and led, but also as a consequence of the type of activity undertaken. Because the nature of their activity was for the most part intellectual, the revolutionists tended to look back to prior history in the quest for the determination of historical precedents rather than attempt to come to grips with the fact that what characterizes revolution is in every case the production of the radically new. Not only the form of their party organization, the replication of bourgeois structures of rulership, but the very content of their activity predisposes the revolutionist to attempt to assimilate events into a sequential continuum: "Since it is his very task to assure the continuity of revolution, he will be inclined to argue in terms of historical precedents, and the conscious and pernicious imitation of past events."[152] Hence the main theoretical tools of the parties were the party programs, "ready-made formulas" for the production of revolutions, which did not advocate action, considered as beginning or creation, but rather the technical application and execution of already existing plans.[153] The conflict between parties and councils in all twentieth-century revolutions is an expression of the conflict between representation and action. For Arendt modern representative systems can be considered democratic to the extent that they theoretically look toward private welfare, but ultimately they are oligarchic to the extent that they do not allow for the expression of public happiness and public freedom.[154] Indeed, such systems must deny that public happiness and public freedom are even actual states of existence to the extent that the former are not capable of accommodating the latter's realization within their structure. Participation must be seen as a burden, and the representative system must look to an end that is not political. The revolutionary parties used councils for their own ends during the revolutions, but they knew perfectly well that once the revolutions were over, the councils would be unnecessary, according to the logic of their own organization, because the councils looked to the impossible ideal of action. Hence, all parties "agreed that the end of government was the welfare of the people, and that the substance of politics was not action but administration."[155] The councils were to be ultimately rejected when their instrumental value was exhausted precisely because they denied this hierarchy of activity.

Contrary to the revolutionary parties, which attempt to purposely produce the revolutionary situation through the practical application of certain fixed theoretical principles generated prior to political action, the system of councils, whose appearance characterizes all genuine revolutions, emerges not out of theory but out of spontaneous practice. For this reason "the council system seems to correspond to and to spring from the very experience of political action."[156] The council system invariably springs up in revolutionary situations as a consequence of the immanent nature of revolution itself, "that is, out of the experiences of action and out of the resulting will of the actors to participate in the further development of public affairs."[157] To the extent that parties and their intellectuals have not understood the nature of political action as radical creation, the appearance of the councils has always been from their perspective unforeseen: "Each time they appeared, they sprang up as the spontaneous organs of the people, not only outside of all revolutionary parties but entirely unexpected by them and their leaders."[158] To the extent that this appearance has contradicted virtually all of the modern era's previous understandings of the nature of politics, the general tendency within intellectual history has been to marginalize or simply ignore the potential of the councils to function as a legitimate and practicable form of political organization. The councils have thus been historically disregarded by historians, political actors, theorists, and the revolutionary tradition itself. All such commentators "failed to understand to what extent the council system confronted them with an entirely new form of government, with a new public space for freedom which was constituted and organized during the course of the revolution itself."[159] Arendt will give herself just this task of comprehending the meaning and significance of the spontaneous emergence of the revolutionary council system, ultimately seeing it as an affirmation of her political ontology, as an expression of the desire for the actualization of the human essence as beginning. She maintains that "it was nothing more or less than this hope for a new form of government that would permit every member of the modern egalitarian society to become a 'participator' in public affairs, that was buried in the disasters of twentieth-century revolutions."[160]

The emergence of revolutionary councils occurred in 1870–1871, as seen in the Paris Commune, in 1905, as seen in the self-organization of workers into soviets, in 1917, as seen in the reorganization of workers' soviets, in 1918–1919, as seen in the German soldier and worker councils, and in 1956, as seen in the new council system in Budapest. Arendt, though, will trace the appearance of the councils back even farther, into the eighteenth century in France and America during the beginning of revolutionary history. The council experience in France was short lived, as the spontaneous rise of a "communal council system" during the revolution was crushed by Robespierre, who attempted to substitute for it party machinery capable of manufacturing identical opinion.[161] The ward system in revolutionary America was more successful than the French council system as a consequence of America's more embedded civic understanding of the goods of public freedom and happiness, as well as the system's achievement of an articulate theoretical expression, as seen primarily in the thought of Thomas Jefferson.[162] For Jefferson the problem with the Constitution was that although it rooted all power in the citizens, it did not give the citizens a means to express this power in the public realm: "the danger was that all power had been given to the people in their private capacity, and there was no space established for them in their capacity of being citizens."[163] According to Jefferson the United States should have been divided into a multitude of wardships, so-called little republics that would provide all citizens with a space for direct participation in public affairs, thus providing a level of democratic involvement not achievable through simple electoral activity. From Arendt's interpretation "the basic assumption of the ward system, whether Jefferson knew it or not, was that no one could be called happy without his share in public happiness, that no one could be called free without his experience in public freedom, and that no one could be called either happy or free without participating or having a share in, public power."[164] If Jefferson was unclear on the precise structure, organization, and substance of the councils, and indeed, this is a recurrent criticism of all theorists of council organization, it was precisely because he was theorizing not just how to reform existing institutions, but rather how to create a radically new form of government. It is for precisely the same reason that Arendt never published detailed analyses of the potential or actual structure of council systems. In John Sitton's words, "her purpose instead is simply to sketch a political structure to illustrate the possibility of realizing alternative public principles: direct democracy, the experience of public freedom and public happiness in the modern world, an arena for proper opinion formation, and a polity not based on the notion of sovereignty."[165]

The very attempt to fabricate in advance the ideal form of the structure that will realize the performative activity must necessarily violate to a certain degree the very essence of this activity. Arendt, though, always aware of this danger, will nevertheless provide some very broad and tenuous formulations regarding council organization and its relation to her political ontology.

For Arendt what is most striking about revolutionary history is the fact that throughout such a diversity of human conditions, precisely the same phenomenon, the appearance of the councils, arose again and again. In each case the members of the councils had no interest in the party system and the machinations of the professional revolutionists who comprised its bureaucracy. What they desired above all was the direct participation of all citizens in the affairs of state. Indeed, council participation actually cut across all party divisions: party membership played no role in the determination of the suitability of political participants, the councils attracting members from all party factions. More important than this integration of diverse partisans, though, was the fact that the councils "were in fact the only political organs for people who belonged to no party."[166] What the councils objected to above all was the production and maintenance of an artificial gap between the revolutionary leaders, who possessed objective knowledge of the historical situation, and the ignorant masses, who were to simply passively apply this knowledge through their directed activity. What the councils affirmed was the general capacity of citizens to think and act for themselves. What is more, precisely because the members of the councils understood that public participation in political affairs – thinking and acting for oneself – was in fact an intrinsic self-expressive good, they also understood that the council system transcended all exclusively instrumental considerations. As spaces of freedom, the councils refused to see themselves as mere temporary organs of the revolution, but rather tried to establish themselves as permanent and enduring political structures. What they aimed at was the radical reconstruction of the nature of politics, which they recognized, in contradistinction to the professional revolutionists, as a necessary and enduring dimension of human existence.

According to Arendt, an analysis of both the 1917 Russian Revolution and the 1956 Hungarian Revolution is capable of producing a general outline of what a political order structured according to the logic of the councils might look like.[167] In both cases the councils sprung up all over the revolutionary field independently of one another: in particular, in

Russia workers', soldiers', and peasants' councils, and in Hungary students', workers', soldiers', and civil servants' councils. Also in both cases it took only between a few days and a few weeks for the councils to spring up, for "accidental proximity" to be transformed into a "political institution."[168] The councils were transformed into a political institution as a consequence of being linked to one another through their mutual integration into a coordinated system that included higher councils on a regional and national level. These higher councils, though, did not have the authority to overwhelm the initial councils and the latter's ability to function as media for the expression of action: "The common object was the foundation of a new body politic, a new type of republican government which would rest on 'elementary republics' in such a way that its own central power did not deprive the constituent bodies of their original power to constitute."[169] Although Arendt's ideal council system would take the form of a hierarchical pyramid composed of both lower and higher councils, this system would escape authoritarianism to the extent that political authority would not be generated from the top or the bottom of the pyramid, but rather from each layer of the pyramid. From the lowest levels political equals would choose among themselves delegates to move above, who would then confront as equals other new delegates at the higher levels, and so on. "Their title rested on nothing but the confidence of their equals, and this equality was not natural but political, it was nothing they had been born with; it was the equality of those who had committed themselves to, and now were engaged in, a joint enterprise."[170] Here, political equality is not associated with a necessary affirmation of a universal and homogeneous capacity – that each can do what the other can – but rather just with a desire to act, and hence solves what Arendt takes to be one of the most serious problems of modern politics: the reconciliation of equality and authority.[171]

Arendt's most detailed historical account of the factual appearance of the council system is the study of the Hungarian Revolution that she undertakes in the essay "Totalitarian Imperialism." For Arendt the Hungarian Revolution was an interruption of the automatic and repetitive motion of totalitarianism, stimulated by nothing other than the attempt by individuals to actualize their creative desire to act in the world. Arendt writes that

if there was ever such a thing as Rosa Luxemburg's "spontaneous revolution" – this sudden uprising of an oppressed people for the sake of freedom and hardly anything else, without the demoralizing chaos of military defeat preceding it, without coup d'état techniques, without a closely knit apparatus of organizers and conspirators, without the undermining propaganda of a revolutionary party, something, that is, which everybody, conservatives and liberals, radicals and revolutionists, had discarded as a noble dream – then we had the privilege to witness it.[172]

The revolution was produced as a consequence of the increasing intensification of a series of spontaneous events: a relatively small student demonstration swelling in size and proceeding to overturn a Stalin statue in Budapest; a group of students departing for a local radio station the next day to attempt to broadcast their program; a large crowd gathering, which the police would attempt to break up; the crowd attacking the police and taking their weapons; the workers leaving the factories to join the crowd; the army being called in to help the police, but instead joining sides with the people and arming them further. In the end, "what had started as a student demonstration had become an armed uprising in less than twenty-four hours."[173]

What marked the revolution was the production of a solidarity among all social strata that were participating, despite the fact that the uprising was initiated by communists, who themselves never resorted to stale dogmas or attempted to raise themselves up as leaders of the people. What was more, the noncommunists did not react against or oppose the uprising simply because it had been begun by communists: "it was as though ideology, of whatever shade and brand, had simply been wiped out of existence and memory the moment the people, intellectuals and workers, communists and non-communists, found themselves together in the streets fighting for freedom."[174] Arendt's account of the Hungarian experience thus points to precisely that phenomenon noted by Jules Michelet in his *History of the French Revolution*. Michelet writes that "I am endeavoring to describe today that epoch of unanimity, that holy period, when a whole nation, free from all party distinction, as yet a comparative stranger to the opposition of classes, marched together under a flag of brotherly love."[175] Indeed, what Arendt saw as the glory of the Hungarian Revolution is in many ways an expression of the anonymous heroism Michelet would locate in the French Revolution, where revolutionary leaders were "wrongfully considered as the sole actors. The fact is, that they rather received than communicated the impulse. The chief actor is the people."[176] The main problem after the Hungarian uprising was not how the people were to establish freedom, for freedom was realized in their very spontaneous acting together, but rather how to institutionalize and hence preserve it. The solution to this problem was found in the creation of a council system, "the same organization which for more than a hundred years has emerged whenever the people have been permitted for a few days, or a few weeks or months, to follow their own political devices without a government (or a party program) imposed from above."[177] What the emergence of the councils demonstrated was not only the extent to which individuals desire political action, but the extent to which they are also capable of channelling this desire into the construction of permanent institutional orders able to actualize this performative desire: "Nothing indeed contradicts more sharply the old adage of the anarchistic and lawless 'natural' inclinations of a people left without the constraint of its government than the emergence of the councils that, wherever they appeared, and most pronouncedly during the Hungarian Revolution, were concerned with the re-organization of the political and economic life of the country and the establishment of a new order."[178] The council system requires "no special conditions for its establishment except the coming together and acting together of a certain number of people on a non-temporary basis."[179] The motivation for this coming together is nothing more than the desire of individuals to express their essence as beings capable of radically beginning. It is for this reason that "the councils say: We want to participate, we want to debate, we want to make our voices heard in public, and we want to have a possibility to determine the political course of our country."[180]

Despite her advocacy of the council system as the form of political organization most conducive to the production of human beginnings, Arendt was not optimistic regarding the potential for the former's successful institutional stabilization, stating at one point that "if you ask me now what prospect it has of being realized, then I must say to you: Very slight, if at all. And yet perhaps, after all – in the wake of the next revolution."[181] Nevertheless, it still seems clear that Arendt did intend to outline in her analysis an actualizable political order. Contrary to those interpreters who maintain that for Arendt the restoration of the revolutionary tradition is not concretely possible – for example Miller, who states that "for Arendt, it is a restoration feasible in memory alone"[182] – her enthusiastic celebration of, for example, the not so distant events of the Hungarian Revolution, in both *On Revolution* and "Totalitarian Imperialism," would seem to suggest that she did believe the council system could function as a practicable form of political ordering. This position would only seem to be strengthened by the fact that elsewhere in her writings she similarly advocates the creation of council-inspired organizations as potential solutions to specific, concrete political problems. On the potential for the practical application of the council system one can look, for example, at certain of her writings regarding the Palestine problem, where it is maintained that "local self-government and mixed Jewish-Arab municipal rural councils, on a small scale and as numerous as possible, are the only *realistic political measures* that can eventually lead to the political emancipation of Palestine."[183] Similarly one can examine her comments regarding the modern nation-state system, which has been according to her rendered obsolete by the development of techniques of absolute destruction. The nation-state system was constructed such that issues of sovereignty could be settled through war, which is no longer possible, in the Global North at least, in the nuclear age. As a new state system Arendt proposes a form of decentralized federalism in which "power moves neither from above nor from below, but is horizontally directed so that the federated units mutually check and control their powers."[184] The model for the new type of state system is said to be, not surprisingly, the council system.[185] In short, Arendt theorizes the council tradition in terms of a specific mode of institutionalization that is able to give a positive expression to the interpenetrative flux of the wills of nonidentical "whos." It is that mode of political objectification that is most appropriate to the democratic mediation of opinions between members of a political We,[186] made for the sake of the radical generation of new political modes and orders, which is considered as a performative and joyous good-in-itself.

In this chapter I have attempted to outline what I take to be certain of the most important elements of Arendt's political theory. I hope at this point that the relation between this attempt and my earlier discussion of the Marcusean understanding of essence has been made clear. To begin with, on an ontological level I believe that both Arendt and Marcuse understand the nature of the specifically human being in quite similar terms. Neither Arendt nor Marcuse attempts to objectively define the human being in terms of its possession of any positive markers or characteristics. Rather, human essence in negatively structured by the capacity for creation. All one can say about the human being is that it is the being that has the ability to institute, to generate new objective and subjective actualities that cannot be logically traced back to any prior determinates. Needless to say, however, both Marcuse and Arendt also realize that the actualization of this essential capacity is not possible outside the specific social context that structures individual life. Being is always and already being-with-others. It is precisely to the extent, though, that individuals are nonidentical, that they cannot be referred to any generic positive content that they all share, that their social existence is marked by a form of conflict. What I have argued in this chapter, however, is that Arendt alone is able to ground democratic political institution precisely in this human difference or division. Whereas Marcuse seems to retreat from the political via his reproduction of Marxian instrumentalism and bureaucratism, locating the human actualization of the capacity for radical creation primarily in the sphere of the social production of use-values, Arendt is able to think the possibility of a specifically political creation, and consequently a specifically political gratification.

# 5 Marcuse Contra Arendt: Dialectics, Destiny, Distinction

In the previous chapter it was suggested that Arendt's theory of a performative political activity oriented toward the creation of the radically new can perhaps function as a model for the development of a political theory that is ultimately able to affirm Marcuse's understanding of the meaning of essence. Specifically, Arendt considers political action to be an intrinsic good-in-itself that looks toward the creative institution of new human actualities, this institution bringing forth a unique type of public joy or happiness. At this point, however, we must reckon with what at first glance appears to be a significant bar to any sort of positive juxtaposition of Marcuse and Arendt on the question of politics and essence, specifically, Arendt's vehement critique of the Marxian philosophical tradition, and especially the Marxian dialectic, which as was suggested earlier is in fact the theoretical foundation of the Marcusean ontology. It is Arendt's reductive understanding of the nature of the Marxian dialectic that in fact produces not only her general hostility to Marx and the Marxian project, but also the most objectionable aspect of her political theory, specifically, her unsustainable attempt to generate impenetrable boundaries between various elements of the human condition. From the standpoint of a dialectical analysis, of course, such an interpretative schema is wholly inadequate for grasping the content of human existence in all of its relational complexity. This chapter will be primarily concerned with evaluating those Arendtian distinctions that have been subject to the most amount of external criticism, those between what Arendt takes to be the three elements of the *vita activa*. The structure of Arendt's organization of human activity takes the form of a hierarchically organized tripartition, the independent value of each triadic moment being defined by its ability to properly facilitate, as opposed to merely contribute to, the expression of human freedom. These three elements are labour, that cyclical movement of regeneration that corresponds to the biological life-process of the organic body; work, that fabrication of human objects that creates an independent and stable world of things marked off against the species, testifying thereby to the unnaturalness of human existence; and action, pluralistic human intercourse mediated by speech and aiming at the initiation of radical beginnings, beginnings whose appearances cannot be traced back to any prior moments in a causal sequence of events. According to Arendt, ultimately neither labour nor work can be identified with freedom, labour to the extent that it destroys plurality by uniting many into one through the reduction of human activity to processes concerned with merely biocyclical regeneration, and work to the extent that as a process of conscious fabrication it is always carried out within an instrumental continuum whose goal is predetermined. In the final instance the political is the only human sphere capable of actualizing the human capacity for initiating beginnings.

If Arendt's ontology of the political is to be affirmed at the same time as Marcuse's ontology of labour, if Arendt's theorization of the nature of performative politics is to indeed be interpreted as assimilable into Marcuse's understanding of essence, then Arendt's rigid categorizations will need to be undone. Arendt's categories, in other words, will need to be dialectized. Many readers of Arendt have already recognized the inadequacy of her mode of schematization, pointing out that human activities are far too complex to be reduced to a simple inclusive category, and in fact always contain a surplus that exceeds the boundaries Arendt constructs. Thus, for example, Seyla Benhabib writes that

> making a meal, the quintessential example of the repetitive, ephemeral labour that serves the needs of the body in Arendt's view, may be an expressive act for a gourmet chef, just as it may be an act of love among two or more individuals. When human activities are considered as complex social relations, and contextualized properly, what appears to be one type of activity may turn out to be another; or the same activity may instantiate more than one action type.[1]

The fluidity of the conceptual content under discussion is perhaps nowhere articulated so well as in Marx's understanding of the nature of the ontological status of human labour. Arendt was certainly aware of this fact. Indeed, Arendt's schematization of the *vita activa* can be specifically comprehended within the context of the Marxian dialectic of labour. The thesis of the present chapter is that Arendt's project of categorization is at least partially a response to what Arendt will identify as the difficulty of the Marxian dialectic, specifically the relation of the dialectic to the great political disaster of the twentieth century, the rise of totalitarianism. Marx is implicated in the rise of totalitarianism to the extent that the formal structure of the dialectical logic reproduces totalitarianism's affirmation of conceptual contingency and historical necessity. Dialectics must thus be countered by distinction. It will be suggested here, however, that recognizing the extent to which Arendt misreads Marx's reconstruction of the dialectic, the extent to which the latter escapes assimilation into the theoretical tendency that Arendt describes, creates the possibility for the transcendence of Arendt's much maligned project of partition. Such a transcendence clears the ground for the establishment of a proximity between Marcuse and Arendt, a proximity that is able to affirm Arendt's political ontology at the same time that it is able to affirm Marcuse's ontology of labour.

## Questioning Distinction: The *Vita Activa* and Marx's Ontology of Labour

As suggested earlier, the political theory of Arendt can be conjoined with Marcuse's project only to the extent that her rigid categorizations are undone. It is quite evident that the Marxian theoretical problematic that Marcuse works within provides a direct challenge to Arendt's affirmation of distinction. Arendt, however, does not provide a critique of those aspects of Marx's thought, which would seem to invalidate her theoretical structure, but rather provides a critique of an imagined content within Marx that in fact produces the initial need for this theoretical structure. Arendt's interpretation of Marx can only be described as highly tendentious, Hanna Pitkin noting that "its detailed formulations are almost always mistaken, sometimes blatantly so."[2] A comprehensive examination of Arendt's critique of Marx is beyond the scope of the present study, but a basic understanding of Arendt's specific criticisms of the function of labour in Marx's philosophy is nevertheless essential to the present discussion.[3] Most simply, Marx's concept of labour is identified as a legitimate object of criticism by Arendt to the extent that she takes his affirmation of the potential for material production to act as a mode for the expression of the human essence as evidence that he associates human nature with the natural and biological movements of her *animal laborans*. Arendt ultimately fails to interpret the Marxian concept on the terms of its own logic, but rather immediately maps it within the universe of her own *vita activa*. There does not seem to be much of a valid ground, however, for this conceptual identification. Arendt, for example, will maintain that proof that Marx's concept of labour conforms to her own can be seen in his description of labour as the human being's "metabolism with nature."[4] To Arendt the invocation of this latter phrase is clear evidence that Marx thought of labour in terms of the physiological circle of production and immediate consumption. This basic misunderstanding of the meaning of labour in Marx is the foundation for Arendt's production of a whole set of misinterpretations of Marx's critical theory. Thus, for example, Marx's value theory is alleged to demonstrate the extent to which Marx is incapable of recognizing the – Arendt's – distinction between labour and work. Arendt notes that Marx theorizes that despite the fact that it leaves nothing behind, labour does in fact have a productivity; specifically, labour is capable of producing a surplus, more than is required for its reproduction. Labour's productivity lies not in labour itself, however, but in a surplus of human labour-power. From the standpoint of this productivity, tangible things are brought into existence only accidentally, as what is really produced is simply life: "Unlike the productivity of work, which adds new objects to the human artifice, the productivity of labour power produces objects only incidentally, and is primarily concerned with the means of its own reproduction … it never 'produces' anything but life."[5] As a consequence of this understanding Marx loses the distinction between labour and work. Under communism "all work would have become labour because all things would be understood, not in their worldly, objective quality, but as results of living labour power and the functions of the life process."[6] Marx valorizes labour not because of the object that it produces, because the object possesses a certain quality, but because it produces a surplus. The distinction between labour and work is erased to the extent that the condition of the worldly object is no longer seen as being a relevant element of the productive process.

Now, even a cursory reading of Marx demonstrates the falsity of Arendt's positions here. Arendt notes that Marx often speaks of labour as the production of life.[7] For Marx, though, life is clearly species-life. The significance of the distinction between mere life and species-life is lost on Arendt to the extent that she interprets the latter as a conceptual representation of a process whereby all individual human trajectories are assimilated into a common stream in order to serve the process that moves the collective species. For Arendt Marx's concept of species-being reduces each individual to the position of a generic and undifferentiated member of the species, into an element of the only humanity fit for participation in a universally construed automatic and necessary life-process.[8] Marx is alleged to abstract from the plurality of individuals a singular noun that absorbs all human beings into one conceptual unity.[9] What all members of the species share under such a condition is a one-sided concern with the production of their merely physical lives. Marx is quite explicit, though, that such a production is actually that which represents the alienation of species-life, the latter always affirming the embedded self-differentiation of the individual. Contrary to Arendt's interpretation, Marx in his account of species-being makes it quite clear that the individual must always remain a particular individual: "It is precisely his particularity which makes him an individual, and a real *individual* social being."[10] Individuals "produce their social being which is no abstract, universal power over against single individuals, but the nature of each individual, his own activity, his own life, his own enjoyment, his own wealth."[11] The subject of species-nature is thus "men, not in the abstract, but as real, living, particular individuals."[12]

Arendt's contention, furthermore, that Marx was not at all concerned with the objects of production fabricated in labour quite clearly contradicts the latter's account of the central role of objectification in labour. Needless to say, for Marx a reflection on the nature of the object is essential to the subject's proper identification of her social power. We know that the first moment of alienation is in fact the alienation of the labourer from the object of her production. Labour of course always produces an object, and hence objectification is the inevitable result of all productive activity: "The product of labour is labour which has been congealed in an object, which has become material: it is the *objectification* of labour."[13] Labour thus realizes itself through being objectified. What is more important to note, however, is that, as we have already seen in chapter 1, the human being does not just alter the nature of the objective world through her participation in such processes; she also alters the subjective nature of herself as a specific human being through the development and refinement of her faculties and capacities. Creative activity not only transfers subjectivity to the object, it also transforms the nature of subjectivity. In the final instance Marx's understanding of human essence is conceptualized as a form of praxis in which the individual, by setting in motion – through activities of labour – conscious processes of creation, and acting communally with her other species-beings, overcomes simultaneously both the nature of the objective world and the nature of herself.

What seems clear, and what Arendt does not realize, is that it is precisely because Marx understands the nature of the specifically human social power to be a form of spontaneous creative expression, resulting in the production of a world of objects, that he values labour. The good of labour for Marx does not lie in the fact that it produces an abstract surplus of labour-power, but in its intrinsic ability to develop and refine human capacities. What Arendt is unable to grasp, or, more precisely, what Arendt refuses to grasp, is that the Marxian concept of labour at once cuts across all three of the dimensions of the *vita activa*. Labour is that activity that, potentially all at once, produces the material required for the physical reproduction of the differentiated and nonidentical members of the species, constructs that objective world of things within which individuals recognize their uniquely human quality, and gives an expression to this quality, which is the performative impulse to initiate beginnings through the spontaneous production of new subjective and objective actualities. For Arendt work cannot be labour to the extent that only the former has a definite beginning and a definite end, and only the former is carried out by subjects who control the process through willing specific intentions. Labour cannot be action because, again, it does not begin anything, does not end, and is not intentional, but also because it is a false plurality that simply reduces all individuals to the same undifferentiated content. Work, finally, cannot be action to the extent that it is performed alone and to the extent that it is always instrumental. What Marx is able to show is that all of these distinctions are false, or at least historically constructed and lacking relevance outside the context of the social formation that he will identify as capitalism.

The activity that Arendt refers to as labour is what Marx refers to as alienated labour. Arendt does not recognize this to the extent that she does not adequately take account of the basic Marxian distinction between alienated and nonalienated modes of productive existence. This latter fact is evident in Arendt's reproduction of the common error that sees a contradiction between Marx's affirmation of labour as the means to the realization of the human essence, and Marx's advocacy of the abolition of labour. She thus asks, "If labour is the most human and most productive of man's activities, what will happen when, after the revolution, 'labour is abolished' in the 'realm of freedom,' when man has succeeded in emancipating himself from it? What productive and what essentially human activity will be left?"[14] We know, of course, that all Marx desires is the abolition of alienated labour, of that repetitive and rhythmic process of production that blunts and denies human capacities, precisely the same process that Arendt will critique and yet bizarrely label a Marxian ideal.

Whereas Arendt abstracts from her present historical context a specific mode of social production, affirming this mode's transhistorical form, Marx will differentiate between such modes on the basis of an analysis of the various embodiments of the social relations of production. Such a historical method of abstraction is able to envisage a form of socialized labour that not only provides the material of life, but also produces a world of objects through creative practice and allows for public deliberation regarding the form and content of social production and consumption. The public and intersubjective dimension of labour here assumes a great significance, to the extent that Arendt will concede that not only do all of the activities of the *vita activa* contain an element of natality,[15] but that working in fact requires the same capacity for creativity as does action. Arendt is quite explicit that spontaneity, the capacity to begin something new, is manifest outside the realm of action: "Spontaneity reveals itself in the productivity of the artist, just as it does with everyone who produces things of the world in isolation from others, and one can say that no production is possible without having first been called into life by this capacity to act."[16] It would seem that objects of work can be in a sense understood, then, as products of a form of creation, a creation that differs from the creation of action only to the extent that, Arendt believes, work is necessarily an independent activity. For Arendt the craftsperson is hostile to the actor and the public world to the extent that the former is not dependent on the fact of human plurality: "In order to be in a position to add constantly new things to the already existing world, he himself must be isolated from the public, must be sheltered and concealed from it."[17] It is of course, though, Marx's point to show that all production, to the extent that it is carried out in manner suitable to the human essence, is in fact social production, the collective realization of species-being: "Activity and consumption, both in their content and in their *mode of existence*, are *social: social* activity and *social* consumption; the *human* essence of nature first exists only for *social* man; for only here does nature exist for him as a *bond* with *man* – as his existence for the other and the other's existence for him – as the life-element of the human world; only here does nature exist as the *foundation* of his own *human* existence."[18] Hence, "the individual *is the social being*. His life, even if it may not appear in the direct form of a *communal* life carried out together with others – is therefore an expression and confirmation of *social life*."[19] Objectification is always species-activity to the extent that its subject is never the private individual alone who labours irrespective of a consideration of the species-existence of other individuals. Work, though, is also distinguished from action, according to Arendt, to the extent that it is carried out within a means-end continuum. Because of the instrumental nature of work, all material production is seen as an expression of domination. Production implies an inherent violence toward the object: the making of a table, for example, involving the killing of a tree, which is justified to the extent that the means of production are undertaken in the service of the realization of a fixed end.[20] Needless to say, however, Marx does not understand production in such terms, quite consciously resisting interpreting the objects of the natural world as the mere stuff of domination. Indeed, objectification, the process by which the sensuous human being both posits and is posited by objects, is in fact the foundation of the unity of human and nonhuman nature. Marx thus believes that "communism, as fully-developed naturalism, equals humanism, and as fully developed humanism equals naturalism."[21] Significantly, this understanding of the relation between concrete human practice and nature will be further developed by Marcuse himself, who will argue, as we will see in chapter 6, that a genuinely humanized existence implies in a real sense the notion of the subjectivization of nature. In the final instance, neither of Arendt's bars blocking the interpenetration of the realms of work and action would seem to hold up to the scrutiny of Marx's understanding of nonreified objectification.

It is disingenuous for Arendt to claim that Marx does not see the human essence in terms of reason (the human as *animal rationale*) or material production (the human as *homo faber*), but in terms of labour (the human as *animal laborans*),[22] precisely because Marx cannot make these distinctions, because labour for him is understood as an activity that both produces objects and develops and refines critical-rational capacities. For Marx labour contains aspects of all three of Arendt's activities of the *vita activa*: labour is necessary for the species' biological reproduction; labour is the creation of a stable, objective reality through the interruption of natural processes; and labour is praxis, is self-development, creativity, and the expression of freedom. In short, Arendt ignores the fact that labour for Marx is always "*purposive* or *rational* labour,"[23] as is straightforwardly revealed when Marx writes that "we are not dealing here with those first instinctive forms of labour which remain on the animal level," but rather, "we presuppose labour in a form in which it is an exclusively human characteristic."[24]

Arendt's unwillingness to affirm the possibility of a uniquely human form of labour refers us to one of her other problematic and often criticized distinctions, that between the political, the site of the actualization of freedom, and the social, the site of merely biological reproduction. Mary McCarthy once pointed out to Arendt that political speech must have a content, that debate must be debate about something, and that precisely this fact functions as a ground for the potential inclusion of so-called social issues in the public sphere.[25] Arendt responds by agreeing with the general proposition that the content of politics is historically variant: "Life changes constantly, and things are constantly there that want to be talked about. At all times people living together will have affairs that belong in the realm of the public – 'are worthy to be talked about in public'. What these matters *are* at any historical *moment* is probably *utterly* different."[26] Despite this concession, Arendt will continue to maintain that there are certain matters that are not subject to debate and hence not political, matters that can indeed be determined with certainty: "Everything which can really be figured out, in the sphere Engels called the administration of things – these are social things in general. That they should then be subject to debate seems to me phony and a plague."[27] An example of one such question that "can really be figured out" is housing: "There shouldn't be any debate about the question that everybody should have decent housing," and, "if it's a question of how many square feet every human being needs in order to be able to breathe and to live a decent life, this is something which we really can figure out."[28] In affirming such a position Arendt will clearly reproduce the administrative logic that her political theory ostensibly attempts to overcome, the logic that maintains that there are spheres of human existence that can be left completely to social engineers, who instrumentally solve problems through the practical application of principles of technical authority. The housing question, for example, presupposes all kinds of political questions that an administration of things would be utterly incapable of answering. In Richard Bernstein's words, "only when we come down to concrete details of what is decent housing, how it is to be financed, how this is to affect the 'allocation of resources,' what priority this is to have, how this relates to 'property rights,' do we face genuine issues of social and political conflict."[29] Indeed, upon reflection it is difficult to identify a single economic or so-called issue of necessity that in itself does not refer to a specific political problematic defined and instituted within the constellation of a specific historical spectrum. Castoriadis, for example, probably does not overstate the case too much when he writes that "the *only* thing that is not defined by the imaginary in human needs for the past three million years is an approximate number of calories per day, including an approximately given qualitative composition," for "every 'productive technique' is such only by reference to the particular 'ends' that determine it and that it, in turn, determines (by circular implication) – that is, social *needs*, needs that are always defined in terms of the imaginary and that could not be defined any other way."[30] What Arendt failed to recognize in formulating the social-political binary is thus that all determinations regarding the institution of policies looking toward the satisfaction of human material wants of existence are in themselves articulated as they are only to the extent that the process of determination is undertaken within the context of historically specific social imaginaries.

## Arendt's Critique of the Dialectic: On the Need for Distinction

It was certainly suggested to Arendt that the inflexibility of her conceptual categories could be potentially undone through dialectical analysis. Arendt once proudly agreed with Albrecht Wellmer that her concern with preserving distinction was a consequence of the lack of Hegelian elements in her thought.[31] After Wellmer had proposed to Arendt a technique to dissolve the rigidity of her distinctions, she responded thusly: "I would say that by these fancy methods you have *eliminated* distinction and have already done this Hegelian trick in which one concept, all of its own, begins to develop into its own *negative. No it doesn't!* And *good* doesn't develop into *bad*, and *bad* doesn't develop into *good*. There I would be adamant."[32] Although Arendt does concede that her distinctions "hardly ever correspond to watertight compartments in the real world,"[33] she is quite clear that human existence nevertheless demands that they be made. For her it is of the utmost importance to maintain distinctions, despite the fact that there is "a silent agreement in most discussions among political and social scientists that we can ignore distinctions and proceed on the assumption that everything can eventually be called anything else, and that distinctions are meaningful only to the extent that each of us has the right 'to define his terms.'"[34]

Such a right to define terms arbitrarily is only possible in a world devoid of common sense and is a manifestation of the individual's retreat from the public world of shared meaning into a strictly private realm. For Arendt, of course, the twentieth-century political phenomenon that is most successful in overcoming the public realm – although it is just as successful in overcoming the private as well – is totalitarianism. The dialectic is implicated in the triumph of totalitarianism to the extent that it provides the theoretical tools for that practical overcoming of distinction that marks the totalitarian experience.

As was the case with Marx, Arendt was far from an adequate reader of Hegel, often, for example, reducing the latter's dialectic to the crude structural stereotype of thesis-antithesis-synthesis.[35] For Arendt the dialectic is a mystical construction that assimilates all human events into its own previously worked-out logic, a logic that claims to hold the key to the formula of universal world history. Indeed, in her mind it is a noncoincidental matter of fact that the periods of prominence for naturalistic philosophies, of which the dialectical philosophy is one, are always immediately followed by religious revivals.[36] To the extent that it allegedly claims an objective knowledge of the functioning of the laws of world history, the dialectic is seen as a form of ideology. Ideology is distinct from opinion "in that it claims to possess either the key to history, or the solution for all the 'riddles of the universe,' or the intimate knowledge of the hidden universal laws which are supposed to rule nature and man."[37] The identifying marker of ideologies is their claim that they are able to solve the problem of history to the extent that they believe they have discovered the proper idea motivating historical movement. The happening of any event occurs as a consequence of the internal logic of the idea, a fundamental premise from which all subsequent movement can be deduced. Needless to say, such processes of assimilation must necessarily deny the spontaneous production of beginnings that characterizes human action: "no ideology which aims at the explanation of all historical events of the past and at mapping out the course of all events of the future can bear the unpredictability which springs from the fact that men are creative, that they can bring forward something so new that nobody ever foresaw it."[38] It is precisely such a denial that for Arendt characterizes the operation of the dialectic: "Dialectical logic, with its process from thesis to antithesis to synthesis which in turn becomes the thesis of the next dialectical movement, is not different in principle, once an ideology gets hold of it; the first thesis becomes the premise and its advantage for ideological explanation is that this dialectical device can explain away all factual contradictions as stages of one identical, consistent movement."[39] For Arendt it is precisely this process of thesis-antithesis-synthesis that Marx adopts from Hegel and incorporates into his methodology.[40]

Arendt argues that "Marx formalizes Hegel's dialectic of the absolute in history as a *development*, as a self-propelled process."[41] Marx read into history an iron law of movement, seeing specifically both politics and philosophy as superstructural manifestations of the struggle between classes. To the extent that he had a political philosophy, it "was based not upon an analysis of action and acting men but, on the contrary, on the Hegelian concern with history."[42] We know that for Arendt nothing can be seen as the end point of action in the same way that a material product can be seen as the end point of fabrication. Marx makes the same mistake as Hegel, believing that freedom can be comprehended as an object to be constructed. If history is the process that looks toward the realization of the product of freedom, then there must come a time when this object is finished, when history ends: "The process of history, as it shows itself in our calendars stretching into the infinity of the past and the future, has been abandoned for the sake of an altogether different kind of process, that of making something which has a beginning as well as an end, whose laws of motion, therefore, can be determined (for instance as dialectical movement) and whose innermost content can be discovered (for instance as class struggle)."[43] It is precisely to the extent that history is considered within an instrumental framework of making that affirms all means that look toward the realization of the end are sanctioned, that the Marxian tradition has so often found itself justifying violence and terror for the sake of freedom. Such a position achieves only its most advanced expression in the development of one form of the political phenomenon that is totalitarianism: "Marxism could be developed into a totalitarian ideology because of its perversion, or misunderstanding, of political action as the making of history."[44]

Arendt is quite explicit: She believes that the origins of totalitarianism can be at least partially traced to a certain "philosophical heresy" that reached its highest theoretical expression in the work of Hegel, and which was practically applied by Marx.[45] This heresy overturned the dominant view of political philosophy at the time, which presumed that positive laws acquired their stabilizing permanence through their derivation from a singular universal law. Under totalitarianism "terror, as the daily execution of an ever-changing universal law of movement, makes all positive law in its relative permanence impossible and drives the whole community into a flood of catastrophes."[46] For the desire for action totalitarianism substitutes the need for insight into the natural laws of historical movement. For this reason dialectical Marxism is a suitable ideological foundation for totalitarianism, as it sees "men as the product of a gigantic historical process racing toward the end of historical time."[47] Subjected to such conditions, "human beings, caught or thrown into the process of Nature or History for the sake of accelerating its movement, can become only the executioners or the victims of its inherent law."[48] Like the dialectic, then, totalitarianism sacrifices human freedom, the concern with spontaneous and radical creation, to historical necessity; indeed, if the pure space of totalitarianism, the concentration camp, is marked by anything, it is its attempt to reduce the human being to a bundle of automatic reactions through cleansing from human life all traces of spontaneity. The effort of totalitarian movements to suppress human spontaneity and creativity is the most advanced historical attack on the human essence, nothing less than an attempt at "the transformation of human nature itself."[49]

The observation of historical necessity, however, is only one element of Arendt's critique of dialectics and totalitarianism, which in fact takes a double-form. The historical law is able to preserve its sense of consistency only to the extent that it is able to eschew distinction: the law is never wrong if it is able to redefine the meaning of categories such that they are capable of being assimilated into its own logic. The dialectic thus incorporates two only apparently contradictory positions, the first presuming that history proceeds along a predetermined axis whose law of movement can be objectively determined in advance of the movement, and the second presuming that all historical objects of consideration can be redefined as the interpreter of historical rationality so desires. The latter position is indeed what makes the former theoretically possible. A history conceived of as "process or stream or development" necessarily must posit "that everything comprehended by it can change into anything else, that distinctions become meaningless because they become obsolete, submerged, as it were, by the historical stream, the moment they have appeared."[50] Dialectics operates according to the principle of historical necessity. Its determinism, though, can only be guaranteed by the conceptual looseness of its categories, by the fact that every object considered by the dialectician has the potential to transform, by its own internal movement, into every other object. Once again, the theoretical principle is seen to be concretely applied in the totalitarian space, which seeks to overcome distinction through the overflowing of the limits of human experience: "The camps are the living laboratories revealing that 'everything is possible,' that humans can create and inhabit a world where the distinctions between life and death, truth and falsehood, appearance and reality, body and soul, and even victim and murderer are constantly blurred."[51] This process is imagined by Arendt in terms of an iron band that squeezes together all bodies into one, individuals being more easily assimilated into the universal history when they are all reduced to the same undifferentiated and generic content.[52] Just as totalitarianism is able to confirm its historical narrative through the manufacturing of reality – for example, the ideology that sees particular human subjects as subhuman is confirmed the moment the camps are able to produce subjects incapable of spontaneity – so too theoretically can the inevitable movement of history be realized through the dialectical ability to create anything through the transcendence of distinction. Arendt makes her distinctions quite self-consciously – she refuses to be dialectical in her analyses to the extent that the dialectic is seen to remain committed to, in a certain sense, totalitarianism, the practical realization of the implacable logic of the Idea.

The affirmation of distinction is made in order to guard against the excesses of the dialectic, the dialectic's presumption of historical universality and its ability to collapse objects into one another – the former is realized precisely as a consequence of the functioning of the latter. We have already suggested, though, that Arendt's critique operates on a highly caricaturized model of the dialectic, one that indeed bears virtually no resemblance to Marx's historical dialectic, and only a slight resemblance to Hegel's ontological dialectic. The question demands to be answered: is there a form of dialectical analysis that escapes the two conditions Arendt criticizes, the two conditions that generate the need for the type of rigorous methodological separation that Arendt calls for? My earlier discussion of Marcuse's application of a reconstructed dialectic, whose outlines can be found in Marx, would seem to suggest that there is, that dialectical analysis can be performed in such a way that it is able to preserve distinction at the same time that it elides assimilation into a universalist historical logic. What is more, though, Marcuse himself will in fact criticize specific applications of the dialectic that assert either of Arendt's two conditions. Marcuse is, just as much as Arendt, concerned with guarding against the affirmation of principles of historical necessity and conceptual arbitrariness. That the former is the case can be seen in Marcuse's critique of Engels's dialectic of nature, and that the latter is the case can be seen in his critique of the dialectical universalism of Norman O. Brown.

## Marcuse's Critique of Nondialectical Dialectics

According to Marcuse it is within the philosophy of Soviet Marxism that the dialectic of nature achieves it most exaggerated form, Stalin's "Dialectical and Historical Materialism" being simply "a paraphrase of Engels's propositions in his *Dialectics of Nature*."[53] When analysed in the light of the dialectical methods of Hegel and Marx, the logical propositions that compose the dialectic of nature "are neither true nor false – they are empty shells."[54] A comprehensive examination of the nature of the Soviet dialectic is not necessary here. It just needs to be noted that it is rejected by Marcuse precisely to the extent that it attempts to present itself as an all-inclusive theory of worldly existence, a theory that is able to delineate the structure of history and assign all historical objects a logical place within this structure. The "hypostatization of dialectic into a universal scientific world outlook"[55] necessitates the abandonment of dialectic's actual concern with history: "The dialectical process thus interpreted is no longer in a strict sense a historical process – it is rather that history is reified into a second nature. Soviet developments thereby obtain the dignity of the objective natural laws by which they are allegedly governed and which, if correctly understood and taken into consciousness, will eventually right all wrongs and lead to final victory over the opposing forces."[56] Here in *Soviet Marxism* Marcuse will even go so far as to delineate a relation between the Bolsheviks' vanguardist political authoritarianism and their adoption of an ahistorical and deterministic dialectic: "As the will of the leadership acts upon the proletariat from above, the theory pronounced by the leadership or endorsed by it assumes rigid determinist forms. The dialectic is petrified into a universal system in which the historical process appears as a 'natural' process and in which objective laws over and above the individuals govern not only the capitalist but also the socialist society."[57] The fundamental error of Soviet Marxism is its positing of a final termination point to history, a termination point toward which all historical occurrences are looking.  It is precisely because for Marcuse there is in fact no such point that there can be no Marxian theory of socialism. Such an idea contradicts the basic principles of authentic, or negative, dialectical thought. According to Marcuse, Marxism is not a slave to the laws of history but aims actually at the latter's abolition.[58]

For him "theory cannot predetermine the laws of freedom," for "the essentially historical character of Marxian theory precludes unhistorical generalizations."[59]

If Hegel will ultimately violate the negativity of his dialectic through situating it within a closed ontological structure that culminates in the positive realization of a teleological Idea, such is in no way the case with Marx. It is precisely this that Arendt fails to recognize. Marx in fact takes Hegel to task for the construction of a speculative and metaphysical concept that overwhelms the concrete multiplicity of the reality it attempts to subsume. In *The Holy Family*, for example, Marx shows how, from the standpoint of metaphysical analysis, reflection on the nature of particular fruits leads to the speculative construction of the general concept of Fruit.[60] This abstract concept of Fruit is consequently taken by speculative analysis to be something real existing outside of the subject, something that constitutes the essence of the particular fruits perceived through sense-perception. In doing this, the subject is "saying, therefore, that to be a pear is not essential to the pear, that to be an apple is not essential to the apple; that what is essential to these things is not their real existence, perceptible to the senses, but the essence that I have abstracted from them and then foisted on them, the essence of my idea – '*Fruit*.'"[61] Particular fruits come to be seen as simply particular forms of existence of the primary mode of being, which is Fruit: "Particular real fruits are no more than *semblances* whose true essence is '*the substance*' – '*Fruit*.'"[62] The distinctions between particular fruits registered by the human sensory apparatus are consequently disregarded as contingent and nonessential.

However, speculative philosophy of this sort must, "if it is to attain some semblance of real content," work its way backward to take account of particular differentiations within the primary substance. "If apples, pears, almonds and strawberries are really nothing but '*the* Substance,' '*the* Fruit,' the question arises: Why does '*the* Fruit' manifest itself to me sometimes as an apple, sometimes as a pear, sometimes as an almond? Why this *semblance of diversity* which so obviously contradicts my speculative conception of *Unity*, '*the* Substance,' '*the* Fruit'?"[63] The answer to the question lies in the fact that substance is conceived not as static matter but as "living, self-differentiating, moving essence."[64] Fruit thus gives itself through its own dynamic motion a multiplicity of differentiated appearances. So, speculative philosophy is able to account for concrete differences in the nature of particular fruits, but only as semblances: particular fruits are ultimately considered not from the standpoint of their concrete, sensuous existence, but from the standpoint of their objective position within the dynamic life-process of the initial abstraction Fruit. Real fruits are spontaneously created out of the activity of the mind, which is capable of comprehending the initial abstraction as the logical starting point of the speculative process. "In the speculative way of speaking, this operation is called comprehending *Substance* as *Subject*, as an *inner process*, as an *Absolute Person*, and this comprehension constitutes the essential character of *Hegel's* method."[65]

Arendt attributes to Marx's method the same metaphysical quality that Marx observes in Hegel's method. There seems, though, to be very little justification for this former criticism. Arendt accuses Marx of completely formalizing the dialectic, of releasing it from any substantive content.[66] To the extent that he achieves this, the dialectic is seen to be able to be applied in any situation. A cursory reading of the basic principles of Marx's methodology, as they are outlined in the *Grundrisse*, demonstrates this to be emphatically not the case.[67] As he was in *The Holy Family*, and as he will be throughout all of his writings, Marx is explicit on the need to reject absolute and universalist modes of abstraction. Abstraction must begin from the simplest, most uncontroversial element of reality, building up from there to more generalized and concrete concepts through the logical examination of the relations and determinations that structure the initial abstraction. Thus, for Marx, although it is not strictly speaking incorrect to simply posit that, for example, country $y$ has a population $x$, it is just an abstraction to the extent that it leaves out a consideration of the further determinations that structure it, for example the composition of classes within the population.[68] One can only analyse and evaluate the nature of the concrete concept after one has logically moved through all of the relations suggested by it. Marxian concepts are not abstract universals that impose a singular meaning on the object, but rather concrete universals saturated by these determinations and relations. Now, according to Marx the most undeniable fact of reality in capitalist society is the existence of an immense accumulation of commodities. This world of immense accumulation thus presents itself as the starting point of dialectical analysis. Hence, in *Capital* Marx moves from an analysis of the commodity to a discussion of use-value and value, to concrete and abstract labour, to money, to the primary circuits of exchange, and so on. Concrete universals are not simply posited but constructed as a consequence of the immanent critical evaluation of simpler concepts. It is here that we arrive at the notion of the labour of the dialectic, "of the working-up of observation and conception into concepts,"[69] an understanding of dialectical analysis far removed from the critical presentation of Arendt, which assumes the necessity of a previously constituted universal concept that moves backward, structuring all simpler concepts according to its own transcendent logic.

Just as he provides a critique of the dialectic as an instrument of historical necessity, so too does Marcuse provide a critique of the dialectic as an absolute effacer of distinction. Very few of Marcuse's commentators have called attention to Marcuse's concern with the need for the preservation of certain boundaries of existence. One of those who does note this concern, though, is Shierry Weber, who points out, for example, that one element of one-dimensionality is "the erasing of distinctions between things that were once in opposition. Integration, the life force, works not through the abolition of distinctions but by rendering them into a meaningful, harmonious whole."[70] Although Weber will exaggerate the extent to which the Marcusean project seeks the integration of distinction into a closed totality, she is nevertheless correct to point out Marcuse's concern with the preservation of separation. This concern is probably nowhere more clearly revealed than in Marcuse's critique of the dialectical practice of Norman O. Brown, particularly as the latter is expressed in the text *Love's Body*. Marcuse will criticize *Love's Body* for surrendering to mysticism and for abandoning the liberatory potential of concrete human practice in the sphere of the political. Brown, in the face of the contradictions of the present social formation, desires the construction of a new whole that is capable of resolving all social division. As a model for this new whole, Brown goes back to the whole of otherworldly myth, which through its illusory synthesizing capacity is able to resolve unequivocally all the contradictions of this world. Brown is quite explicit on this point: the end of mystification and idolatry "is not the abolition of the temple, but the discovery of the true temple: Love's Body."[71] For Brown literalism necessarily leads to reification – it "makes out of everything *things*, these table and chairs, commodities."[72] The only alternative to reification is a move away from literalism, from any theoretical orientation that maintains it is potentially possible to call things by their right names, that it is potentially possible to distinguish between objects. Thus reification has to be denied and mystery affirmed: "Literalism is idolatry of words; the alternative to idolatry is mystery."[73] Literalism is idolatry, a worship of false images. To counter this idolatry Brown turns from literalism to a symbolism capable of evoking the new mystery of Love's Body.

For Marcuse, though, replacing symbolism with symbolism is not enough. Symbolism must in some sense recapture that which it is attempting to symbolize; it must become injected with a certain historical sensibility: "Unless the analysis takes the road of return from the symbolic to the literal, from the illusion to the reality of the illusion, it remains ideological, replacing one mystification by another."[74] The one-sided partiality of reality may indeed constitute its falseness, but it is a falseness that nevertheless produces real effects on the individuals dwelling within this reality. The task of a critical theory is not the outright rejection of the artefacts of the distorted life and a flight into a new irreality, but rather the careful and nuanced interpretation of these artefacts and their potential to contribute to the construction of a future reality. Brown's mistake lies in his total elimination of the "decisive difference between real and artificial, natural and political, fulfilling and repressive boundaries and divisions."[75] Freedom can be actualized only in this life, a life that can never be above contradiction, a life that will always be in some sense mapped by division and boundary. In Brown's understanding, "the solution, the end of the drama of history is the restoration of original and total unity: unity of male and female, father and mother, subject and object, body and soul – abolition of the self, of mine and thine, abolition of the reality principle, of all boundaries."[76] For Marcuse the quest for fulfilment through the attempted overcoming of all mechanisms of differentiation can only result in a radical non-fulfillment: "fulfilment becomes meaningless if everything is one, and one is everything."[77] In *Love's Body* Brown claims to be a dialectician,[78] though his thinking does not extend much further than an unqualified affirmation that in dialectical logic only the whole is the true. Against Marcuse's negative dialectic "Brown envisions an Absolute, a Totality, a Whole which swallows up all parts and divisions, all tensions and all needs, that is to say, all life."[79] Brown's dialectic, in other words, is a manifestation of that theoretical model criticized by Arendt, the model that maintains anything is capable of transforming into anything else. From Marcuse's perspective, though, it is precisely in this sense that the whole is the false. The fight for the true whole, the differentiated whole, is, Marcuse tells us, the work of critical theory. It is a critical theory that attempts to analyse and comprehend the content of the actual, concrete, historical, and antagonistic totality within which all subjects are situated, without appealing to a higher unity capable of resolving all separation.[80] For Marcuse the universal is nothing but an expression of the tension between actuality and potentiality, and thus transcends all of its particular objective realizations. No beautiful object, for example, can ever encompass beauty itself, for the universal here implies a transcending relation, a look beyond particular existence: "Thus the concept of beauty comprehends all the beauty not *yet* realized; the concept of freedom all the liberty not *yet* attained."[81] Because there is no historical point at which the universal could ever be attained, it remains always a goal to be striven for. Such a striving requires the positing of a methodology of distinctive flexibility, a methodology that is able to comprehend historical objects in their relational complexity, but which at the same time does not abandon on principle the affirmation of the need for conceptual separation. It is precisely such a methodology that Arendt does not consider, preferring instead to assimilate all versions of the dialectic into her rigid and ossified model.

To summarize, although there have been many commentators who have criticized Arendt for insisting on the ontological need to construct rigid and impenetrable boundaries between the various activities of the human world, my suggestion in this chapter has been that such commentators have not adequately theorized the philosophical motivation behind this Arendtian project. Earlier, I argued that Arendt is forced to adopt a project of partition to the extent that she understands the dialectical logic as being implicated in the rise of totalitarianism. The dialectical method allegedly affirms on a theoretical plane that which totalitarianism attempts to realize practically in the world of empirical human bodies: it presents us with a logical system that is able to objectively determine the teleological movement of history through the affirmation of the theoretical possibility of its objects of analysis indiscriminately morphing into one another. From the standpoint of both the dialectician and the totalitarian leader, the flow of history can be mapped precisely to the extent that all historical objects escape definition. What I have argued, however, is that Arendt failed to appreciate the subtlety of Marx's dialectic, which in fact is just as concerned with avoiding the sorts of theoretical problems – specifically the problem of historical necessity and the problem of abstract universalism – as the Arendtian methodology is. Had Arendt made the effort to more seriously engage with the Marxian literature, she may very well have been motivated to reevaluate not only her critique of Marx, but also the inflexibility of her conceptual distinctions.

I would like to stress, however, that the inadequacy of Arendt's critique of the dialectic should not invalidate other dimensions of her assessment of Marxism. Most importantly, Arendt continues to provide us with one of the most powerful critiques of Marxian political theory. As I suggested in chapter 2, with the notable exceptions of the *Critique of Hegel's* Philosophy and Right and *The Civil War in France*, Marx fails to present us with a critical theory of politics that is able to affirm his dynamic understanding of creative essence; specifically, he fails to present us with an adequate theory of radical democracy, falling back instead to traditional instrumentalist and managerialist models of political transformation. This error, furthermore, was seen as repeating itself in Marcuse (and Western Marxism more generally). Here at least, Arendt, who theorizes politics as action, as spontaneous collective activity oriented toward the production of radically new beginnings, has much to teach both Marx and Marcuse. Not only is the Marxian dialectic open to such a politics, but to the extent that the former – as opposed to traditional, closed metaphysical systems – looks toward the possibility of allowing for the emergence of new objects of thought, for the sake of the production of new modes of doing and being, it in fact demands it.

Indeed, the potential for the construction of a dialogue between Arendt and the Marxist tradition lies precisely in the fact that each of them is concerned with affirming the historical possibility of human creation. As I have noted, Arendt herself seems to have been dimly aware of this: "When Marx declared he no longer wanted to interpret the world but to change it, he stood, so to speak, on the threshold of a new concept of Being and world, by which Being and world were no longer givens but possible products of man."[82] Arendt, however, was not willing to recognize the degree to which Marx's philosophy was structured so as to allow for the sphere of labour to act as a field for the realization of this possibility for historical creation. Arendt's mistake lay in closing off certain spheres of human activity to potentially performative modes of being. To this degree, Marx's ontology of labour speaks to a certain lack or deficiency in Arendt, just as Arendt's political ontology speaks to a certain lack or deficiency in Marx. The constellative juxtaposition of Arendt and Marcuse, seemingly closed off as a consequence of Arendt's affirmation of the need for distinction, is opened upon the recognition of the unsustainability of this latter project, and a ground is thereby provided for a more meaningful engagement between the Arendtian and Marxist theoretical traditions.

# 6 Marcuse: Reconsidering the Political

In this chapter I will reconsider the political thought of Marcuse in light of those performative elements of the Arendtian political ontology that I previously called attention to. I would like to first, however, once again refer to the original political-theoretical problematic motivating the analysis. In chapter 3 I explored the contradiction between Marcuse's affirmation of essence and his advocacy of a specific form of political practice intended to facilitate the transition to a world capable of actualizing this essence. This contradiction can in a certain sense be traced back to a logical problem inherent in revolutionary strategy. In order for the desire for the realization of the sensibility concerned with essence to arise, the reproduction of the present social formation, to the extent that it produces the contrary system of values, would have to be overcome; however, the overcoming of this social formation requires the action of individuals who are already concerned with the realization of essence, who already feel the need to sublate the existing system of values. Rolf Wiggershaus will recall an instance in which a student questioned Marcuse about the potential forces of radical change in contemporary society:

Instead of addressing this, Marcuse admitted his helplessness in the face of the vicious circle that, in order for the new demands to develop, the mechanisms that reproduced the old demands would first have to be abolished; while, on the other hand, in order to abolish those mechanisms, the demand for them to be abolished would first have to be created. The only solution he could envisage, as he had already mentioned in the essay on tolerance and again – almost to excess – in an interview, 'Professors as State Regents?,' published in *Der Spiegel* several weeks after the Berlin event, was an educational dictatorship."[1]

The production of revolutionary consciousness among the majority of individuals becomes the responsibility of an intellectual elite, a new revolutionary subject that is understood as the primary agent of politics. Before the working classes are to become a subject of political practice, they must first be an object of the intellectual vanguard, the latter unidirectionally imposing its political and organizational strategies upon those social groups external to itself.

It would seem then that Marcuse's pessimism regarding the potential for the spontaneous development of a generalized critical consciousness compels him to advocate the authoritarian institution of an educational dictatorship as the only means of stimulating revolutionary political practice. In criticizing Marcuse's affirmation of such an educational dictatorship, Isaac Balbus will suggest, on the contrary, that the subject's very participation in authoritarian pedagogical processes can itself be seen as evidence of her prior predisposition toward revolutionary consciousness. He asks why the social actor would enter the educational process if she did not already possess a critical reason, if she had not already begun to grapple with the issues of subjectivity: "the voluntary nature of the participation of the social actor in the process of political education presupposes that she be recognized as an active participant in – a subject, not an object of – this process. It presupposes, in other words, that the sensuous social actor be recognized as a rational social theorist."[2] Any form of political education has to recognize the trace of the new sensibility in the social actor, and therefore conduct itself in a manner fitting of this new sensibility: "Successful political education presupposes that the educator has learned to be as 'non-aggressive, erotic, and receptive' as those whom he would educate."[3] The question that demands to be answered, however, is whether it is in fact the case that Marcuse was completely blind to such an understanding, to the fact that their always exists a trace of the essential sensibility, and that this trace can be nurtured and developed through certain forms of democratic practice? When Marcuse is read in the context of the orthodox Marxist tradition, it is surely the vanguardist elements of the former's politics that most clearly shine through. Indeed, more generally, Marcuse reproduces the double-form of Marx's antipolitics: its instrumentalism and its managerialism. There is embedded in Marcuse's writings, though, an alternative understanding of the meaning of politics, an understanding that eschews all instrumental and authoritarian considerations, stressing instead the performative and creative dimensions of political practice. The suggestion of the present work is that a reading of Marcuse in relation to the political theory of Arendt permits the full emergence and development of this understanding. A consideration of the insights of Arendt into the nature of political action allows for a critical reconstruction of the political thought of Marcuse: in particular, it allows us to see in certain of Marcuse's writings on politics an affirmation of a spontaneously developing noninstrumental, nonvanguardist, and nonidentitarian form of political activity that is understood as a type of performance, which is seen as valuable not only to the extent that it motivates a transition from the present society to the future one, but also because its expression is seen as being an intrinsic good bringing forth joy and gratification. Such a reconstruction, therefore, will be the object of this final chapter. Specifically, I will locate the germ of such a politics in Marcuse's early writings on the nature of radical action, and suggest that this germ is further developed in Marcuse's later writings on what he takes to be the biological foundation of socialism, a foundation that is concretely actualized, in a specifically political form, in the theory and practice of the New Left and the council tradition.

## The Theory of the Radical Act

The alternative analysis of Marcuse's political theory must begin with a reading of the concept of the radical act, which was developed in Marcuse's earliest published writings while he was still a student of Heidegger.[4] We know that for Marcuse, Marxism cannot be considered a scientific theory to the extent that it does not expound a truth-system whose validity lies in its ability to appropriate stable empirical knowledge. Philosophy will only become concrete when it takes off from history, when its understanding of potential existence is filtered through the critical analysis of the particular relations and determinations that structure this existence. Such a task presupposes interdisciplinarity: concrete philosophy must make use of other historical intellectual disciplines, for example history, sociology, economics, and more, if it is to fully grasp its reality. According to Marcuse, none of these disciplines is sufficient to grasp reality in itself, however, as none looks to existence as such, the latter category including within itself the contingent modes of political being, economic being, and social being.[5] The theoretical investigations that mark the practice of each are thus enclosed within a circumscribed field of assumptions and presuppositions that attempt to bar the incorporation of external insight. What each discipline aims at is the discovery of a certain content. For Marcuse, though, the truth of historical human existence lies not in the detection, either in reality or in thought, of a certain static state or condition of existence, but in the recognition of the indeterminate truth of human possibility. Philosophy "would miss its mark entirely if it were to attempt to inspect Marxism from the vantage of some transcendent position 'beyond' Marxism, applying the terms of logical closure, universal non-contradiction, and atemporal validity. The truths of Marxism are not truths of knowing, but rather truths of happening."[6] Of special importance here is the concrete happening of the historical subject. Whereas Marcuse primarily identifies this happening as being expressed in processes of creative material production – nonalienated labour – in "Contributions to a Phenomenology of Historical Materialism" and "On Concrete Philosophy," he associates it also with the initiation of political action.

The concrete philosophy capable of comprehending the phenomenon of historical happening is the dialectical philosophy. Again, the dialectic for Marcuse is not reducible to a quasi-scientific theory that is capable of arbitrarily assimilating objects into a previously structured logical framework. The application of such scientific methods are perfectly legitimate within those fields of study that deal with permanent and nonhistorical objects, such as mathematics, but are wholly inappropriate for the analysis of historical spheres of human existence. Contrary to such presumptive methodologies, "the dialectical method sees its object as historical – that is, it regards it in terms of becoming and of transitoriness, as something that has developed in a particular historical situation."[7] What the dialectical method aims at is "doing justice at every moment to the specific, concrete-historical situation of its object."[8] To grasp the concrete-historical situation of the individual subject is above all else to grasp her in the web of social relationships that she acts into and that acts upon her, to grasp her existence as a member of a specific family, class, nationality, society, and more, her existence, in other words, as a member of a community, itself existent only as a consequence of its emergence within a contingent natural and historical context.[9] The subject, then, can only be analysed as a historical subject as opposed to an abstract individual subject. For Marcuse the recognition of the contingency of human existence, represented in the multiplicity of historical subjectivities, implies, just as it does for Arendt, a historical indeterminacy. Although subjects are constrained in their actions as a consequence of their objective situation, the very fact of their objective situation presupposes the capacity for action. To recognize the historical nature of human beingness is to recognize that the present state of the human being could be otherwise, that the capacity to change the form of human existence is always a possibility: "Philosophy, once it has found itself in a situation of contemporaneity with its Dasein, can no longer philosophize as in a vacuum, in generalities 'without qualitative pressure'; existing in reality, it will be forced to take an unequivocal position, to make decisions, to choose its point of view, visibly and tangibly, ready to submit itself to any test."[10] Concrete philosophy is thus the philosophy that is concerned with the ontological possibility of choosing, or better, creating forms of human existence, of acting into the world for the purposes of changing it.

According to Marcuse, Marxism is the "theory of social action, of the historical act."[11] What Marxism is oriented toward is the consideration of the "historical possibility of the radical act – of an act that should clear the way for a new and necessary reality as it brings about the actualization of the whole person."[12] Marcuse follows Marx in pointing out that to be radical is to grasp things by the root, and that the root of humanity is humankind itself.[13] Although all actions alter factual circumstances, not all actions change existences, that is, change the nature of humanity; only the radical act does. To the extent that it is radical, then, the act is an expression of the essentiality of the human subject, which we have already identified as the capacity for creative overcoming. Radical action thus aims at "the decisive realization of the human essence."[14] But if radical action is oriented toward the actualization of essence, and if essence is itself seen as the ability to act radically, to overcome historical existences, then radical action must not be simply concerned with the contingent or arbitrary production of human existences, but rather with the institution of a specific form of human existence, one that is able to generalize and stabilize the capacity for radical action. Indeed, we can recall that it was precisely this that the polis – and later the councils – aimed at in Arendt's thought. In the context of his own historical situation, however, Marcuse identifies the radical act as the self-conscious action of a proletariat that correctly perceives the fundamental nature of its historical condition.

In keeping with the identification of the radical act with the general human essence, Marcuse is here adamant that this act cannot be externally forced upon the actor from an objective exterior position: "Necessity is *immanent* to the radical act. That it must be done precisely here and precisely by this person, means that it cannot, under any circumstances, be forced on the doer from the outside; that the doer *must* – in the sense of an immanent *must* – commit it now because the deed is given along with the doer's very existence."[15] The necessity of the radical act does not here derive from the perception of its place within a causal historical sequence moving toward a determinable and logical terminal point, but rather from the simple fact that the ability to act radically into history is essential to the very nature of the human subject, and that, more than this, this essential ability is incapable of being absolutely effaced. For Marcuse "the possibility of emancipated subjectivity had not yet been entirely lost."[16] In desiring to produce the form of existence that would, from the standpoint of the determinate historical condition, be most successful in overcoming those contingent relations blocking the capacity to act, radical action multiplies both the desire for its realization and the conditions for the realization of this desire through its very exercise. The always-present and necessary need to act is intensified as a consequence of the actualization of this always-present and necessary need.

Again, the radical act always occurs in history. Concrete philosophy can "only approach existence if it seeks out Dasein in the sphere in which its existence is based: as it *acts* in its world in accordance with its historical situation."[17] For Marcuse historical development "is the unfolding of societies as the concrete historical unities propelled by their reproduction and conditioned by their natural environment."[18] To the extent that the human being always exists with and acts with others in society, historical humanity must always be considered as a social-historical humanity. Marcuse believed that in his own historical time and place the consciousness of the subject's position as the bearer of the radical act is achieved through her immanent recognition of herself as a member of a specific class, through class consciousness. Regardless of the accuracy of such an identification, the point to be made is simply that the historical subject always considers herself and her ability to act within an intersubjective context of human community. The subject of historical change is thus not the individual, but the social individual, the subject as comprehended in her determinate communal relations: "Human Dasein, as something historical, is in its essence a being-with with others, and the historical unity is always a unity of being-with-one-another, the constituents of society, are different in the different historical situations and must in each case be demonstrated for a specific situation."[19] Treating the subject seriously requires understanding her in her social situation, neither abstracting her from her society nor reducing her to her society, but recognizing rather that she "exists as an individual only in a particular situation of the surrounding and shared world, in a particular situation of social being."[20] Such a recognition has implications not only for action but for philosophy as well. Not only is action always public action, but for Marcuse all philosophy aimed at grasping the nature of action is itself necessarily public philosophy: "Concrete philosophy will exist in the public realm, because only by so doing can it truly approach existence. Only when, in full public view, it grabs hold of existence in its daily being, in the sphere in which it actually exists, can it effect a movement of this existence toward its truth. Otherwise, only an absolute authority, which is believed unconditionally to be in possession of revealed truth, can call forth such a movement."[21] The critique of philosophical absolutism thus meets the critique of political absolutism. The public nature of concrete philosophy subjects to criticism all those philosophical systems that claim to be in possession of an epistemology capable of divining the objectively revealable structure of reality, while the public nature of radical action ensures that the latter cannot be legitimately identified with tactical or organizational strategies that identify the capacity for the determination of trajectories of action with a privileged historical agent. In both instances publicness counters absolutism and contributes to the preservation of the structure of creative becoming.

## The Affirmation of Socialist Nature

Already we can see in Marcuse's theory of radical action an anticipation of those essential elements of politics that will be identified by Arendt: Action is seen as being concerned with beginnings and creation, this creation is identified with the human essence, action is carried out in public with others, and these others are understood as equals who cannot be treated as political objects. These performative political elements hinted at briefly in Marcuse's account of the radical act will be expanded and concretized in Marcuse's later account of the emergence of a specific form of political activity associated with the appearance of what would come to be known as the New Left, the student movement in particular. It should be noted before proceeding, however, that the presentation of Marcuse's interpretation of the New Left, and later of the council tradition – and indeed, it is of the utmost significance to realize that both Marcuse and Arendt identify these two phenomena as modes for the actualization of the creative capacity – is not meant to suggest that these political phenomena can simply be recuperated in the present. I am concerned with demonstrating, rather, how Marcuse's reading of certain past events can be seen to be informed by his philosophy of radical action, and therefore as gesturing toward the possibility of the construction of a political ontology oriented toward the affirmation of the principle of creation. What political forms may in the present act as media for this affirmation is an entirely different question, one that is beyond the scope of the present work (although I will by way of conclusion attempt to identify certain contemporary political phenomena that can be read through the lens of a Marcuse-Arendt theoretical prism). In any case, what for Marcuse was especially intriguing about the new modes of political activism was the extent to which they not only recognized the fact that the transformation of society required above all else a transformation of human nature, but also that this transformation of human nature could be potentially effected through the very participation of subjects in the political process, a political process that was seen as a performative end-in-itself. Marcuse's two most important engagements with the new political activism, *An Essay on Liberation* and *Counter-revolution and Revolt*, are thus also, along with *Eros and Civilization*, those places where Marcuse will provide the most detailed account of the necessity of a specifically socialist nature.

For Marcuse the institution of socialism entails not just the production of a quantitatively better standard of living for all, but the actual transformation of being, the qualitative transformation of human existence. Socialism requires a change in the very nature of need, which itself is dependent on a change in the nature of human nature. We know that Marcuse, like Arendt, rejects all static interpretations of human nature: "To say that human beings have primary drives does not mean that they cannot change. When I speak of human nature, I mean a nature that can change human beings as whole persons."[22] Hence, "nature is something that must first be created."[23] Indeed, all that can be said about the human essence is its orientation toward creation. For Marcuse the ideal social formation is one in which this capacity for creation becomes generalized and freed from all surplus repressive constraints. The creation of a socialist human nature requires the generation of a form of human need that is organized around the desire for spontaneous and sensuous production, and that rejects the bourgeois construction of need according to principles of accumulation. Marcuse will identify nature in capitalist society as a manifestation of domination, capitalist nature violating both human nature and external nature, preventing both human beings and nonhuman beings from asserting themselves as subjects. Specifically, capitalism "blocks the erotic cathexis (and transformation) of [the human's] environment: it deprives man from finding himself in nature, beyond and this side of alienation; it also prevents him from recognizing nature as a *subject* in its own right – a subject with which to live in a common human universe."[24] To liberate nature is to recover the sensuous aesthetic qualities in nature capable of enhancing the life of nature, both internal and external.

For Marcuse, then, the radical transformation of society has as its prerequisite the radical transformation of nature: "The discovery of the liberating forces of nature and their vital role in the construction of a free society become a new force in social change."[25] As alluded to, Marcuse identifies two moments of nature: human nature, "man's primary impulses and senses as foundation of his rationality and experience," and external nature, "man's existential environment, the 'struggle with nature' in which he forms his society."[26] These two moments, though, cannot be analytically separated as if they were two discrete and simply externally related elements. History is natural history: both internal and external natures are historical objects that cannot be comprehended independently of their metabolic interaction with one another. Marcuse maintains that as a consequence of its historical status, the realization or liberation of nature cannot take the form of a return to some previously achieved historical stage: the meaning of liberation is always achieved in history, and varies accordingly.[27] It would thus be disingenuous to reduce Marcuse's articulation of a "biological foundation for socialism"[28] to a romantic affirmation of an unhistorical state of human existence. Socialism is a biological necessity to the extent that it involves the actualization of essential human possibilities.[29] The biological liberation of humanity depends not upon the return to a condition, but the release of a (double) capacity: the psychological liberation of consciousness and the physiological liberation of the senses, both of which themselves refer to and depend on the liberation or subjectification of external nature and the world of human objects.

Marcuse suggests that the emancipatory project depends on the affirmation of a radical sensuousness, a model of sensuousness in which the senses have an active role to play in the formation and expression of rationality, "that is to say, in shaping the categories under which the world is ordered, experienced, changed."[30] The senses do not merely passively receive objects, although this they certainly do, but also actively synthesize objective data. Such syntheses, though, are not exhausted by the Kantian forms of pure intuition, but other more material ones. Marcuse writes that our world emerges not only in the pure forms of time and space, but also, and *simultaneously*, as a totality of sensuous qualities – object not only of the eye (synopsis) but of *all* human senses (hearing, smelling, touching, tasting). It is this qualitative, elementary, unconscious, or rather preconscious, constitution of the world of experience, it is this primary experience itself which must change radically if social change is to be radical, qualitative change.[31]

Marcuse builds upon and refines Marx's account of human sensuousness as it was presented in the *Economic and Philosophic Manuscripts of 1844*. Marx describes positive communism as (real) humanism, the realization of the human essence. Humanism, though, is in itself naturalism to the extent that the human being is not just situated in nature, but rather is nature.[32] The foundation of the unity of human and nature is objectification, the process by which the sensuous human being both posits and is posited by objects. Objective being is internally related to sensuous being to the extent that the specifically human relation to objects, the fact of objectification, is always a sensuous objectification. Sensuousness "is here an ontological concept within the definition of man's essence."[33]

According to Marcuse, Marx's concept of sensuousness implicitly begins from Kant's account of the nature of sensibility in the *Critique of Pure Reason*, where sensuousness is described as a form of perception in which objects are given to and affect the receptive subject. In Kant's words, "intuition takes place only in so far as the object is given to us. This again is only possible, to man at least, in so far as the mind is affected in a certain way. The capacity (receptivity) for receiving representations through the mode in which we are affected by objects, is entitled *sensibility*."[34] What the account of sensibility demonstrates is the extent to which the human being is dependent upon and unified with the world, the extent to which the human being is irreducible to a subject whose interaction with the world takes as its primary form the exercise of rational mastery over the objects of the earth. The subject is one whose essence is realized in creative material practice, but this practice is both active and passive, the capacity for the spontaneous production of objectivity being itself dependent on the presence of preexisting objects. In Marx's words, "a being who is objective acts objectively, and he would not act objectively if the objective did not reside in the very nature of his being. He creates or establishes only *objects*, *because* he is established by objects - because at bottom he is *nature*."[35] Preexisting objects are taken in by human beings via sensuous receptivity:

Objects can only be given to man in so far as they "affect" to him. Human sensuousness is affectability. Human perception as sensuousness is receptive and passive. It receives what it is given, and it is dependent on and needs this quality of being given. To the extent to which man is characterized by sensuousness he is "posited" by objects, and he accepts these prerequisites through cognition. As a sensuous being he is an affixed, passive, and suffering being.[36]

As a natural being, the human being is characterized by need. The human being's suffering is constituted by its dependency on an otherness, the fact that it requires for the expression of its powers objects that exist outside of the material of itself, and that must be given to it by the world. Marx writes that to "say that man is a *corporeal*, living, real, sensuous, objective being full of natural vigour is to say that he has *real, sensuous, objects* as the objects of his being or of his life, or that he can only *express* his life in real, sensuous objects."[37] Even if Marx does not push this insight far enough, and indeed, in *Eros and Civilization* Marcuse criticizes him for precisely this, his account of human suffering will provide the ground for the recognition of a noninstrumental sensibility. We know that Marx criticizes capitalism for degrading the multiplicity of human sense to that of simply having: "private property has made us so stupid and one-sided that an object is only *ours* when we have it – when it exists for us as capital, or when it is directly possessed, eaten, drunk, worn, inhabited, etc., – in short, when it is *used* by us."[38] Contrarily, socialism represents the emancipation of the multiplicity of human sense; under socialism "the eye has become a *human* eye, just as its *object* has become a social, *human* object – an object emanating from man to man."[39] The senses here orient themselves to the object not in an instrumental or utilitarian manner, but rather for the sake of the object, to the extent that the object is embodied human subjectivity. In this process both the subject is objectified and the object is subjectified: "it is only when the objective world becomes everywhere for man in society the world of man's essential powers – human reality, and for that reason the reality of his *own* essential powers – that all *objects* become for him the *objectification of himself*, become objects which confirm and realize his individuality, become *his* objects: that is *man himself* becomes the object."[40] The establishment of an ethical relation between individuals thus provides the ground for the establishment of an ethical relation between individuals and nature.

In *Counter-revolution and Revolt* Marcuse states explicitly that, in his mind, Marx's writings on sensibility in the *1844 Manuscripts* "espouse the most radical and integral idea of socialism," and that his own account of radical sensuousness will hence take them as its starting point.[41] For Marcuse social change in advanced capitalism is dependent first of all on a change in the human subject's biological reality. Individuals require new instinctual needs, new relations of body and mind: "The individuals who have the power to liberate themselves would not be the same people, the same human beings, who today reproduce the status quo – even if they are the same individuals."[42] Because the individual is a sensuous being oriented toward perceptive appropriation, the multiplicity of potential determinations regarding the structure of human nature are all largely defined in terms of the construction of the system of need: a change in the nature of the species requires a change in the nature of human desire. According to Marcuse, in the present historical social formation the satisfaction of need perpetuates the individual's domination, such that the liberation of the individual requires putting an end to surplus repressive introjection, putting an end to the individual as she is presently constructed. In the context of advanced capitalism, "in a society based on alienated labour, human sensibility is *blunted*: men perceive things only in the forms and functions in which they are given, made, used by the existing society; and they perceive only the possibilities of transformation as defined by, and confined to, the existing society."[43] The aim of social transformation is the liberation of the people, it is true, but a liberation of the people not only from other people, but also from themselves. The individual overcomes herself through the rejection of herself, through the rejection of what the present society has made of her.[44] Marcuse's concept of emancipation thus reveals itself as not an all-too-human one, but one rooted in the very "infrastructure of man," one that succeeds in qualitatively overcoming and reshaping the nature of the species and what it means to be human.[45]

Social revolution, the reinstitutionalization of the structures of political and economic life, therefore presupposes a revolution in sensibility: "the revolution must be at the same time a revolution in perception that will accompany the material and intellectual reconstruction of society, creating the new aesthetic environment."[46] The importance of Marx's *Manuscripts* lay in their recognition of the necessity of this revolution in perception, and their identification of it with the construction of a radical sensibility: "Dialectical materialism finds its truth only when it recognizes the roots of socialism in the sensibility of man, when it recognizes the roots of freedom in man's sensuous needs – the necessity that the political and economic revolution be accompanied by the 'emancipation of the senses.'"[47]

Marx recognizes that the emancipation of the senses will create a new type of individual different than the classed individual "in his very nature, in his physiology."[48] The reconstruction of sensibility according to the logic of essence would render the senses practical and active. Active senses "would develop new modes of seeing, hearing, feeling; they would perceive (and imagine) new forms of the objects of their needs – new potentialities of things, natural as well as technical."[49] Such a reconstruction would emphasize the aesthetic in human production, attempting to in some sense give a form to the definition of socialism as production according to the laws of beauty. We have already seen how Marcuse theorizes such a form of production. Let it here be reaffirmed, though, that such a form would necessarily depend on a restructuring of the relation between internal and external nature. The practical emancipation of the senses would contribute toward not only the creation of a new relation between human and human, but one between humans and the rest of nature as well.

To emancipate the senses is to alter the nature of the subject, the nature of the object, and the nature of each's interpenetration with one another: "the new vision of the senses actively changes the object world to the degree to which the perception of the new forms of things motivates and guides the *praxis* of reconstructing the natural and technical environment."[50] The realization of essence as creation in the sphere of material production is obviously dependent upon the world of objects: "The universe of the emancipated senses is the humanized object world, in man, as species being, has made the object world his own – medium for the development and satisfaction of his needs."[51] To make the object one's own, however, is not to reduce it to the mere stuff of domination, to a thing whose existence is defined by its indeterminate exploitation within the context of human project. Indeed, "the emancipated senses would repel the instrumentalist rationality of capitalism while preserving and developing its achievements."[52] Contrary to Lukács,[53] for Marcuse nature is not just a social category but possesses a subjectivity itself. The subjective elements of nature can be given an expression only when nature is no longer understood as a potential object of domination, only when the material of the natural world is no longer perceived of as a giant commodity market, a source of possessible things. According to Marcuse, when such instrumentalism is transcended, nature would become a subject in its own right: "the object would be experienced as subject to the degree to which the subject, man, makes the object world into a human world."[54]

Marcuse is quite clear, though, that such an understanding of nature as potential subject need not refer to or be dependent upon a teleology: "The idea of the liberation of nature stipulates no such plan or intention in the universe: liberation is the possible plan and intention of human beings, brought to bear upon nature."[55] Human subjects need simply realize that there exist certain forces in nature that have been up to the present dominated and suppressed, and that the establishment of an ethical relation between one another must necessarily include the termination of such domination and suppression. They realize that they have an ethical obligation "in Adorno's words: to help nature 'to open its eyes,' to help it 'on the poor earth to become what perhaps it would like to be.'"[56] According to Marcuse there is a relation here between the understanding of nature as a subject without a teleology and Kant's *purposiveness without purpose*, the correlate of the aesthetic form in art being the aesthetic form in nature. To say that the idea of beauty is applicable to the sphere of external nature as well as to that of art is to recognize that "the aesthetic form, as a token of freedom, is a mode (or moment?) of existence of the human as well as the natural universe, an objective quality."[57] The beautiful within nature is nature's ability to freely form itself according to its own logic, according to its own forces of potentiality.

What is unique about the Marxian philosophy, at least within the Western tradition, is that it "understands nature as a universe which becomes the congenial medium for human gratification to the degree to which nature's *own* gratifying forces and qualities are recovered and released."[58] Marxian philosophy's account of nature is, for Marcuse, an example of the former's reappropriation of the ancient theory of knowledge as recollection, "'science' as the *re*discovery of the true *Forms* of things, distorted and denied in the established reality."[59] Once again, though, this recollection is not the return to some perpetual and ahistorical organization of objects, but is rather the creative synthesis of the fragments found in the distorted life. Such syntheses are organized by the imagination, whose constructions reveal the extent to which the established reality violates the potential of the objects considered. Such a process is thoroughly historical and is, as always, defined by the eternal discrepancy between reality and idea, between what is and what could potentially be. The latter recognition is what prevents the consideration of the affirmation of sensuousness as a call for a simple return to mere animality: "A free society will also be a rational society; history is indeed objective *spirit*. All liberation, no matter how sensuous, how radical, must pay tribute to the brute fact that man is a rational animal, that all his freedom and happiness depend on his consciousness of that which *is* versus that which *can* be, and that the silence of pure sensuousness is transitory: the moment before the renewed transcendence."[60] The question of nature or sensibility can thus be seen to be especially important to Marcuse to the extent that it clearly refers us to the problem of essence, to the fact that creative activity is dependent on the internal relation and interconnection of receptivity, productivity, and joy: "the faculty of being 'receptive,' 'passive,' is a precondition of freedom: it is the ability to see things in their own right, to experience the joy enclosed in them, the erotic energy of nature – an energy which is there to be liberated; nature, too, awaits the revolution! This receptivity is itself the soil of creation."[61]

## Politics and the New Left

The biological dimension of socialism refers to the necessary change in the structure of nature and sensibility that would occur as a reciprocal element of the institution of the former. The question, though, remains: how is this new receptivity to be activated? We can now turn to Marcuse's account of the politics of the New Left. According to Marcuse, it is precisely within those aspects of socialism that are denounced as utopian that lies the authentic truth of socialism, and it is precisely these aspects that the New Left, the student movement in particular, is keeping alive. What the New Left comprehends specifically is that the redefinition of socialism must include the recognition that the former depends for its realization on the creation of a new type of subject: "The student movement has articulated what, in an abstract way, has been known to all of us, namely, that socialism is first of all a new form of human existence."[62] The students' concern with the issue of sensibility is revealed in their understanding of the new individualism, which must first of all be sharply distinguished from all bourgeois or lifestylist understandings of freedom. The new individualism arising out of the theory and practice of the New Left refers us specifically to this problem of personal versus political rebellion, of private versus social liberation. The student opposition is seen as potentially emancipatory only to the extent that it remains concerned with critical education and theory, as opposed to the mere removal of the individual from the established political universe, as opposed to simply "dropping out."[63] Although it is true that social liberation depends on the liberation of the old individual through the construction of the new one, this new individual is never an individual against the whole. As we have already seen, "the individual *is the social being*."[64] The new individual is an individual beyond the bourgeois person and the sphere of abstract right. Instituting the former "means overcoming the bourgeois individual ... while at the same time restoring the dimension of the self, of the privacy which the bourgeois culture had once created."[65] The radical individual is not created through the simple act of rejecting social life, through opting out of society, for "the individual liberation (refusal) must incorporate the *universal* in the particular protest."[66] The radical subject must be cognizant of the fact that in an unfree society no particular individual or group can be free, which is simply another way of saying that the free development of each is the condition for the free development of all: "the subject of this autonomy is never the contingent, private individual as that which he actually is or happens to be; it is rather the individual as a human being who is capable of being free with others."[67] The danger of co-option rests precisely in the affirmation of lifestylism, in the separation of certain cultural phenomena or practices from the political realm. Under such conditions "the 'style' threatens to become what it is – a style, to be picked up or dropped, marketed or phased out, adorning lives radically the same."[68] This phenomenon achieves one of its most advanced expressions in the formation of hippie communes, where liberation is conceptualized as simply "having fun within the Establishment, perhaps also with the Establishment, or cheating the Establishment."[69]

The individualism of the New Left is to be affirmed only to the extent that it transcends such lifestylism. For Marcuse freedom can *only* be attained in the political universe.[70] The revolt of the new radical movements is "a revolt in which the whole organism, the very soul of the human being, becomes political."[71] Here Marcuse quite explicitly rejects those depoliticizing tendencies one finds in those Marxist philosophies, his own included, that understand freedom as being conditional upon the liberation of the individual from the world of politics, that see the institution of socialism as being characterized by the replacement of politics with an administration of things. Marcuse thus returns to a theme developed much earlier, in "The Struggle against Liberalism in the Totalitarian View of the State," in which freedom and political obligation are understood as being potentially reconcilable concepts. They can be brought into line, however, only when individuals are able to consciously recognize their self-fulfilment within the political order,

all identifications of freedom and political obligation being meaningless when this is not the case. In Marcuse's words, "the political obligation of freedom can be only the free practice of the individual himself.
This practice begins with critique and ends with the free self-realization
of the individual in a rationally organized society."[72] Needless to say,
the practice of the New Left in no way approaches the conditions of a
politics of a "rationally ordered society," but it does represent a form of
practical critique, functioning in many ways as a prefiguration or anticipation of such an institutionalized order. Specifically, the New Left's
stress on individualism is formulated within the context of the recognition of the necessity of political action's concern with sensibility.

The theory of radical sensibility must reject all theoretical orienta-
tions that attempt to dissolve the individual into a mere aliquot part of
an economic class. The individual must above all be considered "as a
'natural,' 'objective' being,"[73] as the sensuous subject-object of natural
history. For Marcuse the New Left is to be congratulated to the extent
that it is able to recognize this being and subsequently generate, out
of its negative critique of advanced capitalism, a negative politics that
attempts to develop and affirm a radical sensibility. The truth of the
student movement does not necessarily lie in its positing of certain specific political goals to be achieved, goals that in some sense will always
be structured according to the particular location of the political actors
within a circumscribed social group, but rather in the very form of its
political activity, in its recognition that all politics that proceed according to the principle of radical sensibility must be an essentially negative
or nonidentitarian politics.

In this understanding the New Left must not be considered a new
revolutionary subject, a privileged historical agent in possession
of an objective truth of reality. As we already saw in the discussion
of the radical act, the practical rejection of vanguardism is a correlate of
the philosophical rejection of all singular and unitary ontologies. The
structure of political education is no longer oriented toward the uni-
directional communication of essential positive knowledge when the
existence of the latter is no longer assumed. From the standpoint of the
New Left the political education of the individual proceeds through
the very participation of the individual in political processes that affirm the principles of the new sensibility, specifically the principles
of receptivity, passivity, and joy. We saw in chapter 2 that in *Eros and
Civilization* Marcuse locates the residues of these principles in the content of dream and fantasy, in those forms through which the repressed

instinctual material attempts to return. Marcuse now suggests that the politics of the New Left is oriented toward a concrete recuperation of this content, toward an actualization of an aesthetic education such as was, for example, suggested by Schiller. The political playfulness of the New Left becomes a mode of aesthetic education that further develops and refines the new sensibility through its own practice. Tyson Lewis will note that "for Marcuse, education, or re-education of the senses becomes the fulcrum through which he moves from speculative philosophy to pessimistic cultural critique to political activism in the student movements. Here, education and utopia become tautological categories in the moment of play."[74] For Marcuse "education and revolution are largely synonymous forces which struggle against their reified forms as one-dimensionalizing political apparatuses, corrupting professions and dehumanizing cultural forms."[75] We can begin to see here the rudimentary outlines of an alternative political education oriented toward the spontaneous recuperation of that repressed instinctual content which can never be totally effaced.[76]

At the beginning of this chapter and in chapter 3 I critically identified Marcuse's attempt to escape that revolutionary paradox grounded in the recognition of the mutual dependence of individual and social emancipation via the positing of an educational dictatorship that forces individuals to be free. This tendency, however, can be contrasted with an alternative understanding of political education that affirms the possibility of a democratic self-liberation. Perhaps the clearest expression of this understanding can be found in a lecture Marcuse gave at Brooklyn College in 1968, which has been recently reproduced as part of an important volume on Marcuse and education.[77] Here Marcuse calls education "the teaching and learning of knowledge considered necessary for the protection and enhancement of life,"[78] a life that is considered as an "end-in-itself."[79] Such a protection and enhancement is dependent upon the actualization of "human freedom, which meant, and *still means*, social, political transcendence *beyond the established culture*."[80] The emphasis here on culture, on the totality of lived human experience, refers one to the fact that education must necessarily lead "*beyond the classroom*, beyond the university, *into the political* dimension, and into the *moral*, instinctual dimension."[81] It thus looks to actualize the rational capacities of subjects within a comprehensive sphere of existence that explicitly includes political being. Crucially, though, this political actualization cannot be forced on individuals. Democracy is considered in terms of the self-activity of a population that "*can freely constitute and renew itself* through discussion, education, persuasion, etc."[82] It is thus that "democracy is only to be created,"[83] but created through the conscious participation of political subjects in democratic modes that seek not the homogenous manufacture of identical opinion, but rather the free expression of multiple opinions for the sake of self-creation.

Here, then, Marcuse comes close to thinking about political education in terms similar to those used in what has come to be known as critical pedagogy, particularly the work of Paulo Freire. This fact has indeed been pointed out by Richard Van Heertum, who argues that both Marcuse and Freire recognize the nondetermination of the nature of individuals and their environment, and think education in terms of, not the one-dimensional transmission of objective knowledge, but the stimulation of autonomy by way of the nurturing of those critical faculties that make collective historical change possible.[84] For Freire the actualization of what he takes to be the humanity of individuals is stimulated "through the praxis of their quest for it."[85] The pedagogy of the oppressed aims at the development of a critical consciousness capable both of locating the source of oppression, and stimulating practical action aimed at overcoming this oppression. Crucially, though, this pedagogy "must be forged *with*, not *for*, the oppressed."[86] To act on behalf of the oppressed is to treat them as if they were mere things, which is illegitimate precisely to the degree that the goal of revolutionary praxis needs to be the establishment of freedom, a capacity belonging only to subjects: "the oppressed have been destroyed precisely because their situation has reduced them to things. In order to regain their humanity they must cease to be things and fight as men and women. This is a radical requirement. They cannot enter the struggle as object in order *later* to become human beings."[87] Education is thus "co-intentional," with both teachers and students operating as acting subjects for the sake of the self-development of the humanity of all. In this process a "new person" or a "new being" is created, "no longer oppressor nor longer oppressed, but human in the process of achieving freedom."[88] What is more, Freire's understanding of the human being is not structured by essentialist assumptions that identify the former with certain fixed properties or traits. Humanity, on the contrary, is a project. Like Marcuse, Freire attempts to think the contingent nature of subjective and objective reality (two moments of being that cannot be analytically separated) in terms of a certain transformative potential. Critical pedagogy must thus, from the perspective of the subjective moment, affirm "men and women as beings in the process of *becoming* – as unfinished, uncompleted beings in and with a likewise unfinished reality."[89] The becoming-structure of the individual and world points to the perpetual form of praxis. Individuals act in order to overcome those "limit-situations" that block their historical becoming, but "as reality is transformed and these situations are superseded, new ones will appear, which in turn will evoke new limit-acts."[90] Critical pedagogy thus aims at the autonomous development of a capacity for action that alters both subjective and objective reality within a social-historical context that is never capable of achieving a terminal form.

To return to Marcuse, then, a trace of the need for radical action is always present, and it is precisely this presence that provides the justification for the theorization of a spontaneism that can be activated through educative play. Marcuse laments along with Horkheimer the disappearance of spontaneity as an element of socialist theory, this disappearance being a consequence of socialism's declining concern with the question of individuality.[91] In *An Essay on Liberation* Marcuse is explicit on this point: one cannot search ahead of time for social groups that are capable of assuming the position of historical subject, for revolutionary forces *emerge within processes of change themselves.*[92] A political theory that posits such a spontaneism must reject all strategic and organizational activities that function exclusively within a means-end continuum. The traditional strategies of revolution have been invalidated; "they are simply surpassed by the development of our society," replaced by a critical spontaneity.[93] On the one hand, Marcuse states that certain objective conditions marking the present phase of capitalist development necessitate the generation of new forms of political organization: "The sweeping concentration of power and control in the nationwide political and military Establishment necessitates the shift to decentralized forms of organization, less susceptible to destruction by the engines of repression, and more expressive of the divergent and dispersed nuclei of disintegration."[94] A political opposition is thus needed in which a dysfunction or interruption of one particular place will not produce a correlative dysfunction or interruption of the whole. Subjectively, on the other hand, the necessity of the development of new forms of political activity is required as a consequence of the perception of the nature of the new sensibility, and the inability of vanguardism, and indeed all forms of political instrumentalism, to realize this nature.

Politics must not be a means, but must rather affirm that which it desires to produce. Politics must thus itself affirm the new sensibility and the impulse to creation, and in doing so, posit itself as an end-in-itself.

Marcuse points out that the new sensibility will require a new language if it is to effectively communicate its values. This language, though, "is not, it cannot be, an instrumentalist language, not an instrument of revolution."[95] Marcuse here explicitly repudiates the Leninist understanding of social revolution. An "authentic" Marxism, a Marxism concerned with the realization of the new sensibility as a mode of being that looks toward the affirmation of creative becoming, "is not only guided by the laws of revolutionary pragmatism. It also adheres to the laws of revolutionary morality. Its goal, the liberated individual, must appear in the means to achieve this goal."[96] Marcuse is here specifically applying this insight negatively in the context of singular acts of violence, but it also has a relevance positively with respect to the question of politics. Political acts must contain within themselves that which they are aiming at: "our goals, our values, our own and new morality, our OWN morality, must be visible already in our actions. The new human beings who we want to help to create – we must already strive to be these human beings right here and now."[97] The new politics must thus be a performative and creative politics, to the extent that that which it seeks to create is precisely the human being with the capacity to create. According to Marcuse the new political radicalism knows that "the feeling, the awareness, that the joy of freedom and the need to be free must precede liberation."[98] It knows, in other words, that the object of liberation – the actualization of the creative impulse – must be contained in that political practice that attempts to bring about such liberation, that politics, in other words, must be a negative politics of creativity.

Such a politics stands opposed not only to political vanguardism but to bourgeois forms of political practice as well: "the new radicalism militates against the centralized bureaucratic communist as well as against the semi-democratic liberal organization."[99] Although Marcuse concedes that bourgeois democracy has been historically valuable to the extent that it has developed a system of rights, and hence provided a positive foundation for the affirmation of equality, it is seen as contradictory to the extent that the defence of these rights functions as a justification for the existing state of affairs: "working according to the rules and methods of democratic legality appears as surrender to the prevailing power structure."[100] The identification of right with liberal natural right blocks individuals from recognizing right as a constructed product, as the result of specific political communion, and hence militates against active and transformative political practice, practice aimed at refounding the meaning of right, value, law, and more. For Marcuse it is impossible to imagine a form of parliamentarian opposition that would be capable of maintaining an autonomous existence, of not being swallowed up and destroyed by the dominant political universe. If the New Left is to fulfil its educational and political task, the transformation, or rather, development of consciousness, it must break out of traditional models of what it means to do politics and act politically, despite the fact that from the perspective of the dominant rationality this effort will always appear as "foolish, childish and irrational."[101]

The new politics appears as foolish, childish, and irrational precisely to the extent to which it rejects the understanding, shared by both the dominant socialist and liberal traditions, of political activity as an instrument, as the means to the realization of some extrinsic goal or state, be it the generation of positive communism or the preservation of the individual's abstract right. The new politics' noninstrumentality is revealed in its total character: "It is a total protest, not only against specific shortcomings, but at the same time, a protest against the entire system of values, against the entire system of objectives, against the entire system of performances required and practiced in the established society."[102] What it desires is the establishment of a new system of performances, which it attempts to give a form to in itself. The New Left is unique in that it offers a redefinition of the nature of revolutionary activity, it being no longer concerned with simply seizing economic or political power, but rather with creating new needs and potentialities, and along with these, new modes of production and new institutions.[103] What these new modes of production and new institutions aim at is the negative. To say that the new politics is negative is to say that it comprehends what Arendt would refer to as the joy of action, the joy of initiating beginnings, a form of political being that affirms what Marcuse might refer to in the sphere of labour as creative becoming.

Nowhere will Marcuse articulate more clearly his vision of the new politics than in the following passage from *An Essay on Liberation*:

> And the young also attack the *esprit de sérieux* in the socialist camp: miniskirts against the apparatchiks, rock 'n' roll against Soviet Realism. The insistence that a socialist society can and ought to be light, pretty, playful, that these qualities are essential elements of freedom, the faith in the rationality of the imagination, the demand for a new morality and culture – does this great anti-authoritarian rebellion indicate a new dimension and direction of radical change, the appearance of new agents of radical change, and a new vision of socialism in its qualitative difference from the established societies?[104]

Here Marcuse recognizes precisely that which Arendt does, namely, that what the students understand is that "acting is fun."[105] This recognition is reflected in the plurality of the students' modes of political being, in their aestheticization of the political sphere, in, for example, the performative and carnivalesque forms that their protests will often take. The students will explicitly counterpose the power of the imagination with instrumental reason, this counterposition revealing the strongly aesthetic element at the heart of the students' politics: "art was seen as a productive emancipatory force, as the experience of another (and ordinarily repressed) reality."[106] According to Marcuse "the political dimension can no longer be divorced from the aesthetic."[107] An aesthetic politics is an imaginative politics, a politics that is willing to, to use Marcuse's term, adventure: "If revolution does not contain an element of adventurism, it is worthless. All the rest is organization, labour unions, social democracy, the establishment. Adventure is always beyond."[108] To adventure is to transcend the given reality, which we already know is for Marcuse the essential possibility of human existence. It is, he says, intimately connected with, and perhaps even identical to, the imagination.[109] His juxtaposition here of adventure and politics, his concession that the aesthetic principle is capable of being expressed within the sphere of the political, explicitly posits that which his theory of essence demands: a recognition of the imagination as a necessary element of a concrete political practice oriented toward the affirmation of the new sensibility.

Marcuse's identification of playfulness as a characteristic of the new politics refers us back to his understanding of the pacification of the struggle for existence, of the establishment of a system of nonalienated labour marked by the free play of the individual with the potentialities of the technological apparatus. Indeed, Marcuse suggests that the New Left has redefined the nature of socialism precisely through its redefinition of the relation between the realms of freedom and necessity.[110] Here Marcuse interprets the traditional Marxian conception of this relation as epitomizing "the division of the human existence into labour time and free time, the division between reason, rationality on the one hand, and pleasure, joy, fulfillment on the other hand, the division between alienated and non-alienated labour."[111] What the New Left demands is the restructuring of all human activities, political activities as well as material productive ones, according to an aesthetic logic whose expression is a source of happiness. Given its stress on the aesthetic, which will manifest itself in the practical expression of performativity and the theatrical, it is not surprising that the New Left will make use of laughter as a legitimate political form. For Arendt those subjected to authority must continue to respect this authority if the established relation is to continue, and it is for this reason that, from the standpoint of authority, the most subversive activity is laughter.[112] Marcuse similarly notes that "the all-out fight against the '*esprit de sérieux*' is an indispensable political weapon where the profitable insanity which keeps the Establishment going seems to defy all serious rational argumentation and persuasion."[113] He suggests that "if our politicians are serious, the only adequate opposition to them seems to be defiance of this seriousness, not to accept their standards of discourse and behaviour."[114] And again, even more explicitly, "in the face of the gruesomely serious totality of institutionalized politics, satire, irony, and laughing provocation become a necessary dimension of the new politics."[115] Indeed, such provocations contribute to guarding against what Marcuse considers one of the most dangerous threats facing the new politics: the latter's systematic ritualization. We know, of course, that for Marcuse Marxian concepts are not to be comprehended as elements of a closed system that posits a sacred law of historical development. The very fact of history, rather, demands the permanent critical interrogation of the Marxian conceptual framework: "Not to confront the Marxian concepts with the development of capitalism and not to draw the consequences from this confrontation for the political practice leads to a mechanistic repetition of a 'basic vocabulary,' a petrification of Marxian theory into a rhetoric with hardly any relation to reality."[116] When the New Left ossifies theory, it thus violates the essence of the very principle whose immanent appearance constitutes the outstanding element of certain of its political forms: the creative and performative impulse.

## Spontaneity and the Council Tradition

For Marcuse the values and images of human existence that are produced by the New Left offer a serious challenge to the logic of the capitalist world, to the logic of the performance principle:

> The exhibition of a non-competitive behaviour, the rejection of brutal "virility," the debunking of the capitalist productivity of work, the affirmation of sensibility, sensuality of the body, the ecological protest, the contempt for the false heroism in outer space and colonial wars, the Women's Liberation Movement (where it does not envisage the liberated woman merely as having an equal share in the repressive features of male prerogatives),

the cult of plastic beauty and cleanliness – all these tendencies contribute to the weakening of the Performance Principle.[117]

If these tendencies contribute to the weakening of the performance principle, though, their concrete actualization and generalization requires the positive construction of a new reality principle, a new mode of being realized in a new set of human relations and institutions. Fredric Jameson is correct to note that "Marcuse sees in the new sensibility and the new sexual politics an application of the artistic impulse to the creation of a new life-style itself, to a concrete acting out of the Utopian impulse."[118] These impulses, however, only avoid the flight into narcissism to the extent that they are conscious of themselves not as the expression of an achieved emancipation, but rather as prefigurations of "ultimate concrete social liberation."[119] The question, however, is what would such a concrete social liberation look like?

For reasons similar to Arendt, Marcuse rejects all demands for a precise model of the institutional structure of the future social formation: "The demand is meaningless if it asks for a blueprint of the specific institutions and relationships which would be those of the new society: they cannot be determined a priori; they will develop, in trial and error, as the new society develops."[120] That being said, even if it cannot specify the precise structure of the future society, a critical theory does need to engage with the issue of future potential: "In the theoretical reconstruction of the social process, the critique of current conditions and the analysis of their tendencies necessarily include future-oriented components."[121] The very method of immanent critique, which seeks to demonstrate the object's irrationality by the standards of its own possibility, disallows the jettisoning of the consideration of this latter potential moment. Indeed, for Marcuse this was perhaps one of the limitations of classical Marxian theory: "Marx and Engels refrained from developing concrete concepts of the possible forms of freedom in a socialist society; today, such restraint no longer seems justified."[122] Negative thinking must necessarily contain a positivity; it is "by virtue of its own internal concepts 'positive': oriented toward, and comprehending a future which is 'contained' in the present."[123] In the context of the present discussion, the question is what positive form of institutionalization is potentially capable of providing a concrete ground for the universalization of that performative impulse affirmed by the New Left? Crucially, Marcuse comes up with precisely the same answer to this question as does Arendt.

The key to the determination of the future political form capable of actualizing the substantive concerns of the New Left is to be found in the latter's own political forms, which challenge the organizational logics of revolutionary centralism and liberal parliamentarianism: "As against these forms, what seems to be shaping up is an entirely overt organization, diffused, concentrated in small groups and around local activities, small groups which are highly flexible and autonomous."[124] The New Left "today is the only hope we have," the "true historical heir of the great socialist tradition," to the extent that its forms prefigure "what may in all likelihood be the basic organization of libertarian socialism, namely councils of manual and intellectual workers, soviets," the realization of "organized spontaneity."[125] The relation between certain members of the Frankfurt School and the theory and practice of the council tradition is one that has not been explored in the depth it deserves. Phil Slater, however, will suggest that the late work of Marcuse is an explicit attempt to recuperate certain elements of this latter tradition, and that "Marcuse's spontaneity links up to the anti-Leninist movement of Council Communism."[126] In one of the Frankfurt School's most explicit pronouncements on the subject of the councils as a form of "organized spontaneity," Horkheimer would write that "the modalities of the new society are first found in the process of social transformation. The theoretical conception which, following its first trailblazers, will show the new society its way – the system of workers' councils – grows out of praxis. The roots of the council system go back to 1871, 1905, and other events. *Revolutionary transformation has a tradition that must continue.*"[127] For his part, Marcuse's only detailed elaboration on this theme will occur in an extremely brief, but nevertheless extremely important, discussion in *Counter-revolution and Revolt*.

Contrary to Arendt, Marcuse recognizes perfectly well that the principle of workers' control presupposes the *primacy* of the political over the economic and technical in the sphere of production.[128] The failure to comprehend the political moment in the determination of decisions regarding the organization of social production, to reduce such substantive judgments to merely technical exercises, is to miss precisely that which is unique regarding the theory and practice of the workers' councils. Workers' control presupposes the decentralization and debureaucratization of worker organization, the democratic reorganization of the productive apparatus according to principles of equal self-determination. What is more, however, Marcuse suggests that this form of workers' productive control is capable of being universalized such as to serve as a model of human self-determination more generally. He thus goes on to speak about, not simply workers' councils as an institutional means for the organization of a nonalienated production, but of the councils as an institutional means for the establishment of *self-government*. Organizational decentralization "would recapture a seminal achievement of the revolutionary tradition, namely, the 'councils' ('soviets,' *Räte*) as organizations of self-determination, self-government (or rather preparation for self-government) in local popular assemblies."[129] Here autonomy and self-determination are explicitly linked to the participation of individuals in governmental bodies oriented toward the production of political determinations. The fact of the political function of such bodies is further reinforced by Marcuse's claim that these assemblies collectively constitute the historical heir of the bureaucratic mass party,[130] his claim, that is, that they have a specifically political being.

In this very brief passage Marcuse links together the productive and the political in the theory and practice of the councils. We know that for Marcuse material production is understood as an end-in-itself to the extent that, in its nonalienated modes, it is able to actualize the creative impulse. If the councils provide an institutional ground for the reorganization of labour according to the logic of this impulse, then they also provide an institutional ground for the reorganization of politics according to this same logic. Marcuse maintains that Leftist strategy is dependent on the institution of direct democracy, on "the subjection of all delegation of authority to effective control 'from below.'"[131] Marcuse warns, though, that the logic of the councils cannot succumb to a simple "fetishism of 'below'": "The *immediate* expression of the opinion and will of the workers, farmers, neighbors – in brief, of the people – is not, per se, progressive and a force of social change: it may be the opposite. The councils will be organs of revolution only to the degree to which they represent the people *in revolt*. They are not just there, ready to be elected in the factories, offices, neighborhoods – their emergence presupposes a new consciousness."[132] Here, then, the appearance of the political form is dependent on the appearance of the new sensibility, the sensibility that is specifically concerned with the realization of the human essence. The councils are thus that political form concerned with the actualization of the human capacity for self-overcoming: they become truly revolutionary only when they are bodies occupied by a people "in revolt," a people concerned with the overcoming of the discrepancy between "is" and "ought," between present existence and future.

We can here begin to comprehend the significance of Marcuse's definition of political practice as "the translation of the potential into the actual."[133] The councils are one of the few truly political forms, for they are one of the few that recognize the permanent discrepancy between the potential and the actual. Marcuse thus here moves away from all understandings of the political that comprehend the latter as an instrumental activity looking toward the institution of a static condition of existence capable of indefinitely regulating human affairs, looking toward the creation of an administration of things. Whereas in "Industrialization and Capitalism in the Work of Max Weber" Marcuse had maintained that Weber had erred in identifying technical reason with capitalist reason, suggesting instead that a formal or technical reason could be put in the service of the liberation of humanity,[134] he affirms in *An Essay on Liberation* that there is no technocracy that does not reproduce surplus repression: "Technocracy, no matter how 'pure,' sustains and streamlines the continuum of domination."[135] For Marcuse here, socialist administration is not only no adequate solution to the problem of social harmony, but it is in fact "the exact opposite" of "a true harmony between social and individual needs and goals, between recognized necessity and free development."[136] The establishment of a harmony between the social and the individual is achieved through the construction of a community that is capable of affirming the individual's capacity for creation. Harmony is thus not considered merely as a static or passive worldly order. Indeed, in an unpublished essay co-authored with Franz Neumann, Marcuse would explicitly critique such harmonistic social theories, which are seen to be practically linked with apolitical forms of social administration. Marcuse and Neumann argue that the virtue of classical revolutionary theories lies in their overturning of prior philosophical attempts to stabilize social conflict via the construction of absolutist systems. In revolutionary theory society was a potential object of creation, a creation that refers to "all human relations and institutions, private as well as public."[137] However, the authors will go on to trace socialism's tendency to theoretically neutralize a specifically political creation through its reduction of politics to administration. This tendency is originally located in Saint-Simon's subordination of the political to merely technical economic relations and institutions. Here "the social process is interpreted in terms of the industrial process of technique, and the problem of directing and controlling it becomes a problem of organization and administration, to be treated as a technical task."[138] Such a model of government, the authors suggest, is implicitly dependent on a positive assumption regarding the possibility of the end of history: "The administrative pattern of social change grows out of the conviction that, in the material culture, everything is in order, that production has reached its adequate form, and that all further changes would be but changes within this form, its inherent development, and not changes affecting the form itself."[139] The Enlightenment's original revolutionary concern with the actualization of potentialities is thus overcome since "the conception becomes essentially harmonistic."[140] For Marcuse and Neumann dialectics is necessarily opposed to all such positively harmonistic accounts of social change. In their words, "any harmonistic interpretation of a historical system was only the integration of inherent contradictions which could be resolved only through the destruction of the system."[141]

So, a community marked by a negative as opposed to positive harmony is one that is capable of recognizing the impermanence not only of the individual's existence but of its own as well. This recognition is achieved through the political construction of a system of democratic councils that is always open to the movement of history, always willing to put into question and scrutinize the present existence through the dialectical analysis of this existence's potentialities. To the extent that such a politics looks toward the realization of the human essence, toward creative overcoming, it can thus be comprehended as an end-in-itself. It must be affirmed once again, though, that, as we saw in the case of Arendt, to consider politics as an end-in-itself is not to reject or dismiss as irrelevant all political goals. Marcuse himself will identify the advocacy of the notion of action for the sake of action, found within certain existential philosophies, with fascism. In particular, he responds to Bäumler's claim that "action does not mean 'deciding in favour of' ..., for that presupposes that one knows in favor of what one is deciding; rather, action means 'setting off in a direction,' 'taking sides,' by virtue of a mandate of destiny, by virtue of 'one's own right.'.... It is really secondary to decide in favor of something that I have come to know."[142] For Marcuse such an understanding of the actor and of action, an understanding in which the actor "has not even decided for himself in favour of what he acts," an understanding in which "the goal which gives all human action meaning and value, is secondary," is the height of irrationality.[143] Politics cannot be empty; it must have a substance. Specifically, a performative politics considered as an end-in-itself is one substantively oriented toward the generalization of the performative impulse, to a form of institutionalization which is able to accommodate creative contestation over matters of public concern within a non*ant*agonistic and non–surplus repressive context.

For Marcuse as for Arendt it is this contestation, a permanent condition of human existence given the nonidentity of human subjects, which, when given a so-called pacified expression through democratic institutionalization, functions as a ground for the acting of the historical. Marcuse's recognition of the performative impulse's potential expression through agonistic processes of public deliberation is implied by his nonconcern over the heterogeneity of the composition of the political Left: "The Left is split! The Left is split! Only the Right, which has no ideas to fight for, is united!"[144] Indeed, the forced construction of such a unity is precisely what a surplus repressive political organization aims at. A positive or identitarian politics looks toward the effacement of the creative impulse through the reduction of the diversity of human opinion to the level of the same, to the reproduction of the dominance of a partial interest via both surplus repressive internal, or psychological, and surplus repressive external, or social, repression. Marcuse's negative or nonidentitarian politics aims at the construction of an organization of public life that is capable of giving an expression to the diversity of human opinion, the release of the overcoming capacity of an individual or group serving, through this capacity's agonistic confrontation with equivalent capacities, as the ground for the overcoming capacity of the society as a whole, which now aims not at a partial reproduction of norm or law but at a generalized production of norm or law. Such a politics, to the extent that the capacity for creation is seen as an essential component of human beingness, always aims at the establishment of equality and the overcoming of domination. A performative politics must be a radical participatory and democratic politics; it must attempt to universalize that only (nontedious) universal that, according to Marcuse and Arendt, marks human existence, that is, the ability to begin, create, or overcome.

# Conclusion: From the New Left to Global Justice and from the Councils to Cochabamba

In this text I have attempted to theoretically reconstruct a consistent political ontology capable of affirming the critical theory of the Frankfurt School. I attempted specifically to develop a model of political action that eschews as partial democratic demands that look toward an eventual overcoming of the political sphere via the establishment of a terminal condition of existence. On the contrary, this former model understands democratic politics as a potentially performative good-in-itself, undertaken not just to the extent that it is instrumentally aimed at the actualization of an external end, but also to the extent that its practice is understood to function as a medium for the manifestation of a creative human impulse whose expression brings forth joy and gratification. This possible model for democratic practice was articulated through the critical juxtaposition of the political philosophies of Herbert Marcuse and Hannah Arendt. Although Arendt successfully theorizes the performative nature of what she labels human action, and although Marcuse does the same with respect to human labour, they each end up ultimately restricting the potential scope of creative human expression. I have argued that the juxtaposition of Marcuse and Arendt allows for the emergence of a more fully comprehensive theory of democratic being, one able to affirm the creative capacities of the human being in all of those human spheres in which she is active. Such a juxtaposition allows for both a new appreciation of the emancipatory potential of the political theory of Arendt, which is too often rejected by various theorists of the critical Left, and a re-appreciation of the long-ignored critical theory of Marcuse, which is most often unfairly maligned as being excessively positive, utopian, and conciliatory.

Having attempted to rethink the nature of democratic practice in the context of the political theories of Marcuse and Arendt, I would now like to close this study by noting a few contemporary modes of political activism that can be read as implicitly gesturing toward the affirmation of the political ethic that I have attempted to develop theoretically in this book. The question that would seem to present itself is, what political modes and orders are capable of functioning as media for the acting of political self-creation? Needless to say, although both Marcuse and Arendt found political inspiration in the theory and practice of the New Left and the council tradition, the answer to this question does not lie in the ahistorical repetition of past examples. The possibility of a politics of radical creation must be thought within the context of the social-historical here and now. Although a detailed account of those forms of political activism that might contain the germ of a politics capable of satisfying the performative political aesthetic that I attempt to extract from Marcuse and Arendt is beyond the scope of this work, I would like to nevertheless call attention to some select scholarship that reveals the trace of this aesthetic in various forms of contemporary political practice. The most obvious example is that diverse and fluid web of organizations and groups that has come to be organized under the label of the antiglobalization, or more appropriately, the global justice movement.

One of the most important recent studies of the theory and practice of the global justice movement, which in North America can be roughly traced to the 1994 enactment of the North American Free Trade Agreement and the *Ejército Zapatista de Liberación Nacional* uprising, is David McNally's *Another World Is Possible*. Crucially, McNally will argue that what unites the multiplicity of diverse social movements under the global justice banner is their common struggle against the increasing commodification of social life.[1] Indeed, this fact can be seen as revealing the inherent connection between the critique of commodification and the affirmation of a specific type of human self-activity. Here we can recall Marx's well-known critique of commodity fetishism, which contains a restatement of his early theory of essence. Marx notes that "the mysterious character of the commodity reflects the social characteristics of men's own labour as objective characteristics of the products of labour themselves, as socio-natural properties of these things."[2] A social relation between producers appears as a social relation between objects, a relation outside and independent of the world of individuals. Inversely, the definite social relationship between individuals in the process of production takes on the form of a relation between things.

Objects appear as actors and individuals appear as things. A critique of this reversal, however, can only proceed if one is willing to accept that the proper order affirms individuals as actors, as doers who order the world in some way. Under capitalism, human essence (the ability to act, understood as the creative transformation of the objective and subjective worlds through formative productive activity) has in a sense turned into its opposite. Marx's concept of essence, initially developed in the *1844 Manuscripts* and later appropriated by Marcuse, implies a particular relation between subject and object, between the individual as a possessor of certain social powers that she exercises in order to transform nature for the satisfaction of her indeterminate needs. In a capitalist mode of production the roles played by the human and the object in this relation, the relation by which human nature is realized, is reversed. Thus, for example, a machine is not considered a productive device that the individual needs in order to express her nature, which is spontaneous and creative production, but rather, the human being becomes an object that the machine needs if it is to express its nature, which is its ability to valorize value.

So, commodity fetishism is critiqued for inverting the relationship between subject and object in such a way so as to belie the individual's capacity for action. To the degree that the global justice movement's struggle can be seen as one waged against the dominance of the commodity-form, it can be simultaneously interpreted as a struggle to realize the specifically human capacity to create new forms of doing and being, to realize the Marxian concept of essence that Marcuse attempts to affirm. It is thus not surprising that it often adopts the language of both performativity and self-activity. What characterizes the new movements is the concern with creative self-organization, with the practical realization of "democracy from below": "The emphases on direct action, on participatory democracy (often organized through mass assemblies), and on the festive and celebratory side of political protest distinguish this as a truly popular, not elitist movement."[3] What is crucial to note here is the connection that is established between democracy and festivity. Indeed, the political interventions of many of the new social movements regularly make use of various aesthetic forms, such as dance, music, theatre and so on. In Andrew Boyd and Stephen Duncombe's words, "there is a counter tradition on the Left that has long understood that all politics, at some level, is a kind of theatre. This practice continues on today, particularly in the global justice movements."[4] Such theatrical modes are dismissed as trivial by some, but such a dismissal is only possible if one thinks of politics in purely instrumental terms. What aesthetically structured activism reveals is the recognition, noted already by Arendt, that "acting is fun," that engaging with the world for the purpose of changing it generates a unique type of public happiness, a certain good-in-itself. Indeed, with respect to the new social movement activism, "whether it was the feeling of doing the right thing or being part of a vast democratic civil society, joy re-entered the fold."[5] Political action should contain within itself the content that it seeks to actualize externally. In the words of the Brass Liberation Orchestra, one of the more notable activist groups making use of such aesthetic modes, "culture is a celebration of life and human creativity. We use music and artistic expression as a response to oppressive society, to sustain and build our movements, and as an expression of the world that we want to live in."[6] What such groups recognize is that the actualization of a specifically human life requires more than the satisfaction of certain basic rights or material needs, however necessary the latter may be. Humanity, in addition, "involves imagination, play, culture, sexuality, art, music, architecture, and so on. A culture of liberation must be devoted to the free development and free expression of human creative energies."[7]

This emphasis on human creativity is often expressed in the language of play and carnival. Douglas Torgerson – from whom it will be recalled I borrowed the term performative with respect to the political theory of Arendt – would seem to follow Marcuse's *Essay on Liberation* when he notes that within various environmental movements "carnivalesque gestures abound in various venues, often deliberately designed to counter the tone of tragic seriousness as well as to mock some of the all-too-human incarnations of the administrative mind."[8] Torgerson will go on to give examples of some such gestures seeking to disrupt the identitarian logic of dominant political discourses: "A citizens group stages a funeral for a dead river. Environmentalists at a formal public hearing don humorous hats to underscore their point. Protesters against the clear-cutting of an ancient forest sleep in hammocks that hang from the trees to be logged ... the unarmed *Rainbow Warrior* sails off to confront a modern navy; inflatable dinghies harass mechanized fishing fleets and whaling vessels; irreverent banners hang high from the towers of a supposedly secure nuclear power plant."[9] Such theatrical and playful interventions are theorized as democratic performances. The individual who has done most to think the global justice movement as a form of performance specifically structured by the logic of play, which we will recall is a central concept for Marcuse, is Benjamin Shepard, who notes that "if there was one theme that tied together the divergent themes of the global justice movement – which many first encountered with the Seattle World Trade Organization (WTO) protests in 1999 – it is the overlapping notions of creative play, community building, and carnival."[10]

Shepard, L.M. Bogad, and Duncombe argue that "at its most basic level, play as political performance is about freedom – of the mind and the body – from any number of repressive forces, from the state to the superego."[11] Playful modes of protest do not insist on the mutual exclusivity of means and ends but rather locate the latter in the former, in for example the "joy of protest," there being "motivations and pleasures" inherent in the effort to create new worlds.[12] Although it is argued that traces of such playful political performativity can be located at least as far back as ancient Greece, within the contemporary context they can be traced back to the early work of the AIDS activist group ACT UP: "ACT UP brought that sensibility – a certain sartorial splendour – to every action it did, and in so doing transformed the way activism was conducted."[13] The die-ins, kiss-ins, and zaps of ACT UP served as a model for the development of playful forms of political being in other social spheres, and indeed, Shepard notes that AIDS activism led in this instance to the development of a diverse set of concerns – including poverty, healthcare, immigration, the prison system, welfare, and more[14] – testifying to the degree to which social movements, in overlapping with one another and stimulating activity in additional spheres, recognize the interconnected and dialectical structure of social reality. This structure militates against both participatory exclusivity and the reification of action. Regarding the former, action is not undertaken by a homogenous group of citizens with identical interests and opinions that were formed prior to the group's political self-constitution. On the contrary, activism contains agonistic elements. Creative protest looks "to enter contested space and reach out to either disrupt, cajole, or convert the opposition and the uncommitted/neutral."[15] It is precisely in this process that diverse individuals are, despite their inevitable differences, united – as an Arendtian sort of We – for the purposes of collective action. In this movement the self-identity of the actor is transformed, subjective development being stimulated by their democratic participation. This differential moment of political constitution is noted also by McNally, who argues that "genuine growth is always dialogical – it requires engagement in a dynamic, developing, and open-ended dialogue. Some who feel 'ownership' over the movement may perceive this as a threat. But real democracy comes from below, or not at all. It requires opening up the political space for a multiplicity of voices to be heard and to shape the movement."[16] Regarding the issue of reification, the constant potential of action to overflow its social limits is a consequence of the inability of the creative impulse to achieve a satiated state. This also prevents the ahistorical and romantic fetishization of specific modes of action. Speaking of the 1999 World Trade Organization (WTO) protests, Shepard writes, "While Seattle was the culmination of thousands of protests, pranks, and street parties, it's our responsibility to continue the high jinks, instead of fetishizing its memory. There will never be another Seattle, just as there will not be another Woodstock. So long as we keep proposing alternative, more sustainable models of community building, our new movements will thrive – one prank at a time."[17] The call for the continual diversification and expansion of creative protest is simultaneously a call for the generalization of participation, which in the last chapter I identified as the substantive content motivating a performative politics. Indeed, it is precisely this generalization, I would suggest, which separates the global justice movement from those new reactionary political movements that often make use of apparently similar political modes.

In McNally's words, what the global justice movement recognizes is that "to make history – to change the actual course of world events – is intoxicating, inspiring, and life-transforming."[18] What is especially interesting about McNally's analysis, though, is that he identifies important linkages between the primarily disruptive efforts of the new social movements of the Global North and various political movements in the Global South, movements that often make use of more positive and institutionalized forms of political being. There is thus something of a parallel here between this relation and that between the New Left and the council tradition as theorized by Marcuse and Arendt. I would like to briefly look in particular at one such political phenomenon in the Global South: the well-known Water War in Cochabamba, Bolivia. In 1999 Bolivia, motivated by directives from the World Bank, had for several years been leading the domestic drive toward economic liberalization in Latin America. It was in that year that the state attempted to privatize the water system in the city of Cochabamba, the third largest urban area in the country with around one million inhabitants. The government passed Law 2029, which in effect gave total control of the city's water resources, previously administered by the state agency

SEMAPA, to an international consortium of private corporations. To the surprise of many, there emerged in opposition to the law a massive public opposition that eventually, through the use of a diverse set of political strategies, was able to repel the attempt at privatization and assert public control over the water resources.

The truly revolutionary dimension of the Water War is found not in the object of the struggle, as important as it was, but rather in the struggle's specifically political modes. Resistance to Law 2029 was immediate in Cochabamba, taking the form of various labour actions, street protests, and a mass general strike. What is crucial to note in this case, however, is how the demonstrators positively institutionalized themselves into a democratic decision-making body that served as a model for political self-determination more broadly. The struggle against Law 2029 and the effort to privatize water was eventually generalized, giving rise to a new way of thinking about politics. The movement "grew in meaning to the point where it began to express the belief that decision-making too should be a collective and democratic affair, with wide participation by the population. In this way, there gradually developed a new way of understanding and practicing politics."[19] Specifically, in Bolivia protesters did not simply attempt to occupy or replicate existing governmental institutions, but rather to create a new form of government, a system of mass assemblies that were open to all in such a way so as to actualize popular political power.

Oscar Olivera, one of the more prominent of the Cochabamba water activists, writes that "politics should mean the collective discussion, decision-making, and implementation of solutions for common problems."[20] During the Water War this decision making was executed through civic interaction at various coordinated levels of assembly. Participants – and it is crucial to recognize, remembering Arendt and Michelet, that the movement was composed not of members of a single class or organization, but rather of workers, peasants, indigenous peoples, students, and more – first of all organized themselves into small assemblies based on sector. Here all actors could voice opinions, raise concerns, and advance proposals. At this level "a space was created in which people could participate in the political process by discussing the issues and trying to reach a consensus about what the next step should be."[21] Each of these assemblies chose delegates to send to *Coordinadora* assemblies, where individuals whose interests or social position did not allow them to easily engage with first-level assemblies also met: "These spokespeople were informal representatives who were able to speak insofar as they accurately represented their sector."[22] Here "socially diverse groups – from established unions to neighbourhood organizations and irrigators' committees, from associations of small businessmen and market vendors to workers in small shops, rank-and-file labour groups, young people, and professionals – use the *Coordinadora* to discuss, to deliberate, to decide, and to implement collective agreements."[23] Lastly, decisions made at the *Coordinadora* level required confirmation at the level of the *cabildas*, meetings held in large public spaces and attended by anywhere between 50 and 75,000 people. The *cabildas* were expressions of the belief that all decisions affecting the public needed to be approved by the people, who required a civic forum that allowed them to clearly vocalize their support or opposition. Hence, "at this level of assembly, though representatives addressed the crowds, there was an undercurrent of popular democratic participation and commentary."[24]

The unique structure of the popular assembly system in Bolivia during the Water War would seem to reproduce, on a smaller geographical scale, Hannah Arendt's ideal form of council federalism as discussed in chapter 4. The political composition of this former structure is summarized quite well by Álvaro García Linera: "Neighborhood assemblies, peasant communities, unions, and irrigators' associations; provincial and regional assemblies; state assemblies and town meetings – all of these gave rise to a heirarchized structure that combined assembly-style, deliberative democracy at each horizontal level with representative, assembly-style democracy between each vertical level. This permitted the formation of public opinion among equals at the local level (territorial assembly) and the *cabildo* (town meeting), as well as the executive condensation of opinions at the state level (assembly of local representatives, spokespersons of the *Coordinadora*)."[25] The popular nature of these political modes and orders leads García Linera to identify them as manifestations of a "plebeian democratic politics," as evidence of an "extreme politicization of society" that challenges existing governmental institutions with "alternative systems for the exercise of political power and the conduct of legitimately democratic life."[26] The potential for this specific realization of assembly democracy to serve as a general model for political self-government is recognized also by Olivera. He notes that in this instance the people "briefly replaced the government, the political parties, the prefects, and the state itself with a new type of popular government based on assemblies and town meetings held at the regional and state levels. For one week, the state had been demolished. In its place stood the *self-government* of the poor based on their local and regional organizational struggles."[27] It was an example of "communal self-government based on assemblies and town meetings in which all of us are empowered to discuss social issues, where we all decide on our own course of action, and where we all take responsibility for putting our decisions into practice."[28]

Raquel Gutiérrez-Aguilar sums up the potentially perpetual political form of this type of assembly democracy when she notes that the *Coordinadora* "offer an unsurpassable space for imagination and research into possibilities."[29] Indeed, it was precisely the creative use of imagination, undertaken for the sake of the actualization of nonteleological potentialities, which I identified in this book as being the primary manifestation of the realization of a performative political aesthetic. It is true that the emphases on creativity, joy, play, equality, and democracy that we see in both the global justice movement and the Cochabamba Water War are representative of a "whole new way of doing politics."[30] Political modes and orders that attempt to realize these values are certainly rare, as the vast majority of political activism on both the Right and the Left is mainly driven exclusively by instrumental and identitarian concerns. The existence of such countermovements, however, suggests the possibility of a practical reconceptualization of the very meaning of democracy and politics. In McNally's words, "such movements, if they are organized democratically from below, have the potential to create new forms of organization that prefigure, even if ever so slightly a new way of organizing society."[31] My ultimate suggestion, then, is that the political philosophies of Marcuse and Arendt are not irrelevant to the present historical conjuncture, but in fact can provide a powerful resource for thinking the appearance of these new forms of political being-in-the-world and the possibility of their radically democratic generalization.

# Notes

## Notes to Introduction

1 Chantal Mouffe, *The Democratic Paradox* (London: Verso, 2000), p. 12.
2 Max Horkheimer and Theodor W. Adorno, *Dialectic of Enlightenment*, John Cumming (trans.) (New York: Continuum, 2000).
3 Jeffrey C. Isaac, *Democracy in Dark Times* (Ithaca: Cornell University Press, 1998), p. 24.
4 Julia Kristeva, *Arendt: Life is a Narrative*, Frank Collins (trans.) (Toronto: University of Toronto Press, 2001), p. 50n31 [my emphasis].
5 Elisabeth Young-Bruehl, *Hannah Arendt: For Love of the World* (New Haven: Yale University Press, 1982), p. 80.
6 Theodor Adorno and Herbert Marcuse, "Correspondence on the German Student Movement," Esther Leslie (trans.) *New Left Review* 233 (Jan./Feb. 1999): 135.
7 For example, Jack Woddis maintains that Marcuse cannot be a Marxist precisely because he jettisons the theory of the privileged role of the working class as the agent of socialism. Jack Woddis, *New Theories of Revolution: A Commentary on the Views of Frantz Fanon, Régis Debray and Herbert Marcuse* (New York: International Publishers, 1972), p. 285. For Alasdair MacIntyre, Marcuse is a pre-Marxist thinker who has yet to surpass the critical standpoint of the Young Hegelians. Alasdair MacIntyre, *Marcuse* (London: Fontana, 1970), p. 22. Leszek Kolakowski calls Marcuse a "prophet of semi-romantic anarchism in its most utopian form." Leszek Kolakowski, *Main Currents of Marxism: Its Origins, Growth, and Dissolution*, Vol. III, *The Breakdown*, P.S. Falla (trans.) (Oxford: Clarendon Press, 1978), p. 415. And Morton Schoolman will ultimately see Marcuse as being a theorist of "a radicalized liberal politics." Morton Schoolman,

*The Imaginary Witness: The Critical Theory of Herbert Marcuse* (New York: New York University Press, 1984), p. 320.

8 Herbert Marcuse. "The Foundation of Historical Materialism," in *Studies in Critical Philosophy*, Joris de Bres (trans.) (Boston: Beacon Press, 1972), p. 47.

## Notes to Chapter 1

1 Marcuse, "The Foundation of Historical Materialism," p. 12.
2 For one of the few attempts to note this seemingly obvious fact, see Alkis Kontos, "Through a Glass Darkly: Ontology and False Needs," *Canadian Journal of Political and Social Theory* 33, no. 1 (Winter 1979): 25–45.
3 Herbert Marcuse, "The Concept of Essence," in *Negations: Essays in Critical Theory*, Jeremy J. Shapiro (trans.) (London: Free Association Books, 1988), pp. 43–4.
4 Ibid., p. 47.
5 Rene Descartes, *A Discourse on Method*, John Veitch (trans.) (London: J.M. Dent & Sons, 1929), p. 49.
6 Marcuse, "The Concept of Essence," p. 49.
7 Herbert Marcuse, "A Study on Authority," in *Studies in Critical Philosophy*, Joris de Bres (trans.) (Boston: Beacon Press, 1972), p. 53.
8 Herbert Marcuse, "The Affirmative Character of Culture," in *Negations: Essays in Critical Theory*, Jeremy J. Shapiro (trans.) (London: Free Association Books, 1988), p. 89.
9 Ibid., p. 95.
10 Ibid., p. 107.
11 G.W.F. Hegel, *The Phenomenology of Spirit*, A.V. Miller (trans.) (Oxford: Oxford University Press, 1977), p. 199.
12 Herbert Marcuse, "Sartre's Existentialism," in *Studies in Critical Philosophy*, Joris de Bres (trans.) (Boston: Beacon Press, 1972), p. 162.
13 Marcuse, "The Affirmative Character of Culture," p. 109.
14 Marcuse, "The Concept of Essence," p. 56.
15 Douglas Kellner, *Herbert Marcuse and the Crisis of Marxism* (Berkeley: University of California Press, 1984), p. 54.
16 Marcuse,. "The Concept of Essence," p. 58.
17 Ibid., p. 59.
18 Ibid., p. 57.
19 Herbert Marcuse, "Philosophy and Critical Theory," in *Negations: Essays in Critical Theory*, Jeremy J. Shapiro (trans.) (London: Free Association Books, 1988), p. 134.

20  Max Horkheimer, "Materialism and Metaphysics," in *Critical Theory: Selected Essays*, Matthew J. O'Connell (trans.) (New York: Continuum, 2002), p. 44.

21  Alfred Schmidt, *The Concept of Nature in Marx*, Ben Fowkes (trans.) (London: New Left Books, 1971), p. 41.

22  Theodor W. Adorno, *Negative Dialectics*, E.B. Ashton (trans.) (New York: Seabury Press, 1973), p. 203.

23  Herbert Marcuse, "Freedom and the Historical Imperative," in *Studies in Critical Philosophy*, Joris de Bres (trans.) (Boston: Beacon Press, 1972), p. 216.

24  Herbert Marcuse, *One-Dimensional Man: Studies in the Ideology of Advanced Industrial Society* (Boston: Beacon Press, 1969), p. x.

25  Ibid., p. xi.

26  Marcuse, "Philosophy and Critical Theory," pp. 141–2.

27  Herbert Marcuse, "On Hedonism," in *Negations: Essays in Critical Theory*, Jeremy J. Shapiro (trans.) (Boston: Beacon Press, 1988), p. 180.

28  Ibid., p. 189.

29  Ibid., p. 161.

30  Marcuse, *One-Dimensional Man*, pp. 4–5.

31  Vital needs are the foundation for the satisfaction of all needs and are defined as only those needs that must be satisfied unqualifiedly, including for example, food, water, and shelter. Ibid., p. 5.

32  Ibid., p. 6.

33  Marcuse, "On Hedonism," p. 180. For an account of Marcuse that traces the latter's concept of freedom throughout his work, and which sees it as being rooted in the earlier writings on philosophical ontology, see Peter Lind, *Marcuse and Freedom* (London: Croom Helm, 1985).

34  Herbert Marcuse, *Reason and Revolution: Hegel and the Rise of Social Theory* (Amherst, NY: Humanity Books, 1999), p. 293.

35  Marcuse, "On Hedonism," p. 182.

36  Ibid.

37  Marcuse, "Freedom and the Historical Imperative," p. 214.

38  Ibid., p. 216.

39  Marcuse, "Philosophy and Critical Theory," p. 142.

40  Marcuse, "The Concept of Essence," p. 73.

41  Herbert Marcuse, *Reason and Revolution: Hegel and the Rise of Social Theory* (Amherst: Humanity Books, 1999), p. 126.

42  Ibid., p. 128.

43  G.W.F. Hegel, *The Encyclopaedia Logic*, T.F. Geraets, W.A. Suchting, and H.S. Harris (trans.) (Indianapolis: Hackett, 1991), p. 87.

44  Marcuse, *Reason and Revolution*, p. 130.
45  Ibid., p. 131.
46  Ibid., pp. 135–6.
47  Ibid., p. 136.
48  Ibid., p. 138.
49  Ibid., p. 139.
50  Ibid., p. 142.
51  Adorno, *Negative Dialectics*, p. 153 [my emphasis].
52  Ibid., p. 156.
53  Ibid., p. 167.
54  Marcuse, "The Concept of Essence," p. 67.
55  Ibid., p. 68.
56  Ibid.
57  Marcuse, *Reason and Revolution*, p. 314.
58  Herbert Marcuse, "A Note on Dialectic" in Andrew Feenberg and William
    Leiss (eds.), *The Essential Marcuse: Selected Writings of Philosopher and Social
    Critic Herbert Marcuse* (Boston: Beacon Press, 2007), p. 69.
59  Ibid. Here Marcuse transcends the one-sided critiques of Hegel that focus
    exclusively on the latter's valorization of the Prussian state of his day.
    Marcuse writes, "Hegel, it is true, said that the rational state that reflects
    the idea of philosophy, in other words, the community that confers justice
    in the interest of all, is God on earth. It is possible that he made an error
    with regard to the Prussian state of his time – this is without a shadow of a
    doubt – which he interpreted in much too positive a light. This was not the
    fault of Hegel as dialectician, however, but Hegel as a Prussian citizen."
    Herbert Marcuse. "German Philosophy, 1871–1933," in Richard Wolin and
    John Abromeit (eds.), *Heideggerian Marxism*, Ron Haas (trans.) (Lincoln:
    University of Nebraska Press, 2005), p. 156. The fault of Hegel's dialec-
    tics is to be found elsewhere, namely, in his ahistorical affirmation of the
    totality of Reason: The "conformist character is not Hegel's capitulation
    to external circumstances: on the contrary, it is located in his very concept
    of the dialectic in which the positivity of reason and progress eventually
    prevails." Herbert Marcuse, "The Concept of Negation in the Dialectic,"
    Karl Bogere (trans.) *Telos* 8 (Summer 1971): 130.
60  Adorno, *Negative Dialectics*, p. 27.
61  Ibid.
62  Marcuse, "Philosophy and Critical Theory," p. 154.
63  Quoted in Georges Sorel, *Reflections on Violence*, T. E. Hulme and J. Roth
    (trans.) (London: Collier Books, 1950), p. 137.
64  Marcuse, "The Concept of Essence," p. 72.

65  Ibid., p. 73.

66  Ibid., p. 74.

67  Ibid.

68  Ibid., pp. 78–9.

69  Marcuse, *Reason and Revolution*, p. 65.

70  Marcuse, "On the Philosophical Foundation of the Concept of Labour in Economics," Douglas Kellner (trans.) *Telos*16 (Summer 1973): 36. Given the nature of the present work's primary juxtaposition, it must be remembered that the concept of labour throughout this and the next chapter will be used in a specifically Marxian/Marcusean sense as opposed to an Arendtian one. Arendt's (mis)understanding of the meaning of labour will be discussed in chapter 5.

71  Ibid., p. 11.

72  Ibid., p. 13.

73  Ibid., p. 13.

74  Andrew Feenberg, *Heidegger and Marcuse: The Catastrophe and Redemption of History* (New York: Routledge, 2005), p. 63.

75  Karl Marx, *Economic and Philosophic Manuscripts of 1844*, Martin Milligan (trans.) (Amherst, NY: Prometheus Books, 1988), p. 149.

76  Ibid., p. 149.

77  Ibid., p. 150.

78  Ibid., p. 145.

79  John Locke, *Second Treatise of Government* (Indianapolis: Hackett, 1980), p. 19.

80  Marcuse, "On the Philosophical Foundation of the Concept of Labour in Economics," p. 13.

81  Ibid., p. 10.

82  Ibid., p. 18.

83  Martin Jay, "The Metapolitics of Utopianism," in *Permanent Exiles: Essays on the Intellectual Migration from Germany to America* (New York: Columbia University Press, 1985), p. 9.

84  Herbert Marcuse, "Dialogue with Herbert Marcuse," in Richard Kearney, *Dialogues with Contemporary Continental Thinkers: The Phenomenological Heritage* (Manchester: Manchester University Press, 1984), p. 87.

85  Herbert Marcuse, "Socialist Humanism?" in Erich Fromm (ed.)., *Socialist Humanism: An International Symposium* (New York: Anchor Books, 1966), p. 110.

86  Marcuse, "Philosophy and Critical Theory," p. 144.

87  Marcuse, "On the Philosophical Foundation of the Concept of Labour in Economics," p. 21.

88  Ibid., p. 22.

89  Marcuse, "On the Philosophical Foundation of the Concept of Labour in Economics," p. 22.
90  Marcuse, "Dialogue With Herbert Marcuse," p. 87.
91  Jay, "The Metapolitics of Utopianism," p. 9.
92  Ibid., p. 11.
93  Marcuse, *One-Dimensional Man*, p. 16.
94  Ibid., p. 16.
95  Asher Horowitz, "'By a Hair's Breadth: Critique, Transcendence and the Ethical in Adorno and Levinas," *Philosophy & Social Criticism* 28, no. 2 (2002): 239.
96  Marcuse, *One-Dimensional Man*, p. 238.
97  Herbert Marcuse, "The Problem of Social Change in the Technological Society," in Douglas Kellner (ed.), *Towards a Critical Theory of Society: Collected Papers of Herbert Marcuse*, Vol. 2 (London: Routledge, 2001), p. 56.
98  Marcuse, *One-Dimensional Man*, p. 220.
99  Karl Marx, *Capital: A Critique of Political Economy*, Vol. 3, David Fernbach (trans.) (London: Penguin Books, 1981), p. 959.
100  Ibid., [my emphasis].
101  Schmidt, *The Concept of Nature in Marx*, p. 143.
102  Marcuse, "On the Philosophical Foundation of the Concept of Labour in Economics," p. 14.
103  Ibid., p. 15.
104  Ibid., p. 17.

**Notes to Chapter 2**

1  For Marcuse Prometheus is the hero of the performance principle, symbolizing the dominant rationality against the instincts and senses. Herbert Marcuse, *Eros and Civilization: A Philosophical Inquiry into Freud* (Boston: Beacon Press, 1974), p. 161. The Promethean elements in Marx's thought are to be found, "for example, in the emphasis on the ever more effective development of the productive forces, the ever more productive exploitation of nature, the separation of the 'realm of freedom' from the work world." Herbert Marcuse, "Marxism and Feminism," in Douglas Kellner (ed.), *The New Left and the 1960s: Collected Papers of Herbert Marcuse*, Vol. 3 (London: Routledge, 2005), p. 170.
2  Asher Horowitz, *Ethics at a Standstill*, p. 326.
3  Douglas Kellner will link up Marcuse's Freudian rethinking of libidinal subjectivity with essence when he writes that "against the notion of the rational, domineering subject of modern theory, Marcuse posits a subjectivity that is libidinal and embodied, evolving and developing, while

striving for happiness, gratification and harmony. Such subjectivity is always in process, is never fixed or static, and is thus a creation and goal to be achieved, and is not posited as an absolute metaphysical entity." Douglas Kellner, "Marcuse and the Quest for Radical Subjectivity," in John Abromeit and W. Mark Cobb (eds.), *Herbert Marcuse: A Critical Reader* (New York: Routledge, 2004), p. 89.

4  See, for example, John Fry, *Marcuse – Dilemma and Liberation: A Critical Analysis* (Atlantic Heights, NJ: Humanities Press, 1974), pp. 28–43.

5  We are here, in reading nonrepressive sublimation as a reframing of the theory of negative essence, once again opposed to Jay's reading, which states that whereas Adorno and Horkheimer used psychoanalysis to support the notion of nonidentity, "Marcuse found in Freud, and the later metapsychological Freud to boot, a prophet of identity and reconciliation." Martin Jay, *The Dialectical Imagination: A History of the Frankfurt School of Social Research, 1923–1950* (Berkeley: University of California Press, 1973), p. 107. Again, it is this interpretation of Marcuse that stresses sublation as a form of harmonious reconciliation that must be resisted.

6  Sigmund Freud, "Repression," in James Strachey (ed. and trans.), *On Metapsychology: The Theory of Psychoanalysis* (London: Penguin Books, 1984), p. 147.

7  Marcuse, *Eros and Civilization*, p. 5.

8  Ibid., p. xxvii.

9  Ibid., p. 14.

10  Ibid., p. 257.

11  Ibid., p. 35.

12  Ibid.

13  Ibid., p. 36.

14  The performance principle is defined as the specific historical form of the reality principle governing our age, the age of advanced capitalism; "under its rule society is stratified according to the competitive economic performances of its members." Ibid., p. 44.

15  Ibid., p. 38.

16  Gad Horowitz, *Repression: Basic and Surplus Repression in Psychoanalytic Theory: Freud, Reich, and Marcuse* (Toronto: University of Toronto Press, 1977), p. 151.

17  Marcuse, *Eros and Civilization*, p. 88.

18  Ibid.

19  This piece is also brought up in a similar context by John David Ober in his essay "On Sexuality and Politics in the Work of Herbert Marcuse" in Paul Brienes (ed.), *Critical Interruptions: New Left Perspectives on Herbert Marcuse* (New York: Herder and Herder, 1970), pp. 108–11.

20  Sigmund Freud, "'Civilized' Sexual Morality and Modern Nervous Illness," in James Strachey (ed. and trans.) *The Standard Edition of the Complete Psychological Works of Sigmund Freud*, Vol. 9 (London: Hogarth Press, 1959), p. 181.
21  Gad Horowitz, *Repression*, p. 26.
22  Freud, quoted in Ibid.
23  Ibid., p. 213.
24  Ibid.
25  Ibid., p. 194.
26  Marcuse, *Eros and Civilization*, p. 111.
27  Ibid., p. 124.
28  Marcuse, "On Hedonism," p. 182.
29  Marcuse, *Eros and Civilization*, pp. 223–4.
30  Marcuse, "Philosophy and Critical Theory," p. 154.
31  Marcuse, *Eros and Civilization*, p. 141.
32  Ibid.
33  Marcuse, *Eros and Civilization*, p. 199. Elsewhere Marcuse claims that there are two main aspects of the desexualization that aims at the transformation of the organism into a subject fit for work. On the one hand, there is the blocking of the partial instincts, which "either lose their independence, become subservient to genitality and thereby to reproduction by being made into preliminary stages, or … become sublimated and, if there is resistance, suppressed and tabooed as perversions"; on the other hand, sexuality becomes a private or personal affair through being reduced to love, which Marcuse defines as "the ethical taming and inhibiting of Eros." Herbert Marcuse, "Freedom and Freud's Theory of the Instincts," in *Five Lectures: Psychoanalysis, Politics, Utopia* (Boston: Beacon Press, 1970), p. 9.
34  Marcuse, *Eros and Civilization*, p. 201.
35  Marcuse, "Freedom and Freud's Theory of the Instincts," p. 9 [my emphasis].
36  Marcuse, *Eros and Civilization*, p. 149.
37  Ibid., p. 150.
38  Sigmund Freud, "On Narcissism: An Introduction." in James Strachey (ed. and trans.) *On Metapsychology: The Theory of Psychoanalysis* (London: Penguin Books, 1984, p. 95.
39  Marcuse, *Eros and Civilization*, p. 167.
40  Ibid., p. 170.
41  Sigmund Freud, "The Ego and the Id," in James Strachey (ed. and trans.) *On Metapsychology: The Theory of Psychoanalysis* (London: Penguin Books, 1984), p. 369.
42  Marcuse, *Eros and Civilization*, p. 169.

43  Ibid., pp. 201–2.

44  Marcuse, *One-Dimensional Man*, p. 74.

45  Ibid., p. 75.

46  Ibid., p. 73.

47  Ibid., p. 72.

48  Ibid.

49  Ibid., p. 76.

50  Marcuse, *Eros and Civilization*, p. 202.

51  Marcuse is quite clear on this point: at this higher stage "the libido would not simply reactivate precivilized and infantile stages, but would also transform the perverted content of these stages." Ibid., p 202. He goes on to state that "the reactivation of prehistoric and childhood wishes and attitudes is not necessarily regression; it may well be the opposite – proximity to a happiness that has always been the repressed promise of a better future." Ibid., p. 203.

52  Marcuse, *Eros and Civilization*, p. 205.

53  Ibid.

54  Ibid., p. 206.

55  Ibid., p. 207.

56  Ibid., p. 208. It should be noted, though, that Marcuse perhaps did not give Freud enough credit in this regard. Gad Horowtiz will attempt to argue, for example, that there is more than just a hint in Freud about the possibility of a nonrepressive sublimation. See Horowitz, *Repression*, pp. 185–95.

57  Marcuse, *Eros and Civilization*, p. 206.

58  Gad Horowitz, *Repression*, p. 30.

59  Ibid., p. 145.

60  Ibid., p. 52.

61  Marcuse, *Eros and Civilization*, p. 226.

62  Sigmund Freud, "The Most Prevalent Form of Degradation in Mental Life" in *Collected Papers*, Vol. 4, Joan Riviere (trans.) (London: Hogarth Press, 1950), p. 213.

63  Gad Horowitz, *Repression*, p. 194.

64  Ibid., p. 227.

65  Max Horkheimer and Theodor Adorno, *Dialectic of Enlightenment*, John Cumming (trans.) (New York: Continuum, 2000), p. 105; Marcuse, *Eros and Civilization*, p. 227.

66  Marcuse, *One-Dimensional Man*, p. 237.

67  Marcuse, *Eros and Civilization*, p. 209.

68  Géza Róheim, *The Origin and Function of Culture* (New York: Anchor Books, 1971), p. 96 [my emphasis].

69  Marcuse, *Eros and Civilization*, pp. 209–10.
70  Ibid., p. 43.
71  Ibid., pp. 211–12.
72  Ibid., p. 211.
73  Ibid., p. 204.
74  Ibid., p. 190.
75  Ibid., p. 212 [my emphasis].
76  Ibid.
77  Marcuse, *Eros and Civilization*, p. 212.
78  Ibid., p. 202 [my emphasis].
79  Herbert Marcuse, "Progress and Freud's Theory of Instincts," in *Five Lectures: Psychoanalysis, Politics, Utopia*, Jeremy J. Shapiro and Shierry Weber (trans.) (Boston: Beacon Press, 1970), p. 40.
80  Marcuse, *Eros and Civilization*, p. 84.
81  Ibid., p. 85.
82  Ibid., p. 220.
83  Sigmund Freud, *Civilization and its Discontents*, James Strachey (trans.) (New York:  W.W. Norton and Company, 1989), p. 30n.
84  Marcuse, "Freedom and Freud's Theory of the Instincts," p. 20.
85  See, for example, Freud, *Civilization and Its Discontents*, pp. 70–1.
86  Marcuse, "Freedom and Freud's Theory of the Instincts," p. 12.
87  Marcuse, *Eros and Civilization*, p. 155.
88  Karl Marx, *Grundrisse:  Foundations of the Critique of Political Econcomy*, Martin Nicolaus (trans.) (London:  Penguin Books, 1973), p. 611.
89  Ibid.
90  Ibid.
91  Ibid., p. 611, 712.
92  Marcuse, *Eros and Civilization*, pp. 217–18. For Marcuse "Fourier comes closer than any other utopian socialist to elucidating the dependence of freedom on non-repressive sublimation," which is just another way of saying that nonrepressive sublimation (nonalienated labour) can be made truly free, that is, oriented toward only its own intrinsic expression.
93  Herbert Marcuse, "The End of Utopia," in *Five Lectures: Psychoanalysis, Politics, Utopia*, Jeremy J. Shapiro and Shierry Weber (trans.) (Boston: Beacon Press, 1970), p. 68.
94  Marcuse, "Progress and Freud's Theory of the Instincts," p. 41.
95  Marcuse, *Eros and Civilization*, p. 214.
96  Barbara Lantos, "Work and the Instincts," *International Journal of Psycho-analysis* 24, Pts. 3-4 (1943): 115.

97  Ibid., p. 117.
98  Barbara Lantos, "Metapsychological Considerations on the Concept of Work," *International Journal of Psychoanalysis* 33, Pt. 4 (1952): 442.
99  Ibid.
100  Ibid.
101  Marcuse, *Eros and Civilization*, p. 215.
102  Lantos, "Work and the Instincts," p. 117.
103  See, for example, Marcuse, *Eros and Civilization*, p. 222.
104  Herbert Marcuse, *An Essay on Liberation* (London: Allen Lane, 1969), p. 21.
105  Herbert Marcuse, "The Obsolescence of Marxism," in Nicholas Lobkowicz (ed.), *Marxism and the Western World* (Notre Dame: University of Notre Dame Press, 1967), p. 413.
106  Marcuse, "The End of Utopia," p. 64.
107  Herbert Marcuse, "Karl Popper and the Problem of Historical Laws," in *Studies in Critical Philosophy*, Joris de Bres (trans.) (Boston: Beacon Press, 1972), p. 203.
108  Marcuse, "The End of Utopia," p. 63.
109  Marx, *Grundrisse*, pp. 699–700.
110  Ibid., p. 693.
111  Ibid., p. 701.
112  Ibid.
113  Herbert Marcuse, "The Realm of Freedom and the Realm of Necessity: A Reconsideration," *Praxis* 5, no. 1-2 (969): 22.
114  Ibid., p. 23.
115  Herbert Marcuse, *Soviet Marxism: A Critical Analysis* (New York: Columbia University Press, 1958), p. 257.
116  Moishe Postone, *Time, Labor, and Social Domination: A Reinterpretation of Marx's Critical Theory*, (Cambridge: Cambridge University Press, 1993), p. 7.
117  Ibid., p. 69.
118  Although potentially crucially, as an aside Postone notes that Marcuse is "a partial exception in this regard." Ibid., p. 86n4.
119  Max Horkheimer, "Traditional and Critical Theory," *Critical Theory: Selected Essays*, Matthew J. O'Connell (trans.) (New York: Continuum, 1972).
120  Postone, *Time, Labor, and Social Domination*, p. 108.
121  Ibid., p. 117.
122  Ibid., p. 383.
123  Ibid., p. 372.
124  Ibid., pp. 372–3.

**Notes to Chapter 3**

1 Marcuse, "The Foundation of Historical Materialism," p. 28.

2 Herbert Marcuse, "Theory and Politics: A Discussion with Herbert Marcuse, Juergen Habermas, Heinz Lubasz and Tilman Spengler," *Telos* 38 (Winter 1978–79): 124.

3 Herbert Marcuse, "Letters to Horkheimer" (Nov. 11, 1941), in Douglas Kellner (ed.), *Technology, War, and Fascism: Collected Papers of Herbert Marcuse*, Vol. 1 (New York: Routledge, 1998), p. 233.

4 Marcuse, "On Hedonism," p. 193.

5 Marcuse, *Eros and Civilization*, pp. 71–2.

6 Marcuse, "The End of Utopia," p. 79.

7 Herbert Marcuse, "Cultural Revolution," in Douglas Kellner (ed.), *Towards a Critical Theory of Society: Collected Papers of Herbert Marcuse*, Vol. 2 (London: Routledge, 2001), p. 137.

8 Herbert Marcuse, *Counter-revolution and Revolt* (Boston: Beacon Press, 1972), p. 3.

9 Ibid., p. 74.

10 Karl Marx, *Critique of Hegel's* Philosophy of Right, Annette Jolin and Joseph O'Malley (trans.) (Cambridge: Cambridge University Press, 1970), p. 30.

11 Ibid., p. 31.

12 Miguel Abensour, *Democracy against the State: Marx and the Machiavellian Moment*, Max Blechman and Martin Breaugh (trans.) (Boston: Polity Press, 2010), p. 48.

13 Ibid., p. 53.

14 Ibid., p. 55.

15 Ibid., p. 58.

16 Ibid.

17 Ibid., p. 63.

18 Ibid., p. 68.

19 Ibid., p. 84.

20 Importantly, though, Abensour sees an important shift between the 1843 and the 1871 works. Whereas in 1843 Marx is not yet capable of thinking a politics able to affirm the productive qualities of social division, politics here still looking towards the production of unity (specifically the unity of the *demos*), in 1871 true democracy is thought of as being realized through the exercise of conflict: "Marx rightly comes to think democracy as a form of conflict rather than as a process. Democracy, then, is less the result of a process that brings about a disappearance

of the State, in a largely smooth space devoid of bitterness, than the
determined institution of a space of conflict, a space *against*, an agonistic
stage on which the respective logics of two antagonistic powers pitilessly
attack each other. A struggle without respite here develops between the
becoming independent of the State as form, and the people's life as action." Ibid., p. 94. Absensour will in fact make the suggestion that for Marx
the Commune does not look towards the establishment of a form of
political being capable of institutionalizing the political impulse, but
rather that this impulse reveals itself only its negative confrontation
with the forces of the existing state. Here, "the coming into being of
democracy wouldn't so much take place trough the withering of the state
than it would be constituted in a struggle *against* the state." Ibid.,
p. xxxi.

21  Karl Marx, "The Civil War in France," in Hal Draper (ed.), *Writings on the Paris Commune* (New York: Monthly Review Press, 1971), p. 73.

22  Ibid., p. 76.

23  Absensour, *Democracy against the State*, p. 88.

24  Hal Draper, *Karl Marx's Theory of Revolution*, Vol. 1, *State and Bureaucracy* (New York: Monthly Review Press, 1972), p. 59.

25  Hal Draper, *The 'Dictatorship of the Proletariat' from Marx to Lenin* (New York: Monthly Review Press, 1987), p. 26.

26  Ibid., p. 45.

27  Karl Marx and Friedrich Engels, "Address of the Central Committee to the Communist League," in Robert C. Tucker (ed.), *The Marx-Engels Reader* (New York: W.W. Norton, 1978), p. 502.

28  Ibid., p. 509.

29  Ibid.

30  Ibid.

31  Hence, for example, Bakunin: "They say that this yoke, this dictatorship, is a necessary transitional device for achieving the total liberation of the people: anarchy or freedom, is the *goal*, and the state, or dictatorship, the *means*." Michael Bakunin, *Statism and Anarchy*, Michael S. Schatz (trans.) (Cambridge: Cambridge University Press, 1990), p. 179.

32  Marcuse, *Soviet Marxism*, p. 25.

33  Ibid.

34  Draper, *Karl Marx's Theory of Revolution*, Vol. 1, p. 15.

35  Fredrick Engels, *The Origin of the Family, Private Property and the State* (New York: Pathfinder Press, 1972), p. 159.

36  Ibid., p. 162.

37  Ibid., p. 162.

38  Karl Marx, "After the Revolution: Marx Debates Bakunin," in Robert C. Tucker (ed.), *The Marx-Engels Reader* (New York: W.W. Norton, 1978), p. 545.
39  Ibid. [my emphasis].
40  Frederick Engels, *Socialism: Utopian and Scientific*, Edward Aveling (trans.) (New York: International Publishers, 1998), p. 70.
41  Cornelius Castoriadis, *The Imaginary Institution of Society*, Kathleen Blamey (trans.) (Cambridge: Polity Press, 1987), p. 110.
42  Friedrich Engels, "On Authority," in Robert C. Tucker (ed.), *The Marx-Engels Reader* (New York: W.W. Norton, 1978), p. 732.
43  Marcuse, *Soviet Marxism*, p. 104.
44  Jean Cohen, *Class and Civil Society: The Limits of Marxian Critical Theory* (Amherst: University of Massachusetts Press, 1982), p. 184.
45  Adorno, *Negative Dialectics*, p. 322.
46  Needless to say, it is quite revealing that at one point Marcuse speaks of the fundamental "correctness" of the Leninist paradigm. Herbert Marcuse, "33 Theses," in Douglas Kellner (ed.), *Technology, War, and Fascism: Collected Papers of Herbert Marcuse*, Vol. 1 (New York: Routledge, 1998), p. 227. On Lenin's reproduction of the antipolitical double form in Marx's thought, see especially "What is to be Done?" on the issue of political instrumentality and "State and Revolution" on the issue of political administration, both in Henry M. Christman (ed.), *The Essential Works of Lenin* (New York: Bantam Books, 1971).
47  Kellner, *Herbert Marcuse and the Crisis of Marxism*, p. 69.
48  Herbert Marcuse, "Das Problem der Geschichtlichen Wirklichkeit," in *Schriften: Band I* (Frankfurt: Suhrkamp Verlag, 1978), p. 469.
49  Karl Korsch, *Marxism and Philosophy*, Fred Halliday (trans.) (London: New Left Books, 1970), p. 32.
50  Karl Korsch, "The Present State of the Problem of Marxism and Philosophy: An Anti-Critique," in *Marxism and Philosophy*, Fred Halliday (trans.) (London: New Left Books, 1970), p. 93.
51  Karl Korsch, "Fundamentals of Socialization," in Douglas Kellner (ed.), *Karl Korsch: Revolutionary Theory* (Austin: University of Texas Press, 1977), p. 125.
52  Quoted in Douglas Kellner, "Korsch's Revolutionary Marxism," in Douglas Kellner (ed.), *Karl Korsch: Revolutionary Theory* (Austin: University of Texas Press, 1977), p. 98.
53  Karl Korsch, "On Materialist Dialectic," in Douglas Kellner (ed.), *Karl Korsch: Revolutionary Theory*, Karl-Heinz Otto (trans.) (Austin: University of Texas Press, 1977), p. 141.

54  Ibid., p. 144.
55  Karl Korsch, "The Marxist Dialectic," in Douglas Kellner (ed.), *Karl Korsch: Revolutionary Theory*, Karl-Heinz Otto (trans.) (Austin: University of Texas Press, 1977), p. 136.
56  Karl Korsch, "The Crisis of Marxism," in Douglas Kellner (ed.), *Karl Korsch: Revolutionary Theory*, Otto Koester (trans.) (Austin: University of Texas Press, 1977), p. 172.
57  Karl Korsch, "Why I Am a Marxist," in *Three Essays on Marxism* (New York: Monthly Review Press, 1972), p. 65.
58  Korsch, *Marxism and Philosophy*, p. 55.
59  Korsch, "Why I Am a Marxist," p. 67.
60  Ibid., p. 68.
61  Karl Korsch, "Revolutionary Commune," in Douglas Kellner (ed.), *Karl Korsch: Revolutionary Theory* Andrew Giles-Peters and Karl-Heinz Otto (trans.) (Austin: University of Texas Press, 1977), p. 210.
62  Ibid., p. 211.
63  Korsch, "The Marxist Dialectic," p. 138.
64  Ibid., p. 139.
65  Herbert Marcuse, "On the Problem of the Dialectic," Morton Schoolman and Duncan Smith (trans.) *Telos* 27 (Spring 1976): 24.
66  Andrew Feenberg, *Lukács, Marx and the Sources of Critical Theory* (Totowa: Rowman and Littlefield, 1981), p. 167.
67  Georg Lukács, "The Changing Function of Historical Materialism," in *History and Class Consciousness: Studies in Marxist Dialectics*, Rodney Livingstone (trans.) (Cambridge: MIT Press, 1971), p. 228.
68  Georg Lukács, "Towards a Methodology of the Problem of Organisation," in *History and Class Consciousness: Studies in Marxist Dialectics*, Rodney Livingstone (trans.) (Cambridge: MIT Press, 1971), p. 334.
69  Georg Lukács, "Reification and the Consciousness of the Proletariat," in *History and Class Consciousness: Studies in Marxist Dialectics*, Rodney Livingstone (trans.) (Cambridge: MIT Press, 1971), p. 204.
70  Ibid.
71  Ibid., p. 197.
72  Ibid., p. 152.
73  Georg Lukács, "What is Orthodox Marxism?" in *History and Class Consciousness: Studies in Marxist Dialectics*, Rodney Livingstone (trans.) (Cambridge: MIT Press, 1971), p. 23.
74  Ibid.
75  Marcuse, "On the Problem of the Dialectic," p. 24.

76  Georg Lukács, "Class Consciousness," in *History and Class Consciousness: Studies in Marxist Dialectics*, Rodney Livingstone (trans.) (Cambridge MIT Press, 1971), p. 74.

77  Ibid., p. 76.

78  Georg Lukács, "Towards a Methodology of the Problem of Organisation," p. 303.

79  Georg Lukács, *Lenin: A Study on the Unity of his Thought*, Nicholas Jacobs (trans.) (Cambridge: MIT Press, 1971), p. 24.

80  Georg Lukács, "The Marxism of Rosa Luxemburg," in *History and Class Consciousness: Studies in Marxist Dialectics*, Rodney Livingstone (trans.) (Cambridge: MIT Press, 1971), p. 41.

81  Marcuse, *Counter-revolution and Revolt*, p. 9.

82  Ibid., p. 14.

83  Ibid., pp. 15–16.

84  Herbert Marcuse, "The Reification of the Proletariat," *Canadian Journal of Political and Social Theory* 3, no. 1 (Winter 1979): 20.

85  Herbert Marcuse, "Protosocialism and Late Capitalism: Toward a Theoretical Synthesis Based on Bahro's Analysis," in Ulf Wolter (ed.), *Rudolf Bahro: Critical Responses* (New York: M.E. Sharpe, 1980), p. 38.

86  Herbert Marcuse, "USA: Questions of Organization and the Revolutionary Subject," in Douglas Kellner (ed.), *The New Left and the 1960s: Collected Papers of Herbert Marcuse*, Vol. 3 (London: Routledge, 2005), p. 139.

87  Guy Debord, *The Society of the Spectacle*, Donald Nicholson-Smith (trans.) (New York: Zone Books, 1995), p. 114.

88  Marcuse, *One-Dimensional Man*, p. 208.

89  Marcuse, *Counter-Revolution and Revolt*, pp. 46–7.

90  Ibid., p. 47.

91  Ibid.

92  Herbert Marcuse, "Revolutionary Subject and Self-Government." *Praxis* 5, no. 1-2 (1969): 326.

93  Ibid., p. 327.

94  Ibid., p. 328.

95  Marcuse, *An Essay on Liberation*, p. 54.

96  Joan Alway, *Critical Theory and Political Possibilities: Conceptions of Emancipatory Politics in the Work of Horkheimer, Adorno, Marcuse, and Habermas* (Westport, CT: Greenwood Press, 1995), p. 86.

97  Kellner, *Herbert Marcuse and the Crisis of Marxism*, p. 280.

98  Marcuse, "33 Theses," p. 227.

99  Marcuse, "Protosocialism and Late Capitalism," p. 25. Rudolf Bahro, *The Alternative in Eastern Europe*, David Fernbach (trans.) (London: New Left

Books, 1978). For a short introduction to the main themes of Bahro's book see Rudolf Bahro, "The Alternative in Eastern Europe," David Fernbach and Ben Fowkes (trans.) *New Left Review* 106 (Nov.–Dec. 1977): 3–37.

100 Marcuse, "Protosocialism and Late Capitalism," p. 26.

101 Herbert Marcuse, "The Movement in the New Era of Repression," in Douglas Kellner (ed.), *The New Left and the 1960s: The Collected Papers of Herbert Marcuse*, Vol. 3 (London: Routledge, 2005), p. 145.

102 Marcuse, "The Reification of the Proletariat," p. 21.

103 Ibid.

104 Ibid.

105 Bahro, "The Alternative in Eastern Europe," p. 16.

106 Marcuse, "The Reification of the Proletariat," p. 21.

107 Marcuse, "Protosocialism and Late Capitalism," p. 27.

108 Marcuse, "Freedom and the Historical Imperative," p. 222.

109 Marcuse, "Protosocialism and Late Capitalism," p. 29.

110 Ibid.

111 Herbert Marcuse, "A Revolution in Values," in James A. Gould and Willis H. Truitt (eds.), *Political Ideologies* (New York: Macmillan Company, 1973), p. 332.

112 Marcuse, "Protosocialism and Late Capitalism," p. 40.

113 Ibid., p. 31.

114 Marcuse, *Eros and Civilization*, p. 225. It is not possible to isolate in Marcuse's thought a trajectory moving from one position to the other, from the non- to the justifiability of educational dictatorship. Marcuse would waver between both positions, often within the same period or even the same text. Thus, for example, at around the same time that "The Reification of the Proletariat" and "Protosocialism and Late Capitalism" were written, he would, in an interview with Habermas and others, emphatically advocate discarding the concept of the educational dictatorship. When asked who is to determine what constitutes a better human life, he responds, "That's the one question I refuse to answer. Whoever still doesn't know what a better life is, is hopeless." Marcuse, "Theory and Politics," p. 136. Despite his ambivalence, though, his affirmation of the authoritarian model clearly remains the dominant position in his thought.

115 Marcuse, "Protosocialism and Late Capitalism," p. 32.

116 Herbert Marcuse, "Ethics and Revolution," in Richard T. De George (ed.), *Ethics and Society: Original Essays on Contemporary Moral Problems* (Garden City: Anchor Books, 1966), p. 144.

117 Ibid., p 147.

118 Marcuse, *One-Dimensional Man*, p. 44.

119   Marcuse, "A Study on Authority," p. 135.
120   Herbert Marcuse, "The Obsolescence of the Freudian Concept of Man," in *Five Lectures: Psychoanalysis, Politics, Utopia,* Jeremy J. Shapiro and Shierry Weber (trans.) (Boston: Beacon Press, 1970), p. 50.
121   Herbert Marcuse, "Industrialization and Capitalism in the Work of Max Weber," in *Negations: Essays in Critical Theory,* Jeremy J. Shapiro (trans.) (London: Free Association Books, 1988), p. 215.
122   Marcuse, *Eros and Civilization,* p. 224.
123   Engels, "On Authority," pp. 730–3.
124   Marcuse, *Eros and Civilization,* p. 224.
125   Jeremy J. Shapiro, "One-Dimensionality: The Universal Semiotic of Technological Experience," in Paul Breines (ed.), *Critical Interruptions: New Left Perspectives on Herbert Marcuse* (New York: Herder and Herder, 1970), p. 181.
126   Richard J. Bernstein, "Negativity: Theme and Variations," in *Philosophical Profiles: Essays in a Pragmatic Mode* (Philadelphia: University of Pennsylvania Press, 1986), p. 23.
127   Ibid., pp. 24–5.

## Notes to Chapter 4

1   Hannah Arendt. *The Human Condition* (Chicago: University of Chicago Press, 1998), p. 9.
2   Ibid., p. 11.
3   Hannah Arendt, *The Life of the Mind,* Vol. 1, *Thinking* (San Diego: Harcourt, 1978), p. 19.
4   Ibid., p. 20.
5   Ibid., p. 29.
6   Ibid., p. 36.
7   Arendt, *The Human Condition,* p. 176.
8   Ibid.
9   Ibid., p. 8.
10   Ibid., p. 176.
11   Ibid., p. 177.
12   Ibid., pp. 177–8.
13   Hannah Arendt, "What Is Freedom?" in *Between Past and Future: Eight Exercises in Political Thought* (New York: Penguin Books, 1993), p. 168.
14   Hannah Arendt, "On Violence," in *Crises of the Republic* (New York: Harcourt Brace Jovanovich, 1972), pp. 132–3.
15   Hannah Arendt, "Introduction *Into* Politics," in Jerome Kohn (ed.), *The Promise of Politics* (New York: Schocken Books, 2005), pp. 111–12.

16 Arendt, "What Is Freedom?" p. 171.

17 Arendt, *The Human Condition*, p. 205.

18 Ibid., p. 206.

19 Arendt, "What Is Freedom?" p. 153.

20 As a matter of fact, Seyla Benhabib will suggest a common ground between Marcuse and Arendt on the basis of their appropriation of the Aristotelian concept of praxis, which they, both former students of Heidegger,
felt was missing from the latter's interpretation of Aristotle. Benhabib
writes that "whereas Arendt reread Aristotle to reveal the ontological features of ethical and political action, thus gaining access to the notion of a
'web' of human affairs, Marcuse read Aristotle's concept of praxis in Marxian terms as world-constitutive and historical labouring activity." Seyla
Benhabib, *The Reluctant Modernism of Hannah Arendt* (Thousand Oaks,
CA: Sage Publications, 1996), p. 117. Indeed, on those rare occasions when
readers attempt to construct a relation between Marcuse and Arendt, it is
generally done through the interpretation of each author's critique and
affirmation of human life-activity. Thus also, Kenneth Frampton notes that
Marcuse and Arendt are both concerned with "the problematic cultural
status of play and pleasure in a future labouring society after its hypotheti-
cal liberation from the compulsion of consumption." Kenneth Frampton,
"The Status of Man and the Status of His Objects: A Reading of *The Human
Condition*," in Melvyn A. Hill (ed.), *Hannah Arendt: The Recovery of the Public World* (New York: St. Martin's Press, 1979), p. 121. Andrew Feenberg,
meanwhile, will understand both Arendt's rereading of Kant's aesthetic
theory and Marcuse's radical politics of technology as being efforts to
affirm an active and aestheticized politics: "There is a certain similiarity
between Marcuse's project and that of Arendt. Is it a coincidence that both
these Heidegger students affirm the disclosive power of art and attempt to
transpose it to the political domain by drawing on Kant's third *Critique*?"
Feenberg. *Heidegger and Marcuse*, p. 96.

21 Dana Villa, *Arendt and Heidegger: The Fate of the Political* (Princeton:
Princeton University Press, 1996), p. 25.

22 Ibid., p. 47.

23 Arendt, *The Human Condition*, p. 187.

24 See, for example, Martin Jay, "'The Aesthetic Ideology' as Ideology: Or
What Does It Mean to Aestheticize Politics?" in *Force Fields: Between Intellectual History and Cultural Critique* (New York: Routledge, 1993).

25 Arendt, *The Human Condition*, p. 229.

26 James T. Knauer, "Motive and Goal in Hannah Arendt's Concept of Political Action," *American Political Science Review* 74, no. 3 (Sept. 1980): 733.

27  Douglas Torgerson, "Farewell to the Green Movement? Political Action and the Green Public Sphere," *Environmental Politics* 9, no. 4 (Winter 2000): 3.

28  Ibid.

29  Ibid., p. 4.

30  Douglas Torgerson, *The Promise of Green Politics: Environmentalism and the Public Sphere* (Durham, NC: Duke University Press, 1999), pp. 154–55.

31  Arendt, "What Is Freedom?" p. 151.

32  Ibid.

33  Arendt, "Introduction *Into* Politics," p. 193.

34  Ibid.

35  Hannah Arendt, "The Eggs Speak Up," in Jerome Kohn (ed.), *Essays in Understanding, 1930–1954: Formation, Exile, and Totalitarianism* (New York: Schocken Books, 1994), pp. 280–1.

36  Arendt, "Introduction *Into* Politics," p. 193.

37  Arendt, "What Is Freedom?" p. 152.

38  For an account of the theory of the principle's foundation in Montesquieu see Hannah Arendt, "Montesquieu's Revision of the Tradition," in Jerome Kohn (ed.), *The Promise of Politics* (New York: Schocken Books, 2005), pp. 63–9.

39  Hannah Arendt, "Introduction *Into* Politics," p. 113.

40  Arendt, "What Is Freedom?" p 167. For Augustine's critique of the necessity of historical repetition and his affirmation of the possibility of the new see Saint Augustine, *The City of God*, Marcus Dods (trans.) (New York: The Modern Library, 1950), Bk. 12, Ch. 20.

41  Hannah Arendt, "Understanding and Politics (The Difficulties of Understanding)," in Jerome Kohn (ed.), *Essays in Understanding, 1930–1954: Formation, Exile, Totalitarianism* (New York: Schocken Books, 1994), p. 321.

42  Arendt, *The Human Condition*, p. 178.

43  Ibid., p. 179.

44  Bonnie Honig, "Toward an Agonistic Feminism: Hannah Arendt and the Politics of Identity." in Judith Butler and Joan W. Scott (eds.), *Feminists Theorize the Political* (New York: Routledge, 1992), p. 219.

45  Arendt, "Understanding and Politics (The Difficulties of Understanding)," p. 309.

46  Arendt, *The Life of the Mind: Thinking*, p. 46.

47  Arendt, *The Human Condition*, p. 188.

48  Arendt, "What Is Freedom?" p. 154.

49  Arendt, *The Human Condition*, p. 180.

50  Hannah Arendt, "The Concept of History," in *Between Past and Future: Eight Exercises in Political Thought* (New York: Penguin Books, 1993), p. 51.

51  Ibid.
52  Arendt, "Introduction *Into* Politics," p. 175.
53  Hannah Arendt, "Truth and Politics," in *Between Past and Future: Eight Exercises in Political Thought* (New York: Penguin Books, 1993), p. 233.
54  Ibid., p. 242.
55  Arendt, "On Violence," p. 143. For Arendt, of course, power is to be firmly distinguished from strength, violence, authority, and force. Strength refers to the energy of movement inherent in a singular object or person (ibid.), violence to the instrumental use of implements designed to multiply strength (ibid., p. 145), authority to the voluntary recognition of the legitimacy of a relation of obedience (ibid., p. 144), and force to the quanta of energy released by natural or social movements (ibid., pp. 143–4).
56  Ibid., p. 179.
57  Arendt, "Introduction *Into* Politics," p. 167.
58  Ibid., p. 168.
59  Arendt, *The Human Condition*, pp. 199–200.
60  Ibid., p. 201.
61  Lisa Jane Disch, *Hannah Arendt and the Limits of Philosophy* (Ithaca: Cornell University Press, 1994), p. 44. Disch, though, will suggest that Arendt fails to outline the specific ways in which such a communicative articulation could take place (ibid., p. 44). I will attempt to show that this is not the case in my discussion of Arendt's appropriation of the council tradition that follows.
62  Arendt, "Introduction *Into* Politics," p. 93.
63  Arendt, *The Life of the Mind: Willing*, p. 200.
64  Arendt, "What Is Freedom?" p. 151.
65  Ibid., p. 146.
66  Ibid.
67  Ibid., p. 149.
68  Hannah Arendt, "On Humanity in Dark Times: Thoughts about Lessing" in *Men in Dark Times*, Clara and Richard Winston (trans.) (San Diego: Harcourt Bruce & Company, 1968), p. 9.
69  Arendt, "What Is Freedom?" p. 160.
70  Ibid., p. 162.
71  Ibid., p. 161.
72  Ibid.
73  Arendt, "Introduction *Into* Politics," pp. 186–7.
74  Arendt, *The Human Condition*, p. 184. Interestingly enough, Engels will produce almost an identical formulation when he writes that "history is made in such a way that the final result always arises from conflicts

between many individual wills, of which each again has been made what it is by a host of particular conditions of life. Thus there are innumerable intersecting forces, an infinite series of parallelograms of forces which give rise to one resultant – the historical event. This may again itself be viewed as the product of a power which works as a whole, *unconsciously* and without volition. For what each individual wills is obstructed by everyone else, and what emerges is something that no one willed." Friedrich Engels, "Letter to Joseph Bloch," in Robert C. Tucker (ed.), *The Marx-Engels Reader* (New York: W. W. Norton), p. 761.

75 Arendt, "The Concept of History," p. 84.

76 Arendt, *The Human Condition*, p. 185.

77 Ibid., p. 190.

78 Ibid.

79 Hannah Arendt, "The Ex-Communists," in Jerome Kohn (ed.), *Essays in Understanding, 1930–1954: Formation, Exile, and Totalitarianism* (New York: Schocken Books, 1994), p. 397. Needless to say, though, the fact that the consequences of actions cannot be completely controlled in no way implies that individuals are not responsible for the outcomes of the processes they initiate. On this point see Hanna Pitkin, *The Attack of the Blob: Hannah Arendt's Concept of the Social* (Chicago: University of Chicago Press, 1998), pp. 198–200.

80 Arendt, *The Human Condition*, p. 237.

81 Hannah Arendt, "'What Remains? The Language Remains': A Conversation with Günter Gaus," in Jerome Kohn (ed.), *Essays in Understanding, 1930–1954: Formation, Exile, and Totalitarianism*, Joan Stambough (trans.) (New York: Schocken Books, 1994), p. 23.

82 Arendt, *The Human Condition*, p. 245.

83 Ibid., p. 234.

84 Arendt, "What Is Freedom?" p. 164.

85 Ibid., p. 163.

86 Ibid., p. 164.

87 Arendt, *The Human Condition*, p. 235.

88 Arendt, "What Is Freedom?" p. 165; Hannah Arendt, *On Revolution* (New York: The Viking Press, 1965), p. 152.

89 Arendt, *The Human Condition*, p. 41.

90 Arendt, "On Violence," p. 109.

91 Arendt, "The Concept of History," p. 42.

92 Hannah Arendt, "The Tradition of Political Thought," in Jerome Kohn (ed.), *The Promise of Politics* (New York: Schocken Books, 2005), p. 43.

93 Arendt, "The Concept of History," p. 41.

94  Arendt, *The Human Condition*, p. 95.

95  Arendt, "The Concept of History," p. 47.

96  See, for example, Sheldon Wolin, "Hannah Arendt: Democracy and the Political," in Lewis P. Hinchman and Sandra K. Hinchman (eds.), *Hannah Arendt: Critical Essays* (Albany: State University of New York Press, 1994).

97  Benhabib, *The Reluctant Modernism of Hannah Arendt*, p. 127.

98  Ibid., p. 130.

99  Arendt, "Introduction *Into* Politics," p. 119.

100  Indeed, for Arendt the motivating principle of action in a republic is equality, and hence laws in a republic take a restricting form: "they are designed to restrict the strength of each citizen so that room may be left for the strength of his fellow citizens." Hannah Arendt, "The Great Tradition I: Law and Power," in *Social Research* 74, no. 3 (Fall 2007): 726. This is simply another way of saying that not just an exceptional few, but all, should be allowed to act.

101  Pitkin, *The Attack of the Blob*, p. 114.

102  Leon Botstein, "Hannah Arendt: Opposing Views," in *Partisan Review* 45, no. 3 (1978): 379.

103  Hannah Arendt, *Eichmann in Jerusalem: A Report on the Banality of Evil* (New York: Penguin Books, 1994), p. 12.

104  Arendt, *The Human Condition*, p. 197 [my emphasis].

105  Ibid.

106  Arendt, "The Concept of History," p. 72.

107  Maurizio Passerin d'Entrèves, *The Political Philosophy of Hannah Arendt* (London: Routledge, 1994), pp. 76–7.

108  Eric Hobsbawm, "Hannah Arendt on Revolution," in *Revolutionaries: Contemporary Essays* (London: Quartet Books, 1973), p. 202.

109  Recent years have seen a dramatic increase in the volume of scholarship concerned with exploring the relationship between Arendt and Benjamin. See, for example, Raluca Eddon, "Arendt, Scholem, Benjamin: Between Revolution and Messianism," in *European Journal of Political Theory* 5, no. 3 (Fall 2006): 261–79; Annabel Herzog, "Illuminating Inheritance: Benjamin's Influence on Arendt's Political Storytelling," in *Philosophy and Social Criticism* 26, no. 5 (Sept. 2000): 1–27; and Robert Lee-Nichols, "Judgment, History, Memory: Arendt and Benjamin on Connecting Us to Our Past," in *Philosophy Today* 50, no. 3 (Fall 2006): 307–23.

110  For both Benjamin and Arendt, revolutions are major as opposed to minor events. "Major events crystallize the tensions within a situation, and present us with a kind of historical monad, the congealed essence of an entire era." James Miller, "The Pathos of Novelty: Hannah Arendt's

Image of Freedom in the Modern World," in Melvyn A. Hill, *Hannah Arendt: The Recovery of the Public World* (New York: St. Martin's Press, 1979), p. 182.

111 Miller, "The Pathos of Novelty," p. 183. On Miller's interpretation, though, although the memory of the revolutionary tradition must be preserved, its actual restoration is not seen as being concretely possible: "for Arendt, it is a restoration feasible in memory alone" (ibid., p. 198). In all but Arendt's very latest period, however, this is clearly not the case, as can be seen, for example, in her advocacy of Jewish councils as a practical form of organization and her celebration of the institutions of the Hungarian revolution, which will be discussed subsequently.

112 d'Entrèves, *The Political Philosophy of Hannah Arendt*, pp. 31–2.

113 Hannah Arendt, "Walter Benjamin," in *Men in Dark Times*, Harry Zohn (trans.) (San Diego: Harcourt Brace and Company, 1968), pp. 205–6.

114 Arendt, *On Revolution*, p. 13.

115 Arendt, *On Revolution*, p. 22.

116 Ibid., p. 23.

117 Ibid., p. 22.

118 Ibid.

119 Ibid., p. 25.

120 Ibid., p. 27.

121 Ibid., p. 36.

122 Ibid., p. 37. Thomas Paine, *The Rights of Man* (New York: Penguin Books, 1984), p. 161.

123 Arendt, "Truth and Politics," p. 263 [my emphasis].

124 Arendt, *On Revolution*, p. 115.

125 Ibid., pp. 124–5.

126 Hannah Arendt, "Thoughts on Politics and Revolution," in *Crises of the Republic* (New York: Harcourt Brace Jovanovich, 1972), p. 201.

127 Ibid., p. 202.

128 Arendt, "On Violence," pp. 117–18.

129 Arendt, "Thoughts on Politics and Revolution," p. 203.

130 Ibid.

131 Arendt, "On Violence," p. 124.

132 Arendt, *On Revolution*, p. 174.

133 Arendt, *The Life of the Mind*, Vol. 2, *Willing*, p. 203.

134 Arendt *On Revolution*, p. 175.

135 Ibid., pp. 202–3.

136 Ibid., pp. 203–4.

137 Ibid., p. 205.

138  Ibid., p. 226.
139  Ibid., p. 238.
140  Ibid., p. 222.
141  Ibid., p. 223.
142  Elisabeth Young-Bruehl, *Why Arendt Matters* (New Haven: Yale University Press, 2006), p. 131.
143  Arendt, "The Tradition of Political Thought," p. 47.
144  Ibid.
145  Arendt, *On Revolution*, p. 251.
146  Arendt, "Thoughts on Politics and Revolution," p. 216.
147  Arendt, *On Revolution*, pp. 260–1.
148  For a good and detailed account of the process by which the Bolshevist political system neutralized the revolutionary potential of the soviets see Maurice Brinton, *The Bolsheviks & Workers' Control, 1917–1921* (London: Solidarity, 1970).
149  Arendt, *On Revolution*, p. 261.
150  Ibid., p. 263.
151  Ibid., p. 275.
152  Ibid., p. 264.
153  Ibid., p. 267.
154  Ibid., p. 273.
155  Ibid., p. 277.
156  Arendt, "Thoughts on Politics and Revolution," pp. 231–2.
157  Ibid., p. 231.
158  Arendt, *On Revolution*, p. 252.
159  Ibid., p. 253.
160  Ibid., p. 268.
161  Ibid., pp. 249–50.
162  For an account of the radical democratic nature of Jefferson's political thought see Richard Matthews, *The Radical Politics of Thomas Jefferson: A Revisionist View* (Lawrence: University Press of Kansas, 1984).
163  Arendt, *On Revolution*, p. 256.
164  Ibid., pp. 258–9.
165  John F. Sitton, "Hannah Arendt's Argument for Council Democracy," in Lewis P. Hinchman and Sandra K. Hinchman (eds.), *Hannah Arendt: Critical Essays* (Albany: State University of New York Press, 1994), p. 308.
166  Arendt, *On Revolution*, p. 267.
167  Ibid., p. 270.
168  Ibid., p. 271.
169  Ibid.

170  Ibid., p. 282.

171  Ibid., p 283. Needless to say, though, any citizens who do not want to act do not have to, as individuals still maintain a negative liberty to be free from politics. The fact that Arendt, though, will label those who do participate in public affairs political elites has not surprisingly fueled criticism of her and her political theory as elitist. Phillip Hansen is right to point out, however, that it is quite clear that the category of political elite is open to all, and that one is self-selected on the basis of nothing other than one's desire for public freedom and happiness. Phillip Hansen, *Hannah Arendt: Politics, History and Citizenship* (Stanford: Stanford University Press, 1993), p. 190. Jeffrey Isaac similarly notes that Arendt's elites are just those citizens with a genuine interest in participation, and that her advocacy of political "elitism" is nothing but an expression of her democratic pluralism. Jeffrey C. Isaac, *Arendt, Camus, and Modern Rebellion* (New Haven: Yale University Press, 1992), pp. 153–5.

172  Hannah Arendt, "Totalitarian Imperialism: Reflections on the Hungarian Revolution," in *Journal of Politics* 20, no. 1 (Feb. 1958): 8.

173  Ibid., p. 26.

174  Ibid., p. 27.

175  Jules Michelet, *History of the French Revolution*, Charles Cocks (trans.) (Chicago: University of Chicago Press, 1967), p. 13.

176  Ibid., p. 12.

177  Arendt, "Totalitarian Imperialism," p. 28. For an account of the specific structure of the council system in Hungary, see ibid., pp. 28–33. It should be noted here that for Arendt the councils had a dual political and economic role: Revolutionary councils fulfilled political functions and Workers' councils economic ones. Arendt, though, will ultimately question whether economic life can in fact be ordered according to principles of self-rule. She maintains that for this reason the two council forms should be kept strictly apart, and that she will deal only with the Revolutionary councils (ibid., p. 29). This hostility toward economic concerns, even when they are quite clearly tied up with issues of freedom and politics, manifests itself throughout all of Arendt's theoretical work, and in fact forms the basis for the most legitimate critiques of Arendt's affirmation of the revolutionary council tradition. See, for example, Sitton, "Hannah Arendt's Argument for Council Democracy," pp. 468–72; Mike McConkey, "On Arendt's Vision of the European Council Phenomenon: Critique from an Historical Perspective," *Dialectical Anthropology* 16, no. 1 (Mar. 1991): 24–7; and John Medearis, "Lost or Obscured? How V. I. Lenin, Joseph Schumpeter, and Hannah Arendt Misunderstood the Council Movement," *Polity* 36, no. 3 (Apr. 2004): 468–72.

178  Arendt, *On Revolution*, p. 275.

179  Arendt, "Totalitarian Imperialism," p. 31.

180  Arendt, "Thoughts on Politics and Revolution," p. 232.

181  Ibid.

182  Miller, "The Pathos of Novelty," p. 198.

183  Hannah Arendt, "To Save the Jewish Homeland: There Is Still Time," in Ron H. Feldman (ed.), *The Jew as Pariah: Jewish Identity and Politics in the Modern Age* (New York: Grove Press, 1978), p. 192 [my emphasis].

184  Arendt, "Thoughts on Politics and Revolution," p. 230.

185  Ibid., p. 231.

186  It should be noted, however, that with the publication in 1971 of "Thinking and Moral Considerations" (Hannah Arendt, "Thinking and Moral Considerations," in *Responsibility and Judgment*, ed. Jerome Kohn [New Haven: Schocken Books, 2003]), there is a shift in the nature of Arendt's account of judgment, which is no longer understood in terms of an active exercise oriented toward the mediation of opinion for the sake of the stimulation of action, but rather as a retrospective and contemplative consideration of past deeds. For an excellent account of the nature of this shift, which is seen to be rooted in an alleged impasse of the will, in the philosophical tradition's incapability of affirming radical creation, see Ronald Beiner, "Hannah Arendt on Judging," in *Lectures on Kant's Political Philosophy*, ed. Ronald Beiner (Chicago: University of Chicago Press, 1992). Although Arendt did not live to complete what would have been her major work on judgment, the third volume of *The Life of the Mind*, much can be gleaned from her lectures on Kant's third critique. Hannah Arendt, *Lectures on Kant's Political Philosophy*, ed. Ronald Beiner (Chicago: University of Chicago Press, 1992).

## Notes to Chapter 5

1  Benhabib, *The Reluctant Modernism of Hannah Arendt*, p. 131.

2  Pitkin, *The Attack of the Blob*, p. 115.

3  For faithful reconstructions of Arendt's often scattered and not quite systematic critique of Marx, see Margaret Canovan, *Hannah Arendt: A Reinterpretation of Her Political Thought* (Cambridge: Cambridge University Press, 1992), pp. 63–98, and Bikhu Parekh, "Hannah Arendt's Critique of Marx," in Melvyn A. Hill (ed.), *The Recovery of the Public World* (New York: St. Martin's Press, 1979), pp. 73–83.

4  Arendt, *The Human Condition*, p. 99.

5  Ibid., p. 88.

6  Ibid., p. 99.

7  Ibid., p. 88n20.

8  Ibid., p. 116.

9  Ibid., pp. 324–5.

10  Marx, *Economic and Philosophic Manuscripts of 1844*, p. 105.

11  Karl Marx, "On James Mill," in David McLellan (ed.), *Karl Marx: Selected Writings* (Oxford: Oxford University Press, 2000), p. 125.

12  Ibid.

13  Marx, *Economic and Philosophic Manuscripts of 1844*, p. 71.

14  Hannah Arendt, "Tradition and the Modern Age," in *Between Past and Future: Eight Exercises in Political Thought* (New York: Penguin Books, 1993), p. 24.

15  Arendt, *The Human Condition*, p. 9.

16  Arendt, "Introduction *Into* Politics," p. 128.

17  Arendt, "The Crisis in Culture," in *Between Past and Future: Eight Exercises in Political Thought* (New York: Penguin Books, 1993), p. 217.

18  Marx, *Economic and Philosophic Manuscripts of 1844*, p. 104.

19  Ibid., p. 105.

20  Arendt, "The Eggs Speak Up," p. 283.

21  Marx, *Economic and Philosophic Manuscripts of 1844*, p. 102.

22  Hannah Arendt, "From Hegel to Marx," in Jerome Kohn (ed.), *The Promise of Politics* (New York: Schocken Books, 2005), p. 79; and Arendt, "Tradition and the Modern Age," p. 22.

23  Parekh, "Hannah Arendt's Critique of Marx," p. 84.

24  Karl Marx, *Capital,* Vol. 1 (London: Penguin Books, 1976), pp. 284–5.

25  Hannah Arendt, "On Hannah Arendt," in Melvyn A. Hill (ed.), *Hannah Arendt: the Recovery of the Public World* (New York: St. Martin's Press, 1979), p. 316.

26  Ibid.

27  Ibid., p. 317.

28  Ibid., pp. 318–19.

29  Richard Bernstein, "ReThinking the Social and the Political," in *Philosophical Profiles: Essays in a Pragmatic Mode* (Philadelphia: University of Pennsylvania Press, 1986), p. 253.

30  Castoriadis, *The Imaginary Institution of Society*, p. 265. Indeed, elsewhere Castoriadis will specifically maintain that Arendt "commits an enormous blunder" in not recognizing that "the social question is a political question." Cornelius Castoriadis, "Does the Idea of Revolution Still Make Sense," David Ames Curtis (trans.) *Thesis Eleven* 26, no. 1 (1990): 125.

31  Arendt, "On Hannah Arendt," p. 325.

32  Ibid., pp. 326–7.

33 Arendt, "On Violence," p. 146. This comment is made in the context of the distinctions made between violence, strength, force, and authority.

34 Hannah Arendt, "What Is Authority?" in *Between Past and Future: Eight Exercises in Political Thought* (New York: Penguin Books, 1993), p. 95.

35 See, for example, Arendt, *The Life of the Mind: Willing*, p. 49.

36 Hannah Arendt, "Religion and the Intellectuals," in Jerome Kohn (ed.), *Essays in Understanding, 1930–1954: Formation, Exile, and Totalitarianism* (New York: Schocken Books, 1994), p. 230.

37 Hannah Arendt, *The Origins of Totalitarianism* (San Diego: Harcourt, 1968), p. 159.

38 Ibid., p. 458.

39 Ibid., p. 469.

40 Arendt, "From Hegel to Marx," p. 74.

41 Ibid.

42 Arendt, "The Concept of History," pp. 78–9.

43 Ibid., p. 79.

44 Arendt, "The Ex-Communists," p. 396.

45 Arendt, "The Great Tradition I," p. 719.

46 Ibid., p. 720.

47 Hannah Arendt, "On the Nature of Totalitarianism: An Essay in Understanding," in Jerome Kohn (ed.), *Essays in Understanding, 1930–1954: Formation, Exile, and Totalitarianism* (New York: Schocken Books, 1994), p. 341.

48 Ibid., p. 349.

49 Arendt, *The Origins of Totalitarianism*, p. 458.

50 Arendt, "What Is Authority?" p. 101.

51 Benhabib, *The Reluctant Modernism of Hannah Arendt*, p. 65.

52 See, for example, Arendt, *The Origins of Totalitarianism*, p. 466.

53 Marcuse, *Soviet Marxism*, p. 143.

54 Ibid.

55 Ibid., p. 144.

56 Ibid., p. 145.

57 Ibid., p. 149.

58 Marcuse, "Karl Popper and the Problem of Historical Laws," p. 203.

59 Marcuse, *Soviet Marxism*, p. 142.

60 Karl Marx and Frederick Engels, *The Holy Family, or Critique of Critical Criticism: Against Bruno Bauer, and Company*, Richard Dixon and Clemens Dutt (trans.) (Moscow: Progress Publishers, 1975), p. 72.

61 Ibid.

62 Ibid.

63  Ibid., p. 73.
64  Ibid.
65  Ibid., p. 75.
66  Arendt, "From Hegel to Marx," p. 75.
67  Marx, *Grundrisse*, pp. 100–1.
68  Marx, *Grundrisse*, p. 100.
69  Ibid., p. 101.
70  Shierry M. Weber, "Individuation as Praxis," in Paul Breines (ed.), *Critical Interruptions: New Left Perspectives on Herbert Marcuse* (New York: Herder and Herder, 1970): p. 34.
71  Norman O. Brown, *Love's Body* (New York: Vintage Books, 1966), p. 244.
72  Ibid.
73  Ibid.
74  Herbert Marcuse, "Love Mystified: A Critique of Norman O. Brown," in *Negations: Essays in Critical Theory* (London: Free Association Books, 1988), p. 235.
75  Ibid., p. 237.
76  Ibid., p. 234.
77  Ibid., p. 237.
78  Brown, *Love's Body*, p. 154.
79  Marcuse, "Love Mystified," p. 241.
80  Ibid., p. 243.
81  Marcuse, *One-Dimensional Man*, p. 214.
82  Hannah Arendt, "What Is Existential Philosophy?" in Jerome Kohn (ed.), *Essays in Understanding, 1930–1954: Formation, Exile, and Totalitarianism* (New York: Schocken Books, 1994), p. 171.

## Notes to Chapter 6

1  Rolf Wiggershaus, *The Frankfurt School: Its History, Theories, and Political Significance*, Michael Robertson (trans.) (Cambridge: MIT Press, 1995), p. 623. The interview Wiggershaus cites is Herbert Marcuse, "Professoren als Staats-regenten?: Spiegel-Gespräch mit dem Philosophen Professor Herbert Marcuse," *Der Spiegel* 35 (Aug. 21, 1967): 112–18. Here, Marcuse claims that with respect to any revolutionary activity, "the intellectuals could and should carry out the preparatory work. I believe that the revolution tends towards an educational dictatorship which would abolish [*aufheben*] itself in its fulfillment" (ibid., p. 116, [my translation]).
2  Isaac D. Balbus, "The Missing Dimension: Self-Reflexivity and the 'New Sensibility,'" in John Bokina and Timothy J. Lukes (eds.), *Marcuse: From*

*the New Left to the Next Left* (Lawrence:  University Press of Kansas, 1994), p. 111.

3  Ibid., p. 112.

4  A brief word on Marcuse's much discussed relation to Heidegger may here be necessary. Generally speaking, the degree to which Marcuse's philosophical problematic can be grounded in his early attempt to establish a phenomenological Marxism is greatly exaggerated. Marcuse's engagement with Heidegger was primarily motivated by the former's perception of a gap within Marxist philosophy in the late 1920s. In particular, his theoretical utilization of the early Heidegger was aimed at injecting Marxism with a conscious concern for concrete problems of human existence considered in terms of autonomous subjectivity and action, a concern sorely lacking in those strains of Marxism influenced by the theory and practice of the Second International. In Morton Schoolman's words, "From the outset, Heidegger was to be received favorably only to the degree that he contributed to solving the problem and eliminating the void, in effect, to the degree that his philosophy made a definite contribution to Marxist theory and practice." Morton Schoolman, *The Imaginary Witness*, p. 4. Marcuse would state that he and certain of his contemporaries "saw in Heidegger what we had first saw in Husserl, a new beginning, the first radical attempt to put philosophy on really concrete foundations – philosophy concerned with human existence, the human condition." Herbert Marcuse, "Heidegger's Politics: An Interview," in Richard Woling and John Abromeit (eds.), *Heideggerian Marxism* (Lincoln: Nebraska University Press, 2005), pp. 165–6. However, despite Marcuse's recognition of what he considered to be the specific virtues of Heidegger – the understanding of subjectivity as being-in-the-world, as situated in time, and as oriented toward the actualization of possibility via authentic action – he never overlooked the more objectionable aspects of the latter's thought, such as the dismissal of the merely ontic dimensions of human life, the critique of the levelling tendencies of *das Man*, and the one-sided decisionism unattached to any concrete ethical standards. The elements that would crystallize into Marcuse's mature critique of Heidegger, in which the former would claim that there is nothing in the latter's analysis of the individual subject worth saying yes to (Marcuse, "Heidegger's Politics," p. 170), can already be identified in those early essays that allegedly look toward the construction of a Heideggerian-Marxism. Marcuse, however, was inclined to overlook these objectionable aspects of fundamental ontology for the sake of the affirmation of the principle of radical choice. Marcuse's complete turn away from Heidegger, however, was stimulated not simply by Heidegger's turn to National Socialism, but by the discovery of Marx's *Paris Manuscripts*:

it was no longer necessary to extract from Heidegger a content required to supplement Marx, as it was now provided by Marx himself. Marcuse, in fact, will make this explicit in an interview with Habermas and others, where he states that the question of Heidegger versus Marx for him disappeared after the publication of the *Manuscripts*. Marcuse, "Theory and Politics," p. 125. In sum, although it may be tempting to locate within Marcuse's critical theory a substantive phenomenological heritage, especially in the present context, where the effort is being made to read Marcuse in light of another of Heidegger's students, such an interpretation must nevertheless be strongly resisted.

5  Herbert Marcuse, "On Concrete Philosophy," in Richard Wolin and John Abromeit (eds.), Matthew Erlin (trans.) *Heideggerian Marxism* (Lincoln: University of Nebraska Press, 2005), p. 45.

6  Herbert Marcuse, "Contributions to a Phenomenology of Historical Materialism," in Richard Wolin and John Abromeit (eds.), Eric Oberle (trans.) *Heideggerian Marxism* (Lincoln: University of Nebraska Press, 2005), p. 1.

7  Marcuse, "Contributions to a Phenomenology of Historical Materialism," p. 17.

8  Ibid., p. 20.

9  Marcuse, "On Concrete Philosophy," p. 37.

10  Ibid., p. 47.

11  Marcuse, "Contributions to a Phenomenology of Historical Materialism," p. 1.

12  Ibid.

13  Karl Marx, "Contribution to the Critique of Hegel's *Philosophy of Right*: Introduction," in Robert C. Tucker (ed.), *The Marx-Engels Reader* (New York: W.W. Norton, 1978), p. 60.

14  Marcuse, "Contributions to a Phenomenology of Historical Materialism," p. 4.

15  Ibid., p. 5.

16  Michael Werz, "The Fate of Emancipated Subjectivity," in John Abromeit and W. Mark Cobb (eds.), *Herbert Marcuse: A Critical Reader* (New York: Routledge, 2004), p. 212.

17  Marcuse, "On Concrete Philosophy," p. 47.

18  Marcuse, "Contributions to a Phenomenology of Historical Materialism," p. 7.

19  Marcuse, "On Concrete Philosophy," p. 49.

20  Ibid., p. 50.

21  Ibid., p. 47.

22  Marcuse, "Theory and Politics," p. 133.

23  Ibid.

24  Marcuse, *Counter-revolution and Revolt*, p. 60.

25  Ibid., p. 59.

26  Ibid.

27  Ibid., p. 60.

28  "A Biological Foundation for Socialism?" is the title of the first chapter of *An Essay on Liberation*. Marcuse, *An Essay on Liberation*, pp. 7–22.

29  Herbert Marcuse, "Liberation from the Affluent Society," in Douglas Kellner (ed.), *The New Left and the 1960s: The Collected Papers of Herbert Marcuse*, Vol. 3 (London: Routledge, 2005), p. 77.

30  Marcuse, *Counter-revolution and Revolt*, p. 63.

31  Ibid.

32  Marx, *Economic and Philosophic Manuscripts of 1844*, pp. 102–3.

33  Marcuse, "The Foundation of Historical Materialism," p. 18.

34  Immanuel Kant, *Critique of Pure Reason*, Norman Kemp Smith (trans.) (London: Macmillan, 1958), B33.

35  Marx, *Economic and Philosophic Manuscripts of 1844*, pp. 153–4.

36  Marcuse, "The Foundations of Historical Materialism," p. 19.

37  Marx, *Economic and Philosophic Manuscripts of 1844*, p. 154.

38  Ibid., p. 106.

39  Ibid.

40  Ibid., p. 108.

41  Marcuse, *Counter-Revolution and Revolt*, p. 64.

42  Ibid., p. 46.

43  Ibid., p. 70.

44  Marcuse, *An Essay on Liberation*, p. 17.

45  Ibid., p. 4.

46  Ibid., p. 37.

47  Marcuse, "Cultural Revolution," pp. 134–5.

48  Marcuse, *Counter-revolution and Revolt*, p. 64.

49  Marcuse, "Cultural Revolution," p. 131.

50  Ibid.

51  Ibid., p. 137.

52  Marcuse, *Counter-revolution and Revolt*, p. 64.

53  See, for example, Lukács, "The Changing Function of Historical Materialism," p. 234: "Nature is a societal category. That is to say, whatever is held to be natural at any given stage of social development, however this nature is related to man and whatever form his involvement with it takes, i.e. nature's form, its content, its range and its objectivity are all socially conditioned."

54 Marcuse, "Cultural Revolution," p. 132.
55 Marcuse, *Counter-revolution and Revolt*, p. 66.
56 Ibid.
57 Ibid., p. 87.
58 Ibid., p. 67. Marcuse will, though, qualify his account, maintaining that in the present reality, priority should definitely be given to the alleviation of specifically human suffering: "In the face of the suffering inflicted by man on man, it seems terribly 'premature' to campaign for universal vegetarianism or synthetic foodstuffs" (ibid.) Nevertheless, individuals should still make a consistent and genuine effort to reduce natural, especially animal, suffering.
59 Ibid., pp. 69–70.
60 Marcuse, "Cultural Revolution," p. 149.
61 Marcuse, *Counter-revolution and Revolt*, p. 74.
62 Marcuse, "The Realm of Freedom and the Realm of Necessity," p. 24.
63 Herbert Marcuse, "The Problem of Violence and the Radical Opposition," in *Five Lectures: Psychoanalysis, Politics, Utopia*, Jeremy J. Shapiro and Shierry Weber (trans.) (Boston: Beacon Press, 1970), p. 88.
64 Marcuse, "The Foundation of Historical Materialism," p. 34.
65 Marcuse, *Counter-revolution and Revolt*, p. 48.
66 Ibid., p. 49.
67 Herbert Marcuse, "Repressive Tolerance," in Paul Connerton (ed.), *Critical Sociology* (Harmondsworth: Penguin, 1976), pp. 304–5.
68 Russell Jacoby, "Reversals and Lost Meanings," in Paul Breines (ed.), *Critical Interruptions: New Left Perspectives on Herbert Marcuse* (New York: Herder and Herder, 1970), p. 65.
69 Marcuse, *Counter-revolution and Revolt*, p. 50.
70 Ibid.
71 Herbert Marcuse, "Ecology and the Critique of Modern Society," in *Capitalism, Nature, Socialism* 3, no. 3 (Sept. 1992): 37.
72 Herbert Marcuse, "The Struggle against Liberalism in the Totalitarian View of the State," in *Negations: Essays in Critical Theory*, Jeremy J. Shapiro (trans.) (London: Free Association Books, 1988), p. 40.
73 Marcuse, "Cultural Revolution," p. 127.
74 Tyson Lewis, "Utopia and Education in Critical Theory," in *Policy Futures in Education* 4, no. 1 (2006): 15. Lewis, though, will not adequately grasp the nonidentical in Marcuse, thus suggesting that Marcuse's project is ultimately concerned with a passive recuperation of a prior instinctual content for the sake of the construction of a positive utopia.

75  Richard Kahn, "For a Marcusian Ecopedagogy," in Douglas Kellner, Tyson Lewis, Clayton Pierce, and K. Daniel Choi (eds.), *Marcuse's Challenge to Education* (Lanham: Rowman & Littlefield, 2009), p. 90.

76  Only recently has the question of education become a major concern of readers of Marcuse. The most substantial attempt to extract from Marcuse an aesthetic pedagogy is undertaken by Charles Reitz in his *Art, Alienation, and the Humanities*. See as well the essays collected in a special issue of *Policy Futures in Education* 4, no. 1 (2006) devoted exclusively to Marcuse and critical pedagogy, and in Douglas Kellner, Tyson Lewis, Clayton Pierce, K. Daniel Choi (eds.), *Marcuse's Challenge to Education* (Lanham: Rowman & Littlefield, 2009). Also especially notable in this respect is Balbus, "The Missing Dimension," pp. 106–17.

77  Herbert Marcuse, "Lecture on Education, Brooklyn College, 1968," in Douglas Kellner, Tyson Lewis, Clayton Pierce, K. Daniel Choi (eds.), *Marcuse's Challenge to Education* (Lanham: Rowman & Littlefield, 2009).

78  Ibid., p. 33.

79  Herbert Marcuse, "Lecture on Higher Education and Politics, Berkeley, 1975," in Douglas Kellner, Tyson Lewis, Clayton Pierce, K. Daniel Choi (eds.), *Marcuse's Challenge to Education* (Lanham: Rowman & Littlefield, 2009), p. 40.

80  Marcuse, "Lecture on Education, Brooklyn College, 1968," p. 35.

81  Ibid.

82  Ibid., p. 37.

83  Ibid., p. 38.

84  Richard Van Heertum, "Moving from Critique to Hope: Critical Interventions from Marcuse to Freire," in Douglas Kellner, Tyson Lewis, Clayton Pierce, K. Daniel Choi (eds.), *Marcuse's Challenge to Education* (Lanham: Rowman & Littlefield, 2009), p. 105.

85  Paulo Freire, *Pedagogy of the Oppressed*, Myra Bergman Ramos (trans.) (New York: Continuum, 2005), p. 45.

86  Ibid., p. 48.

87  Ibid., p. 68.

88  Ibid., p. 49.

89  Ibid., p. 84.

90  Ibid., p. 100.

91  Max Horkheimer, *Eclipse of Reason* (London: Continuum, 2004), p. 97.

92  Marcuse, *An Essay on Liberation*, p. 79.

93  Herbert Marcuse, "Reflections on the French Revolution," in Douglas Kellner (ed.), *The New Left and the 1960s: The Collected Papers of Herbert Marcuse*, Vol. 3 (London: Routledge, 2005), p. 45.

94   Marcuse, *Counter-revolution and Revolt*, p. 42.

95   Marcuse, *An Essay on Liberation*, p. 33.

96   Herbert Marcuse, "Murder Is Not a Political Weapon," in Douglas Kellner (ed.), *The New Left and the 1960s: The Collected Papers of Herbert Marcuse*, Vol. 3 (London: Routledge, 2005), p. 178.

97   Herbert Marcuse, "On the New Left," in Douglas Kellner (ed.), Jeffrey Herf (trans.) *The New Left and the 1960s: The Collected Papers of Herbert Marcuse*, Vol. 3. (London: Routledge, 2005), p. 123.

98   Marcuse, *An Essay on Liberation*, p. 89.

99   Ibid.

100  Ibid., p. 65.

101  Marcuse, "On the New Left," p. 125.

102  Marcuse, "Reflections on the French Revolution," p. 44.

103  Marcuse, "The Failure of the New Left," in Douglas Kellner (ed.), Biddy Martin (trans.) *The New Left and the 1960s: The Collected Papers of Herbert Marcuse*, Vol. 3 (London: Routledge, 2005), p. 183.

104  Marcuse, *An Essay on Liberation*, p. 26.

105  Arendt, "Thoughts on Politics and Revolution," p. 203.

106  Marcuse, "The Failure of the New Left," p. 184.

107  Marcuse, "Cultural Revolution," p. 157.

108  Marcuse, "Marcuse Defines His New Left Line," p. 116.

109  Ibid.

110  Marcuse. "The Realm of Freedom and the Realm of Necessity," p. 22.

111  Ibid.

112  Arendt, "On Violence," p. 144.

113  Marcuse, "Cultural Revolution," p. 155.

114  Herbert Marcuse, "Beyond One-Dimensional Man," in Douglas Kellner (ed.), *Towards a Critical Theory of Society: Collected Papers of Herbert Marcuse*, Vol. 2 (London: Routledge, 1998), p. 116.

115  Marcuse, *An Essay on Liberation*, pp. 63–4.

116  Marcuse, *Counter-Revolution and Revolt*, pp. 33–4.

117  Ibid., p. 31.

118  Fredric Jameson, *Marxism and Form: Twentieth-Century Dialectical Theories of Literature* (Princeton, NJ: Princeton University Press), p. 111.

119  Ibid., pp. 111–12.

120  Marcuse, *An Essay on Liberation*, p. 86. For Arendt's critique of the tendency to interpret the task of political theory in terms of the fabrication of utopian blueprints see, for example, Arendt, *The Human Condition*, pp. 220–30.

121  Marcuse, "Philosophy and Critical Theory," p. 145.

122  Marcuse, *An Essay on Liberation*, p. 5.

123  Ibid., p. 87.

124  Marcuse, "On the New Left," p. 126.

125  Ibid.

126  Phil Slater, *Origin and Significance of the Frankfurt School: A Marxist Perspective* (London: Routledge & Kegan Paul, 1977), p. 91.

127  Max Horkheimer, "The Authoritarian State," in Andrew Arato and Eike Gebhardt (eds.), *The Essential Frankfurt School Reader* (New York: Continuum, 1982), p. 104.

128  Marcuse, *Counter-revolution and Revolt*, p. 44.

129  Ibid.

130  Ibid.

131  Ibid., p. 45.

132  Ibid.

133  Marcuse, *An Essay on Liberation*, p. 79.

134  Marcuse, "Industrialization and Capitalism in the Work of Max Weber," p. 223.

135  Marcuse, *An Essay on Liberation*, p. 56.

136  Ibid., p. 88.

137  Herbert Marcuse and Franz Neumann, "Theories of Social Change," in Douglas Kellner (ed.), *Technology, War, and Fascism: Collected Papers of Herbert Marcuse*, Vol. 1 (London: Routledge, 1998), p. 110.

138  Ibid., p. 126.

139  Ibid.

140  Ibid., p. 127.

141  Ibid., p. 131.

142  Quoted in Marcuse, "The Struggle Against Liberalism in the Totalitarian View of the State," pp. 33–4.

143  Marcuse, "The Struggle against Liberalism in the Totalitarian View of the State," p. 34.

144  Marcuse, "On the New Left," p. 126.

## Notes to Conclusion

1  David McNally, *Another World Is Possible: Globalization & Anti-Capitalism* (Winnipeg: Arbeiter Ring, 2006), p. 341.

2  Marx, *Capital*, Vol. 1, pp. 164–5.

3  McNally, *Another World is Possible*, p. 24.

4  Andrew Boyd and Stephen Duncombe, "The Manufacture of Dissent: What the Left Can Learn from Las Vegas," *Journal of Aesthetics & Protest* 1, no. 3 (June 2004), www.joapp.org/new3/duncombeboyd.html.

5  Benjamin Shepard, "Joy, Justice, and Resistance to the New Global Apartheid," in Benjamin Shepard and Ronald Hayduk (eds.), *From ACT UP to the WTO: Urban Protest and Community Building in the Era of Globalization* (London: Verso, 2002), p. 390.

6  Brass Liberation Orchestra, "Points of Unity and Vision," October 2004, retrieved Dec. 2, 2010, from www.brassliberation.org/pov.php.

7  McNally, *Another World Is Possible*, p. 354.

8  Torgerson, *The Promise of Green Politics*, p. 93.

9  Ibid.

10  Benjamin Shepard, "If I Can't Dance: Play, Creativity, and Social Movements" (PhD Diss., City University of New York, 2006), p. 572.

11  Benjamin Shepard, L.M. Bogad, and Stephen Duncombe, "Performing vs. the Insurmountable: Theatrics, Activism, and Social Movements," in *Liminalities* 4, no. 3 (Oct. 2008): 2.

12  Ibid., p. 5.

13  Benjamin Shepard, "Introductory Notes on the Trail from ACT UP to the WTO," in Benjamin Shepard and Ronald Hayduk (eds.), *From ACT UP to the WTO: Urban Protest and Community Building in the Era of Globalization* (London: Verso, 2002), p. 12. For a specifically Arendtian account of the activism of ACT UP see Mark Reinhardt, *The Art of Being Free: Taking Liberties with Tocqueville, Marx, and Arendt* (Ithaca, NY: Cornell University Press, 1997), pp. 166–78.

14  Shepard, "Introductory Notes on the Trail from ACT UP to the WTO," p. 13.

15  Shepard, Bogad, and Duncombe, "Performing vs. the Insurmountable," p. 14.

16  McNally, *Another World Is Possible*, pp. 338–9.

17  Shepard, "Joy, Justice, and Resistance to the New Global Apartheid," p. 393.

18  McNally, *Another World Is Possible*, p. 15.

19  Raquel Gutiérrez-Aguilar, "The Coordinadora: One Year After the Water War," in Oscar Olivera, *Cochabamba!: Water War in Bolivia* (Cambridge: South End Press, 2004), p. 55.

20  Oscar Olivera, *Cochabamba!: Water War in Bolivia* (Cambridge: South End Press, 2004), p. 21.

21  Ibid., pp. 37–8.

22  Ibid., p. 38.

23  Gutiérrez-Aguilar, "The Coordinadora," p. 56.

24  Olivera, *Cochabamba!* p. 38.

25  Álvaro García Linera, "The Multitude," in Oscar Olivera, *Cochabamba!: Water War in Bolivia* (Cambridge: South End Press, 2004), p. 81.

26  Ibid., pp. 81–2.

27  Olivera, *Cochabamba!* p. 125.

28  Ibid., p. 127.
29  Gutiérrez-Aguilar, "The Coordinadora," p. 61.
30  McNally, *Another World Is Possible*, p. 18.
31  Ibid., p. 367.

# References

Abensour, Miguel. *Democracy against the State: Marx and the Machiavellian Moment.* Translated by Max Blechman and Martin Breaugh. Boston: Polity Press, 2010.

Abromeit, John. "Herbert Marcuse's Critical Encounter with Martin Heidegger: 1927–1933." In *Herbert Marcuse: A Critical Reader*, edited by John Abromeit and W. Mark Cobb, 131–51. New York: Routledge, 2004.

Adorno, Theodor. "The Idea of Natural History." Translated by Bob Hullot-Kentor. *Telos* 60 (Summer 1984): 111–24.

Adorno, Theodor. *Minima Moralia: Reflections from Damaged Life.* Translated by E.F.N. Jephcott.. London: Verso, 1974.

Adorno, Theodor. *Negative Dialectics.* Translated by E.B. Ashton. New York: Seabury Press, 1973.

Adorno, Theodor. "A Portrait of Walter Benjamin." In *Prisms*, translated by Samuel and Shierry Weber, 227–42. London: Neville Spearman, 1976.

Adorno, Theodor, and Walter Benjamin. *The Complete Correspondence, 1928–1940.* Edited by Henri Lonitz. Translated by Nicholas Walker. Cambridge: Harvard University Press, 1999.

Adorno, Theodor, and Herbert Marcuse. "Correspondence on the German Student Movement." Translated by Esther Leslie. *New Left Review* 233 (Jan./Feb. 1999): 123–6.

Agger, Ben. *The Decline of Discourse: Reading, Writing and Resistance in Postmodern Capitalism.* New York: Falmer Press, 1990.

Agger, Ben. *The Discourse of Domination: From the Frankfurt School to Postmodernism.* Evanston, IL: Northwestern University Press, 1992.

Agger, Ben. "Marcuse in Postmodernity." In *Marcuse: From the New Left to the Next Left*, edited by John Bokina and Timothy J. Lukes, 27–40. Lawrence: University Press of Kansas, 1994.

Alway, Joan. *Critical Theory and Political Possibilities: Conceptions of Emancipatory Politics in the Work of Horkheimer, Adorno, Marcuse, and Habermas*. Westport, CT: Greenwood Press, 1995.

Ansell-Pearson, Keith. *Nietzsche Contra Rousseau: A Study of Nietzsche's Moral Political Thought*. Cambridge: Cambridge University Press, 1991. http://dx.doi.org/10.1017/CBO9780511554490.

Arendt, Hannah. "The Concept of History: Ancient and Modern." In *Between Past and Future: Eight Exercises in Political Thought*, 41–90. New York: Penguin Books, 1993.

Arendt, Hannah. "The Crisis in Culture." In *Between Past and Future: Eight Exercises in Political Thought*, 197–226. New York: Penguin Books, 1993.

Arendt, Hannah. "The Eggs Speak Up." In *Essays in Understanding, 1930–1954: Formation, Exile, and Totalitarianism*, edited by Jerome Kohn, 270–84. New York: Schocken Books, 1994.

Arendt, Hannah. *Eichmann in Jerusalem: A Report on the Banality of Evil*. New York: Penguin Books, 1994.

Arendt, Hannah. "The Ex-Communists." In *Essays in Understanding, 1930–1954: Formation, Exile, and Totalitarianism*, edited by Jerome Kohn, 391–400. New York: Schocken Books, 1994.

Arendt, Hannah. "From Hegel to Marx." In *The Promise of Politics*, edited by Jerome Kohn, 40–62. New York: Schocken Books, 2005.

Arendt, Hannah. "The Great Tradition I: Law and Power." *Social Research* 74, no. 3 (Fall 2007): 713–26.

Arendt, Hannah. *The Human Condition*. Chicago: University of Chicago Press, 1998.

Arendt, Hannah. "Introduction *Into* Politics." In *The Promise of Politics*, edited by Jerome Kohn, 93–200. New York: Schocken Books, 2005.

Arendt, Hannah. *Lectures on Kant's Political Philosophy*. Edited by Ronald Beiner. (Chicago: University of Chicago Press, 1992).

Arendt, Hannah. *The Life of the Mind.* Vol. 1, *Thinking*. San Diego: Harcourt, 1978.

Arendt, Hannah. *The Life of the Mind.* Vol. 2, *Willing*. San Diego: Harcourt, 1978.

Arendt, Hannah. "Lying in Politics: Reflections on the Pentagon Papers." In *Crises of the Republic*, 1–48. New York: Harcourt Brace Jovanovich, 1972.

Arendt, Hannah. "Mankind and Terror." In *Essays in Understanding, 1930–1954: Formation, Exile, and Totalitarianism*, edited by Jerome Kohn and translated by Robert and Rita Kimber, 297–306. New York: Schocken Books, 1994.

Arendt, Hannah. "Montesquieu's Revision of the Tradition." In *The Promise of Politics*, edited by Jerome Kohn, 63–9. New York: Schocken Books, 2005.

Arendt, Hannah. "On Hannah Arendt." In *Hannah Arendt: The Recovery of the Public World*, edited by Melvyn A. Hill., 301–39. New York: St. Martin's Press, 1979.

Arendt, Hannah. "On Humanity in Dark Times: Thoughts on Doris Lessing." In *Men in Dark Times*, translated by Clara and Richard Winston, 3–32. San Diego: Harcourt Brace & World, 1968.

Arendt, Hannah. "On the Nature of Totalitarianism: An Essay in Understanding." In *Essays in Understanding, 1930–1954: Formation, Exile, and Totalitarianism*, edited by Jerome Kohn, 328–60. New York: Schocken Books, 1994.

Arendt, Hannah. *On Revolution*. New York: Viking Press, 1965.

Arendt, Hannah. "On Violence." In *Crises of the Republic*, 103–84. New York: Harcourt Brace Jovanovich, 1972.

Arendt, Hannah. *The Origins of Totalitarianism*. San Diego: Harcourt, 1968.

Arendt, Hannah. "Preface: The Gap between Past and Future." In *Between Past and Future: Eight Exercises in Political* Thought, 3–13. New York: Penguin Books, 1993.

Arendt, Hannah. "Religion and the Intellectuals." In *Essays in Understanding, 1930–1954: Formation, Exile, and Totalitarianism*, edited by Jerome Kohn, 228–31. New York: Schocken Books, 1994.

Arendt, Hannah. "Rosa Luxemburg: 1871–1919." In *Men in Dark Times*, translated byHarry Zohn, 33–56. San Diego: Harcourt Brace & World, 1968.

Arendt, Hannah. "Social Science Techniques and the Study of Concentration Camps." In *Essays in Understanding, 1930–1954: Formation, Exile, and Totalitarianism*, edited by Jerome Kohn, 232–47. New York: Schocken Books, 1994.

Arendt, Hannah. "Some Questions of Moral Philosophy." In *Responsibility and Judgment*, edited by Jerome Kohn, 49–146. New York: Schocken Books, 2003.

Arendt, Hannah. "Thinking and Moral Considerations." In *Responsibility and Judgment*, edited by Jerome Kohn, 159–89. New York: Schocken Books, 2003.

Arendt, Hannah. "Thoughts on Politics and Revolution." In *Crises of the Republic*, 199–234. New York: Harcourt Brace Jovanovich, 1972.

Arendt, Hannah. "To Save the Jewish Homeland: There Is Still Time." In *The Jew as Pariah: Jewish Identity and Politics in the Modern Age*, edited by Ron H. Feldman, 83–106. New York: Grove Press, 1978.

Arendt, Hannah. "Totalitarianism Imperialism: Reflections on the Hungarian Revolution." *Journal of Politics* 20, no. 1 (Feb. 1958): 5–43. http://dx.doi.org/10.2307/2127387.

Arendt, Hannah. "Tradition and the Modern Age." In *Between Past and Future: Eight Exercises in Political Thought* , 17–41. New York: Penguin Books, 1993.

Arendt, Hannah. "The Tradition of Political Thought." In *The Promise of Politics*, edited by Jerome Kohn, 40–62. New York: Schocken Books, 2005.

Arendt, Hannah. "Truth and Politics." In *Between Past and Future: Eight Exercises in Political Thought*, 22–64. New York: Penguin Books, 1993.

Arendt, Hannah. "Understanding and Politics (The Difficulties of Understanding)." In *Essays in Understanding, 1930–1954: Formation, Exile, and Totalitarianism*, edited by Jerome Kohn, 307–27. New York: Schocken Books, 1994.

Arendt, Hannah. "Walter Benjamin." In *Men in Dark Times*, translated by Harry Zohn, 153–206. San Diego: Harcourt Brace and World, 1968.

Arendt, Hannah. "What Is Authority?" In *Between Past and Future: Eight Exercises in Political Thought*, 91–142. New York: Penguin Books, 1993.

Arendt, Hannah. "What Is Existential Philosophy?" In *Essays in Understanding, 1930–1954: Formation, Exile, and Totalitarianism*, edited by Jerome Kohn and translated by Robert and Rita Kimber, 163–87. New York: Schocken Books, 1994.

Arendt, Hannah. "What Is Freedom?" In *Between Past and Future: Eight Exercises in Political Thought*, 143–72. New York: Penguin Books, 1993.

Arendt, Hannah. "'What Remains? The Language Remains': A Conversation with Günter Gaus." In *Essays in Understanding, 1930–1954: Formation, Exile, and Totalitarianism*, edited by Jerome Kohn and translated by Joan Stambough, 1–23. New York: Schocken Books, 1994.

Arendt, Hannah, and Karl Jaspers. *Hannah Arendt Karl Jaspers: Correspondence, 1926–1969*. Edited by Lotte Kohler and Hans Saner. Translated by Robert and Rita Kimber. (New York: Harcourt Brace Jovanovich, 1992).

Aristotle. *Nichomachean Ethics*. Translated by Terence Irwin. Indianapolis: Hackett, 1999.

Augustine. *The City of God*. Translated by Marcus Dods. New York: Modern Library, 1950.

Bahro, Rudolf. "The Alternative in Eastern Europe." Translated by David Fernbach and Ben Fowkes. *New Left Review* 106 (Nov.-Dec. 1977): 3–38.

Bahro, Rudolf. *The Alternative in Eastern Europe*. Translated by David Fernbach. London: New Left Books, 1978.

Bakan, Mildred. "Hannah Arendt's Concepts of Labour and Work." In *Hannah Arendt: The Recovery of the Public World*, edited by Melvyn A. Hill, 49–66. New York: St. Martin's Press, 1979.

Bakunin, Michael. *Statism and Anarchy*. Translated by Michael S. Schatz. Cambridge: Cambridge University Press, 1990. http://dx.doi.org/10.1017/CBO9781139168083.

Balbus, Isaac D. "The Missing Dimension: Self-Reflexivity and the 'New Sensibility.'" In *Marcuse: From the New Left to the Next Left*, edited by John Bokina and Timothy J. Lukes, 106–17. Lawrence: University of Press of Kansas, 1994.

Balibar, Etienne. "(De)Constructing the Human as Human Institution: A Reflection on the Coherence of Hannah Arendt's Practical Philosophy."*Social Research* 74, no. 3(Fall 2007): 727–38.

Beiner, Ronald. ""Hannah Arendt on Judging" in Hannah Arendt." In *Lectures on Kant's Political Philosophy*, edited by Ronald Beiner, 89–156. Chicago: University of Chicago Press, 1992.

Benhabib, Seyla. *The Reluctant Modernism of Hannah Arendt*. Thousand Oaks: Sage, 1996.

Benjamin, Walter. *The Origin of German Tragic Drama*. Translated by John Osborne. London: Verso, 1998.

Benjamin, Walter. "The Storyteller." In *Illuminations: Essays and Reflections*, edited by Hannah Arendt and translated by Harry Zohn, 83–110. New York: Schocken Books, 1968.

Benjamin, Walter. "Theses on the Philosophy of History." In *Illuminations: Essays and Reflections,* edited by Hannah Arendt and translated by Harry Zohn, 253–64. New York: Schocken Books, 1968.

Bernstein, Richard J. "Negativity: Theme and Variations." In *Marcuse: Critical Theory and the Promise of Utopia*, edited by Robert Pippen, Andrew Feenberg, and Charles P. Webb, 13–28. South Hadley: Bergin & Garvey 1988.

Bernstein, Richard J. "ReThinking the Social and the Political." In *Philosophical Profiles: Essays in a Pragmatic Mode*, 111–30. Philadelphia: University of Pennsylvania Press, 1986.

Birmingham, Peg. "The An-Archic Event of Natality and the 'Right to Have Rights.'" *Social Research* 74, no. 3 (Fall 2007): 763–76.

Biskowski, Lawrence J. "Politics versus Aesthetics: Arendt's Critiques of Nietzsche and Heidegger." *Review of Politics* 57, no. 1 (Winter 1995): 59–89.

Blatter, Sidonia, and Irene M. Marti. "Rosa Luxemburg and Hannah Arendt: Against the Destruction of the Political Spheres of Freedom." Translated by Senem Saner. *Hypatia* 20, no. 2 (Spring 2005): 83–101.

Bookchin, Murray. "Beyond Neo-Marxism." *Telos* 36 (Summer 1978): 5–28.

Botstein, Leon. "Hannah Arendt: Opposing Views." *Partisan Review* 45, no. 3 (1978): 368–80.

Bowen-Moore, Patricia. *Hannah Arendt's Philosophy of Natality*. New York: St. Martin's Press, 1989.

Boyd, Andrew, and Stephen Duncombe. "The Manufacture of Dissent: What the Left Can Learn from Las Vegas." *Journal of Aesthetics & Protest* 1, no. 3 (June 2004): 34–47.

Brass Liberation Orchestra. "Points of Unity and Vision." October 2004. Retrieved Dec. 2, 2010, from www.brassliberation.org/pou.php.

Breines, Paul. "From Guru to Spectre: Marcuse and the Implosion of the Movement." In *Critical Interruptions: New Left Perspectives on Herbert*

*Marcuse*, edited by Paul Breines, 1–21. New York: Herder and Herder, 1970.

Brinton, Maurice. *The Bolsheviks & Workers' Control, 1917–1921*. London: Solidarity, 1970.

Brown, Norman O. "Dionysus in 1990." In *Apocalypse and/or Metamorphosis*, 179–200. Berkeley: University of California Press, 1991.

Brown, Norman O. *Life against Death: The Psychoanalytic Meaning of History*. Hanover, NH: Wesleyan University Press, 1985.

Brown, Norman O. *Love's Body*. New York: Vintage Books, 1966.

Brown, Norman O. "A Reply to Herbert Marcuse." In *Herbert Marcuse. Negations: Essays in Critical Theory*, 243–7. London: Free Association Books, 1988.

Buck-Morss, Susan. *The Origin of Negative Dialectics: Theodor W. Adorno, Walter Benjamin, and the Frankfurt Institute*. New York: Free Press, 1977.

Bundschuh, Stephan. "The Theoretical Place of Utopia: Some Remarks on Herbert Marcuse's Dual Anthropology." In *Herbert Marcuse: A Critical Reader*, edited by John Abromeit and W. Mark Cobb, 152–62. New York: Routledge, 2004.

Canovan, Margaret. "The Contradictions of Hannah Arendt's Political Thought." *Political Theory* 6, no. 1 (Feb. 1978): 5–26. http://dx.doi. org/10.1177/009059177800600102.

Canovan, Margaret. *Hannah Arendt: A Reinterpretation of Her Political Thought*. Cambridge: Cambridge University Press, 1992. http://dx.doi.org/10.1017/CBO9780511521300.

Canovan, Margaret. *The Political Thought of Hannah Arendt*. London: J. M. Dent & Sons, 1974.

Castoriadis, Cornelius. "Does the Idea of Revolution Still Make Sense?" *Thesis Eleven* 26, no. 1 (1990): 123–38. http://dx.doi.org/10.1177/072551369002600109.

Castoriadis, Cornelius. *The Imaginary Institution of Society*. Translated by Kathleen Blamey. Cambridge: Polity Press, 1987.

Cobb, W. Mark. "Diatribes and Distortions: Marcuse's Academic Reception." In *Herbert Marcuse: A Critical Reader*, edited by John Abromeit and W. Mark Cobb., 163–87. New York: Routledge, 2004.

Cohen, Jean. *Class and Civil Society: The Limits of Marxian Critical Theory*. Amherst: University of Massachusetts Press, 1982.

Colletti, Lucio. "From Hegel to Marcuse." In *From Rousseau to Lenin: Studies in Ideology and Society*, translated by John Merrington and Judith White, 111–40. New York: Monthly Review Press, 1972.

Curtis, Kimberly F. "Aesthetic Foundations of Democratic Politics in the Work of Hannah Arendt." In *Hannah Arendt and the Meaning of Politics*, edited by

Craig Calhoun and John McGowan, 27–52. Minneapolis: University of Minnesota Press, 1997.

d'Entrèves, Maurizio Passerin. *The Political Philosophy of Hannah Arendt*. London: Routledge, 1994.

Debord, Guy. *The Society of the Spectacle*. Translated by Donald Nicholson-Smith. New York: Zone Books, 1995.

Descartes, Rene. *A Discourse on Method*. Translated by John Veitch. J.M. Dent & Sons, 1929.

Disch, Lisa Jane. *Hannah Arendt and the Limits of Philosophy*. Ithaca, NY: Cornell University Press, 1994.

Dossa, Shiraz. *The Public Realm and the Public Self: The Political Theory of Hannah Arendt*. Waterloo, Ontario: Wilfred Laurier University Press, 1989.

Draper, Hal. *The 'Dictatorship of the Proletariat' from Marx to Lenin*. New York: Monthly Review Press, 1987.

Draper, Hal. *Karl Marx's Theory of Revolution*. Vol. 1, *State and Bureaucracy*. New York: Monthly Review Press, 1972.

Eddon, Raluca. "Arendt, Scholem, Benjamin: Between Revolution and Messianism." *European Journal of Political Theory* 5, no. 3 (Fall 2006): 261–79. http://dx.doi.org/10.1177/1474885106064661.

Engels, Friedrich. "Letter to Joseph Bloch." In *The Marx-Engels Reader*, edited by Robert C. Tucker, 760–5. New York: W. W. Norton and Company, 1978.

Engels, Friedrich. "On Authority." In *The Marx-Engels Reader*, ed. Robert C. Tucker, 730–3. New York: W. W. Norton, 1978.

Engels, Friedrich. *The Origin of the Family, Private Property and the State*. New York: Pathfinder Press, 1972.

Engels, Frederick. *Socialism: Utopian and Scientific*. Translated by Edward Aveling. New York: International, 1998.

Feenberg, Andrew. *Heidegger and Marcuse: The Catastrophe and Redemption of History*. New York: Routledge, 2005.

Feenberg, Andrew. "Heidegger and Marcuse: The Catastrophe and Redemption of Technology." In *Herbert Marcuse: A Critical Reader*, edited by John Abromeit and W. Mark Cobb, 67–80. New York: Routledge, 2004.

Feenberg, Andrew. *Lukács, Marx and the Sources of Critical Theory*. Totowa, N.J.: Rowman and Littlefield, 1981.

Frampton, Kenneth. "The Status of Man and the Status of His Objects: A Reading of *The Human Condition*." In *Hannah Arendt: The Recovery of the Public World*, edited by Melvyn A. Hill, 101–30. New York: St. Martin's Press, 1979.

Freud, Sigmund. "Beyond the Pleasure Principle,." In *On Metapsychology: The Theory of Psychoanalysis*, edited and translated by James Strachey, 269–338. London: Penguin Books, 1984.

Freud, Sigmund. *Civilization and its Discontents*. Translated by James Strachey. New York: W. W. Norton and Company, 1989.

Freud, Sigmund. "'Civilized' Sexual Morality and Modern Nervous Illness." In *The Standard Edition of the Complete Psychological Works of Sigmund Freud*, Vol. 9, edited and translated by James Strachey, 179–204. London: Hogarth Press, 1959.

Freud, Sigmund. *The Complete Introductory Lectures of Psychoanalysis*. Translated by James Strachey. New York: W. W. Norton, 1966.

Freud, Sigmund. "The Ego and the Id." In *On Metapsychology: The Theory of Psychoanalysis*, edited and translated by James Strachey, 341–406. London: Penguin Books, 1984.

Freud, Sigmund. *Five Lectures on Psychoanalysis*. Edited and translated by James Strachey. New York: W. W. Norton, 1952.

Freud, Sigmund. "The Most Prevalent Form of Degradation in Mental Life." In *Collected Papers*, Vo. IV, translated by Joan Riviere, 203–16. London: The Hogarth Press, 1950.

Freud, Sigmund. "Mourning and Melancholia." In *On Metapsychology: The Theory of Psychoanalysis*, edited and translated by James Strachey, 245–68. London: Penguin Books, 1984.

Freud, Sigmund. "Negation." In *On Metapsychology: The Theory of Psychoanalysis*, edited and translated by James Strachey, 439–41. London: Penguin Books, 1984.

Freud, Sigmund. *New Introductory Lectures on Psychoanalysis*. Edited by James Strachey. (London: Penguin Books, 1973).

Freud, Sigmund. "On Narcissism: An Introduction." In *On Metapsychology: The Theory of Psychoanalysis*, edited and translated by James Strachey, James, 65–97. London: Penguin Books, 1984.

Freud, Sigmund. "An Outline of Psychoanalysis." In *The Standard Edition of the Complete Psychological Works of Sigmund Freud*, Vol. 23, edited and translated by James Strachey, 141–208. London: Hogarth Press, 1964.

Freud, Sigmund. "Repression." In *On Metapsychology: The Theory of Psychoanalysis*, edited and translated by James Strachey, 145–58. London: Penguin Books, 1984.

Freud, Sigmund. *Three Essays on the Theory of Sexuality*. Translated by James Strachey. London: Hogarth Press, 1970.

Fromm, Erich. "The Crisis in Psychoanalysis." In *The Crisis in Psychoanalysis: Essays on Freud, Marx, and Social Psychology*, 11–41. New York: Henry Holt and Company, 1970.

Fry, John. *Marcuse – Dilemma and Liberation: A Critical Analysis*. Atlantic Highlands, NJ: Humanities Press, 1974.

Fuss, Peter. "Hannah Arendt's Conception of Political Community." In *Hannah Arendt: The Recovery of the Public World*, edited by Melvyn A. Hill, 157–76. New York: St. Martin's Press, 1979.

García Linera, Álvaro. "The Multitude. In Oscar Olivera, *Cochabamba!: Water War in Bolivia*, edited by Oscar Olivera, pp. 65–86. Cambridge: South End Press, 2004.

Garsten, Bryan. "The Elusiveness of Arendtian Judgment." *Social Research* 74, no. 4 (Winter 2007): 1071–1108.

Geoghegan, Vincent. *Reason and Eros: The Social Theory of Herbert Marcuse.* London: Pluto Press, 1981.

Gramsci, Antonio. "The Modern Prince." In *Selections from the Prison Notebooks*, edited and translated by Quinton Hoare and Geoffrey Nowell Smith, 123–205. New York: International Publishers, 1971.

Gramsci, Antonio. "The Study of Philosophy." In *Selections from the Prison Notebooks*, edited and translated by Quinton Hoare and Geoffrey Nowell Smith, 125–209. New York: International Publishers, 1971.

Gramsci, Antonio. "Unions and Councils." In *Pre-Prison Writings*, edited by Richard Bellamy and translated by Virginia Cox, 115–20. (Cambridge: Cambridge University Press, 1994).

Gutiérrez-Aguilar, Raquel. "The Coordinadora: One Year after the Water War." In Oscar Olivera. *Cochabamba!: Water War in Bolivia*, edited by Oscar Olivera, 53–64. Cambridge: South End Press, 2004.

Habermas, Jürgen. "Psychic Thermidor and the Rebirth of Radical Subjectivity." In *Habermas and Modernity*, edited by Richard J. Bernstein, 67–77. Cambridge: MIT Press, 1985.

Hansen, Phillip. *Hannah Arendt: Politics, History and Citizenship.* Stanford: Stanford University Press, 1993.

Hegel, G.W.F. *The Encyclopaedia Logic.* Translated by T.F. Garaets, W.A. Suchting, and H.S. Harris . Indianapolis: Hackett, 1991.

Hegel, G.W.F. *The Phenomenology of Spirit.* Translated by A.V. Miller. Oxford: Oxford University Press, 1977.

Heidegger, Martin. *Being and Time.* Translated by John Macquarrie and Edward Robinson. Albany: State University of New York Press, 1996.

Held, David. *Introduction to Critical Theory: Horkheimer to Habermas.* Berkeley: University of California Press, 1980.

Herzog, Annabel. "Illuminating Inheritance: Benjamin's Influence on Arendt's Political Storytelling." *Philosophy and Social Criticism* 26, no. 5 (Sept. 2000): 1–27. http://dx.doi.org/10.1177/019145370002600501.

Hobsbawm, Eric. "Hannah Arendt on Revolution." In *Revolutionaries: Contemporary Essays*, 201–8. London: Quartet Books, 1973.

Hohendahl, Peter Uwe. *Prismatic Thought: Theodor W. Adorno.* Lincoln: University of Nebraska Press, 1995.

Honig, Bonnie. "Arendt, Identity, and Difference." *Political Theory* 16, no. 1 (Feb. 1988): 77–98. http://dx.doi.org/10.1177/0090591788016001005.

Honig, Bonnie. *Political Theory and the Displacement of Politics*. Ithaca: Cornell University Press, 1993.

Honig, Bonnie. "The Politics of Agonism: A Critical Response to 'Beyond Good and Evil: Arendt, Nietzsche, and the Aestheticization of Political Action' by Dana Villa." *Political Theory* 21, no. 3 (Aug. 1993): 528–33. http://dx.doi.org/10.1177/0090591793021003010.

Honig, Bonnie. "Toward an Agonistic Feminism: Hannah Arendt and the Politics of Identity." In *Feminists Theorize the Political*, edited by Judith Butler and Joan W. Scott, 215–35. New York: Routledge, 1992.

Horkheimer, Max. "The Authoritarian State." In *The Essential Frankfurt School Reader*, edited by Andrew Arato and Eike Gebhardt., 95–118. New York: Continuum, 1982.

Horkheimer, Max. *Eclipse of Reason*. London: Continuum, 2004.

Horkheimer, Max. "Materialism and Metaphysics." In *Critical Theory: Selected Essays*, translated by Matthew J. O'Connell, 10–46. New York: Continuum, 2002.

Horkheimer, Max. "Traditional and Critical Theory." In *Critical Theory: Selected Essays*, translated by Matthew J. O'Connell, 188–243. New York: Continuum, 2002.

Horkheimer, Max, and Theodor W. Adorno. *Dialectic of Enlightenment*. Translated by John Cumming. New York: Continuum, 2000.

Horowitz, Asher. "'By a Hair's Breadth: Critique, Transcendence and the Ethical in Adorno and Levinas." *Philosophy and Social Criticism* 28, no. 2 (2002): 213–48. http://dx.doi.org/10.1177/0191453702028002803.

Horowitz, Asher. *Ethics at a Standstill: History and Subjectivity in Levinas and the Frankfurt School*. Pittsburgh: Duquesne University Press, 2008.

Horowitz, Gad. *Repression: Basic and Surplus Repression in Psychoanalytic Theory: Freud, Reich, and Marcuse*. Toronto: University of Toronto Press, 1977.

Isaac, Jeffrey C. *Arendt, Camus, and Modern Rebellion*. New Haven, CT: Yale University Press, 1992.

Isaac, Jeffrey C. *Democracy in Dark Times*. Ithaca, NY: Cornell University Press, 1998.

Jacobitti, Suzanne. "Hannah Arendt and the Will." *Political Theory* 16, no. 1 (Feb. 1988): 53–76. http://dx.doi.org/10.1177/0090591788016001004.

Jacoby, Russell. "Reversals and Lost Meanings." In *Critical Interruptions: New Left Perspectives on Herbert Marcuse*, edited by Paul Breines, 60–73. New York: Herder and Herder, 1970.

Jameson, Fredric. *Late Marxism: Adorno or the Persistence of the Dialectic*. London: Verso, 1990.

Jameson, Fredric. *Marxism and Form: Twentieth-century Dialectical Theories of Literature*. Princeton: Princeton University Press, 1971.

Jay, Martin. "'The Aesthetic Ideology' as Ideology: Or What Does It Mean to Aestheticize Politics?" In *Force Fields: Between Intellectual History and Cultural Critique*, 71–83. New York: Routledge, 1993.

Jay, Martin. *The Dialectical Imagination: A History of the Frankfurt School of Social Research, 1923–1950*. Berkeley: University of California Press, 1973.

Jay, Martin. "Hannah Arendt: Opposing Views." *Partisan Review* 45, no. 3 (1978): 348–67.

Jay, Martin. *Marxism and Totality: The Adventures of a Concept from Lukács to Habermas*. Berkeley: University of California Press, 1984.

Jay, Martin. "The Metapolitics of Utopianism." In *Permanent Exiles: Essays on the Intellectual Migration from Germany to America*, 3–13. New York: Columbia University Press, 1985.

Jay, Martin. "Reflections on Marcuse's Theory of Critical Remembrance." In *Marcuse: Critical Theory and the Promise of Utopia*, edited by Robert Pippen, Andrew Feenberg, and Charles P. Webel, 29–44. South Hadley: Bergin & Garvey Publishers, 1988.

Kahn, Richard. "The Educative Potential of Ecological Militancy in an Age of Big Oil: Towards a Marcusean Pedagogy." *Policy Futures in Education* 4, no. 1 (2006): 31–44. http://dx.doi.org/10.2304/pfie.2006.4.1.31.

Kant, Immanuel. *Critique of Judgment*. Translated by J.H. Bernhard. New York: Hafner Press, 1951.

Kant, Immanuel. *Critique of Pure Reason*. Translated by Norman Kemp Smith. London: Macmillan Co. Ltd, 1958.

Kateb, George. *Hannah Arendt: Politics, Conscience, Evil*. Totowa, NJ: Rowman & Allanheld, 1984.

Katz, Barry. *Herbert Marcuse and the Art of Liberation*. London: Verso, 1982.

Kellner, Douglas. *Herbert Marcuse and the Crisis of Marxism*. Berkeley: University of California Press, 1984.

Kellner, Douglas. "Herbert Marcuse's Reconstruction of Marxism." In *Marcuse: Critical Theory and the Promise of Utopia*, edited by Robert Pippen, Andrew Feenberg, and Charles P. Webel, 169–88. South Hadley: Bergin & Garvey, 1988.

Kellner, Douglas. "Korsch's Revolutionary Marxism." In *Karl Korsch: Revolutionary Theory*, edited by Douglas Kellner, 3–113. Austin: University of Texas Press, 1977.

Kellner, Douglas. "Marcuse and the Quest for Radical Subjectivity." In *Herbert Marcuse: A Critical Reader*, edited by John Abromeit and W. Mark Cobb, 81–99. New York: Routledge, 2004.

Knauer, James T. "Motive and Goal in Hannah Arendt's Concept of Political Action." *American Political Science Review* 74, no. 3 (Sept. 1980): 721–33. http://dx.doi.org/10.2307/1958153.

Kolakowski, Leszek. *The Breakdown*. Vol. 3 of *Main Currents of Marxism: Its Origins, Growth, and Dissolution*. Translated by P.S. Falla. Oxford: Clarendon Press, 1978.

Kontos, Alkis. "Through a Glass Darkly: Ontology and False Needs." *Canadian Journal of Political and Social Theory* 33, no. 1 (Winter 1979): 25–45.

Korsch, Karl. "The Crisis of Marxism." In *Karl Korsch: Revolutionary Theory*, edited by Douglas Kellner and translated by Otto Koester, 167–76. Austin: University of Texas Press, 1977.

Korsch, Karl. "Fundamentals of Socialization." In *Karl Korsch: Revolutionary Theory*, edited by Douglas Kellner, 124–33. Austin: University of Texas Press, 1977.

Korsch, Karl. *Marxism and Philosophy*. Translated by Fred Halliday. London: New Left Books, 1970.

Korsch, Karl. "The Marxist Dialectic." In *Karl Korsch: Revolutionary Theory*, edited by Douglas Kellner and translated by Karl-Heinz Otto, 135–40. Austin: University of Texas Press, 1977.

Korsch, Karl. "On Materialist Dialectic." In *Karl Korsch: Revolutionary Theory*, edited by Douglas Kellner and translated by Karl-Heinz Otto, 140–4. Austin: University of Texas Press, 1977.

Korsch, Karl. "The Present State of the Problem of Marxism and Philosophy: An Anti-Critique." In *Marxism and Philosophy*, translated by Fred Halliday, 89–128. London: New Left Books, 1970.

Korsch, Karl. "Revolutionary Commune." In *Karl Korsch: Revolutionary Theory*, edited by Douglas Kellner, translated by Andrew Giles-Peters and Karl-Heinz Otto, 199–211. Austin: University of Texas Press, 1977.

Korsch, Karl. "Why I am a Marxist." In *Three Essays on Marxism*, 60–71. New York: Monthly Review Press, 1972.

Kristeva, Julia. *Hannah Arendt: Life is a Narrative*. Translated by Frank Collins. Toronto: University of Toronto Press, 2001.

Lantos, Barbara. "Metapsychological Considerations on the Concept of Work." *International Journal of Psychoanalysis* 33, no. 4(1952): 439–43.

Lantos, Barbara. "Work and the Instincts." *International Journal of Psychoanalysis* 24, Pts. 3 and 4, (1943): 114–19.

Lee-Nichols, Robert. "Judgment, History, Memory: Arendt and Benjamin on Connecting Us to Our Past." *Philosophy Today* 50, no. 3 (Fall 2006): 397–23.

Lenin, V.I. "State and Revolution." In *The Essential Works of Lenin*, edited by Henry M. Christman, 271–364. New York: Bantam Books, 1971.

Lenin, V.I. "What Is to Be Done?" In *The Essential Works of Lenin*, edited by Henry M. Christman, 53–176. New York: Bantam Books, 1971.

Lewis, Tyson. "Utopia and Education in Critical Theory." *Policy Futures in Education* 4, no. 1 (2006): 6–17. http://dx.doi.org/10.2304/pfie.2006.4.1.6.

Lind, Peter. *Marcuse and Freedom*. London: Croom Helm, 1985.

Lipshires, Sidney. *Herbert Marcuse: From Marx to Freud and Beyond*. Cambridge: Schenkman, 1974.

Locke, John. *Second Treatise of Government*. Indianapolis: Hackett, 1980.

Lukács, Georg. "The Changing Function of Historical Materialism." In *History and Class Consciousness: Studies in Marxist Dialectics*, translated by Rodney Livingstone, 223–55. Cambridge: MIT Press, 1971.

Lukács, Georg. "Class Consciousness." In *History and Class Consciousness: Studies in Marxist Dialectics*, translated by Rodney Livingstone, 46–82. Cambridge: MIT Press, 1971.

Lukács, Georg. *Lenin: A Study on the Unity of His Thought*. Translated by Nicholas Jacobs. Cambridge: MIT Press, 1971.

Lukács, Georg. "The Marxism of Rosa Luxemburg." In *History and Class Consciousness: Studies in Marxist Dialectics*, translated by Rodney Livingstone, 27–45. Cambridge: MIT Press, 1971.

Lukács, Georg. "Reification and the Consciousness of the Proletariat." In *History and Class Consciousness: Studies in Marxist Dialectics*, translated by Rodney Livingstone, 83–222. Cambridge: MIT Press, 1971.

Lukács, Georg. "Towards a Methodology of the Problem of Organisation." In *History and Class Consciousness: Studies in Marxist Dialectics*, translated by Rodney Livingstone, 295–342. Cambridge: MIT Press, 1971.

Lukács, Georg. "What Is Orthodox Marxism?" In *History and Class Consciousness: Studies in Marxist Dialectics*, translated by Rodney Livingstone, 1–26. Cambridge: MIT Press, 1971.

Luxemburg, Rosa. *The Accumulation of Capital*. Translated by Agnes Schwarzschild. London: Routledge, 2003.

Luxemburg, Rosa. "Leninism or Marxism." In *The Russian Revolution and Leninism or Marxism*, 81–108. Ann Arbor: University of Michigan Press, 1961.

Luxemburg, Rosa. *The Mass Strike, the Political Party and the Trade Unions*. New York: Harper Torchbooks, 1971.

Luxemburg, Rosa. "The Russian Revolution." In *The Russian Revolution and Leninism or Marxism*, 25–80. Ann Arbor: University of Michigan Press, 1961.

MacIntyre, Alasdair. *Marcuse*. London: Fontana, 1970.

Marcuse, Herbert. "33 Theses." In *Technology, War, and Fascism: Collected Papers of Herbert Marcuse*, Vol. 1, edited by Douglas Kellner and translated by John Abromeit, 217–27. New York: Routledge, 1998.

Marcuse, Herbert. *The Aesthetic Dimension: Toward a Critique of Marxist Aesthetics*. Boston: Beacon Press, 1977.

Marcuse, Herbert. "The Affirmative Character of Culture." In *Negations: Essays in Critical Theory*, translated by Jeremy Shapiro, 88–133. London: Free Association Books, 1988.

Marcuse, Herbert. "Beyond One-Dimensional Man." In *Towards a Critical Theory of Society: Collected Papers of Herbert Marcuse*, Vol. 2, edited by Douglas Kellner, 107–20. London: Routledge, 2001.

Marcuse, Herbert. "The Concept of Essence." In *Negations: Essays in Critical Theory*, translated by Jeremy Shapiro, 43–87. London: Free Association Books, 1988.

Marcuse, Herbert. "The Concept of Negation in the Dialectic." *Telos* 1971 8 (Summer 1971): 130–2. http://dx.doi.org/10.3817/0671008130.

Marcuse, Herbert. "Contributions to a Phenomenology of Historical Materialism." In *Heideggerian Marxism*, edited by Richard Wolin and John Abromeit, translated by Eric Oberle, 1–32, Lincoln: University of Nebraska Press, 2005.

Marcuse, Herbert. *Counter-revolution and Revolt*. Boston: Beacon Press, 1972.

Marcuse, Herbert. "Cultural Revolution." In *Towards a Critical Theory of Society: Collected Papers of Herbert Marcuse*, Vol. 2, edited by Douglas Kellner., 121–62. London: Routledge, 2001.

Marcuse, Herbert. "Das Problem der Geschichtlichen Wirklichkeit." In *Schriften*, Vol. 1, 469–87. Frankfurt: Suhrkamp Verlag, 1978.

Marcuse, Herbert. "Dialogue with Herbert Marcuse." In *Dialogues with Contemporary Continental Thinkers: The Phenomenological Heritage*, edited by Richard Kearney, 71–88. Manchester: Manchester University Press, 1984.

Marcuse, Herbert. "Ecology and the Critique of Modern Society." *Capitalism, Nature, Socialism* 3, no. 3 (Sept. 1992): 29–38. http://dx.doi.org/10.1080/10455759209358500.

Marcuse, Herbert. "The End of Utopia." In *Five Lectures: Psychoanalysis, Politics, Utopia*, translated by Jeremy J. Shapiro and Shierry Weber , 62–82. Boston: Beacon Press, 1970.

Marcuse, Herbert. *Eros and Civilization: A Philosophical Inquiry into Freud*. Boston: Beacon Press, 1974.

Marcuse, Herbert. *An Essay on Liberation*. London: Allen Lane, 1969.

Marcuse, Herbert. "Ethics and Revolution." In *Ethics and Society: Original Essays on Contemporary Moral Problems*, edited by Richard T. De George, 133–47. Garden City, NY: Anchor Books, 1966.

Marcuse, Herbert. "The Failure of the New Left." In *The New Left and the 1960s: Collected Papers of Herbert Marcuse*. Vol. 3, edited by Douglas Kellner and translated by Biddy Martin, 183–91. London: Routledge, 2005.

Marcuse, Herbert. "The Foundation of Historical Materialism." In *Studies in Critical Philosophy*, translated by Joris de Bres, 1–48. Boston: Beacon Press, 1972.

Marcuse, Herbert. "Freedom and Freud's Theory of the Instincts." In *Five Lectures: Psychoanalysis, Politics, Utopia*, translated by Jeremy J. Shapiro and Shierry Weber, 1–27. Boston: Beacon Press, 1970.

Marcuse, Herbert. "Freedom and the Historical Imperative." In *Studies in Critical Philosophy*, translated by Joris de Bres, 209–23. Boston: Beacon Press, 1972.

Marcuse, Herbert. "German Philosophy, 1871-1933." In *Heideggerian Marxism*, edited by Richard Wolin and John Abromeit, translated by Ron Haas, 151–64. Lincoln: University of Nebraska Press, 2005.

Marcuse, Herbert. *Hegel's Ontology and the Theory of Historicity*. Translated by Seyla Benhabib. Cambridge: MIT Press, 1987.

Marcuse, Herbert. "Heidegger and Marcuse: A Dialogue in Letters." In *Technology, War and Fascism: Collected Papers of Herbert Marcuse*, Vol. 1, edited by Douglas Kellner and translated by Richard Wolin, 263–7. London: Routledge, 1998.

Marcuse, Herbert. "Heidegger's Politics: An Interview." In *Heideggerian Marxism*, edited by Richard Wolin and John Abromeit, 165–75. Lincoln: University of Nebraska Press, 2005.

Marcuse, Herbert. "The Ideology of Death." In *The Meaning of Death*, edited by Herman Feifel, 64–75. New York: McGraw-Hill, 1959.

Marcuse, Herbert. "Industrialization and Capitalism in the Work of Max Weber." In *Negations: Essays in Critical Theory*, translated by Jeremy J. Shapiro, 133–51. London: Free Association Books, 1988.

Marcuse, Herbert. "Karl Popper and the Problem of Historical Laws." In *Studies in Critical Philosophy*, translated by Joris de Bres, 191–208. Boston: Beacon Press, 1972.

Marcuse, Herbert. "Lecture on Education, Brooklyn College, 1968." In *Marcuse's Challenge to Education*, edited by Douglas Kellner, Tyson Lewis, Clayton Pierce, and K. Daniel Choi, 33–8. Lanham, MD: Rowman & Littlefield, 2009.

Marcuse, Herbert. "Lecture on Higher Education and Politics, Berkeley, 1975." In *Marcuse's Challenge to Education*, edited by Douglas Kellner, Tyson Lewis, Clayton Pierce, and K. Daniel Choi, 39–44. Lanham, MD: Rowman & Littlefield, 2009.

Marcuse, Herbert. "Letters to Horkheimer." In *Technology, War, and Fascism: Collected Papers of Herbert Marcuse*, Vol. 1, edited by Douglas Kellner and translated by Benjamin Gregg, 231–60.  New York: Routledge, 1998.

Marcuse, Herbert. "Liberation from the Affluent Society." In *The New Left and the 1960s: Collected Papers of Herbert Marcuse*, Vol. 3, edited by Douglas Kellner, 76–86. London: Routledge, 2005.

Marcuse, Herbert. "Love Mystified: A Critique of Norman O. Brown." In *Negations: Essays in Critical Theory* , pp. 227–43. London: Free Association Books, 1988.

Marcuse, Herbert. "Marcuse Defines His New Left Line." In *The New Left and the 1960s: Collected Papers of Herbert Marcuse*, Vol. 3, edited by Douglas Kellner, pp. 100–17. London: Routledge, 2005.

Marcuse, Herbert. "Marxism and Feminism." In *The New Left and the 1960s: Collected Papers of Herbert Marcuse*, Vol. 3, edited by Douglas Kellner, pp. 165–72. London: Routledge, 2005.

Marcuse, Herbert. "The Movement in the New Era of Repression." In *The New Left and the 1960s: Collected Papers of Herbert Marcuse*, Vol. 3, edited by Douglas Kellner, pp. 142–53. London: Routledge, 2005.

Marcuse, Herbert. "Murder Is Not a Political Weapon." In *The New Left and the 1960s: Collected Papers of Herbert Marcuse*, Vol. 3, edited by Douglas Kellner and translated by Jeffrey Herf, pp. 177–9. London: Routledge, 2005.

Marcuse, Herbert. "My Disillusionment with Heidegger." In *Heideggerian Marxism*, edited by Richard Wolin and John Abromeit, and translated by Richard Wolin, p. 176. Lincoln: University of Nebraska Press, 2005.

Marcuse, Herbert. "A Note on Dialectic." In *The Essential Marcuse: Selected Writings of Philosopher and Social Critic Herbert Marcuse*, edited by Andrew Feenberg and William Leiss, pp. 63–71. Boston: Beacon Press, 2007.

Marcuse, Herbert. "The Obsolescence of the Freudian Concept of Man." In *Five Lectures: Psychoanalysis, Politics, Utopia*, translated by Jeremy J. Shapiro and Shierry Weber, pp. 44–61. Boston: Beacon Press, 1970.

Marcuse, Herbert. "The Obsolescence of Marxism." In *Marxism and the Western World*, edited by Nicholas Lobkowicz, pp. 409–17. Notre Dame: University of Notre Dame Press, 1967.

Marcuse, Herbert. "On Concrete Philosophy." In *Heideggerian Marxism*, edited by Richard Wolin and John Abromeit, and translated by Matthew Erlin, pp. 34–52. Lincoln: University of Nebraska Press, 2005.

Marcuse, Herbert. *One-Dimensional Man: Studies in the Ideology of Advanced Industrial Society*. Boston: Beacon Press, 1969.

Marcuse, Herbert. "On Hedonism." In *Negations: Essays in Critical Theory*, translated by Jeremy J. Shapiro, pp. 159–200. London: Free Association Books, 1988.

Marcuse, Herbert. "On the New Left." In *The New Left and the 1960s: Collected Papers of Herbert Marcuse*, Vol. 3, edited by Douglas Kellner, pp. 122–7. London: Routledge, 2005.

Marcuse, Herbert. "On the Philosophical Foundation of the Concept of Labour in Economics." Translated by Douglas Kellner. *Telos* 16 (Summer 1973): 9–37 .

Marcuse, Herbert. "On the Problem of the Dialectic." Translated by Morton Schoolman and Duncan Smith. *Telos*.27 (Spring 1976): 3–11. (trans.).

Marcuse, Herbert. "Philosophy and Critical Theory." In *Negations: Essays in Critical Theory*, translated by Jeremy J. Shapiro, pp. 134–58. London: Free Association Books, 1988.

Marcuse, Herbert. "The Problem of Social Change in the Technological Society." In *Towards a Critical Theory of Society: Collected Papers of Herbert Marcuse*, Vol. 2, edited by Douglas Kellner, pp. 35–58. London: Routledge, 2001.

Marcuse, Herbert. "The Problem of Violence and the Radical Opposition." In *Five Lectures: Psychoanalysis, Politics, Utopia*, translated by Jeremy J. Shapiro and Shierry Weber, pp. 83–94. Boston: Beacon Press, 1970.

Marcuse, Herbert. "Professoren als Staats-regenten?: Spiegel-Gespräch mit dem Philosophen Professor Herbert Marcuse." *Der Spiegel* 35 (Aug. 21, 1967): 112–18.

Marcuse, Herbert. "Progress and Freud's Theory of the Instincts." In *Five Lectures: Psychoanalysis, Politics, Utopia*, translated by Jeremy J. Shapiro and Shierry Weber, pp. 28–43. Boston: Beacon Press, 1970.

Marcuse, Herbert. "Protosocialism and Late Capitalism: Toward a Theoretical Synthesis Based on Bahro's Analysis." In *Rudolf Bahro: Critical Responses*, edited by Ulf Wolter, pp. 24–48. New York: M.E. Sharpe, 1980.

Marcuse, Herbert. "The Realm of Freedom and the Realm of Necessity: A Reconsideration." *Praxis* 5, no. 1-2 (1969): 20–25.

Marcuse, Herbert. *Reason and Revolution: Hegel and the Rise of Social Theory*. Amherst, NY: Humanity Books, 1999.

Marcuse, Herbert. "Reflections on the French Revolution." In *The New Left and the 1960s: Collected Papers of Herbert Marcuse*, Vol. 3, edited by Douglas Kellner, pp. 40–5. London: Routledge, 2005.

Marcuse, Herbert. "The Reification of the Proletariat." *Canadian Journal of Political and Social Theory* 3, no. 1 (Winter 1979): 20–3.

Marcuse, Herbert. "Repressive Tolerance." In *Critical Sociology*, edited by Paul Connerton., pp. 301–29. Harmondsworth: Penguin, 1976.

Marcuse, Herbert. "Revolutionary Subject and Self-Government." *Praxis* 5, no. 1-2 (1969):32—9.

Marcuse, Herbert. "A Revolution in Values." In *Political Ideologies*, edited by James A. Gould and Willis H. Truitt, pp. 331–6. New York: Macmillan Company, 1973.

Marcuse, Herbert. "Sartre's Existentialism." In *Studies in Critical Philosophy*. Translated by Joris de Bres, pp. 157–90. Boston: Beacon Press, 1972.

Marcuse, Herbert. "Socialist Humanism?" In *Socialist Humanism: An International Symposium*, edited by Erich Fromm, pp. 107–17. New York: Anchor Books, 1966.

Marcuse, Herbert. *Soviet Marxism: A Critical Analysis*. New York: Columbia University Press, 1958.

Marcuse, Herbert. "The Struggle Against Liberalism in the Totalitarian View of the State." In *Negations: Essays in Critical Theory*, translated by Jeremy J. Shapiro, pp. 3–42. London: Free Association Press, 1988.

Marcuse, Herbert. "A Study on Authority." In *Studies in Critical Philosophy*, translated by Joris de Bres, pp. 49–156. Boston: Beacon Press, 1972.

Marcuse, Herbert. "Theory and Politics: A Discussion with Herbert Marcuse, Juergen Habermas, Heinz Lubasz and Tilman Spengler." *Telos* 38 (Winter 1978–1979): 124–53.

Marcuse, Herbert. "USA: Questions of Organization and the Revolutionary Subject." In *The New Left and the 1960s: Collected Papers of Herbert Marcuse*, Vol. 3, edited by Douglas Kellner, 137–41. London: Routledge, 2005.

Marcuse, Herbert, and Franz Neumann. "Theories of Social Change." In *Technology, War, and Fascism: Collected Papers of Herbert Marcuse*, Vol. 1, edited by Douglas Kellner, pp. 107–37. London: Routledge, 1998.

Martel, James. "'Amo: Volu ut sis': "Love, Willing, and Arendt's Reluctant Embrace of Sovereignty." *Philosophy and Social Criticism* 34, no. 3 (March 2008): 287–313. http://dx.doi.org/10.1177/0191453707087254.

Marx, Karl. "After the Revolution: Marx Debates Bakunin." In *The Marx-Engels Reader*, edited by Robert C. Tucker., pp. 542–8. New York: W. W. Norton, 1978.

Marx, Karl. *Capital: A Critique of Political Economy*. Vol. 1. Translated by Ben Fowkes. London: Penguin Books, 1976.

Marx, Karl. *Capital: A Critique of Political Economy*. Vol. 3. Translated by David Fernbach. London: Penguin Books, 1981.

Marx, Karl. "The Civil War in France." In *Writings on the Paris Commune*, edited by Hal Draper, pp. 51–101. New York: Monthly Review Press, 1971.

Marx, Karl. "Contribution to the Critique of Hegel's *Philosophy of Right*: Introduction." In *The Marx-Engels Reader*, edited by Robert C. Tucker., pp. 16–25. New York: W. W. Norton, 1978.

Marx, Karl. *Critique of Hegel's Philosophy of Right*. Translated by Annette Jolin and Joseph O'Malley. Cambridge: Cambridge University Press, 1970.

Marx, Karl. *Economic and Philosophic Manuscripts of 1844*. Translated by Martin Milligan. Amherst, NY: Prometheus Books, 1988.

Marx, Karl. *Grundrisse: Foundations of the Critique of Political Economy*. Translated by Martin Nicolaus. London: Penguin Books, 1973.

Marx, Karl. "On James Mill." In *Karl Marx: Selected Writings*, edited by David McLellan, pp. 114–24. Oxford: Oxford University Press, 2000.

Marx, Karl, and Friedrich Engels. "Address of the Central Committee to the Communist League." In *The Marx-Engels Reader*, edited by Robert C. Tucker, pp. 366–73. New York: W. W. Norton, 1978.

Marx, Karl, and Friedrich Engels. *The German Ideology*. Amherst, NY: Prometheus Books, 1983.

Marx, Karl, and Frederick Engels. *The Holy Family, or Critique of Critical Criticism: Against Bruno Bauer, and Company*. Translated by Richard Dixon and Clemens Dutt. Moscow: Progress Publishers, 1975.

Matthews, Richard. *The Radical Politics of Thomas Jefferson*. Lawrence: University Press of Kansas, 1984.

Mattick, Paul. *Critique of Marcuse: One-Dimensional Man in Class Society*. London: Merlin, 1972.

McConkey, Mike. "On Arendt's Vision of the European Council Phenomenon: Critique from an Historical Perspective." *Dialectical Anthropology* 16, no. 1 (Mar. 1991): 15–31. http://dx.doi.org/10.1007/BF00247767.

McNally, David. *Another World is Possible: Globalization & Anti-Capitalism*. Winnipeg: Arbeiter Ring, 2006.

Medearis, John. "Lost or Obscured? How V.I. Lenin, Joseph Schumpeter, and Hannah Arendt Misunderstood the Council Movement." *Polity* 36, no. 3 (Apr. 2004): 447–76.

Michelet, Jules. *History of the French Revolution*. Translated by Charles Cocks. Chicago: University of Chicago Press, 1967.

Miller, James. "The Pathos of Novelty: Hannah Arendt's Image of Freedom in the Modern World." In *Hannah Arendt: The Recovery of the Public World*, edited by Melvyn A. Hill, pp. 177–208. New York: St. Martin's Press, 1979.

Mouffe, Chantal. *The Democratic Paradox*. London: Verso, 2000.

Nietzsche, Friedrich. *The Birth of Tragedy*. Translated by Douglas Smith. Oxford: Oxford University Press, 2000.

Nietzsche, Friedrich. *On the Advantage and Disadvantage of History in Life*. Translated by Peter Preuss. Indianapolis: Hackett, 1980.

Nietzsche, Friedrich. *On the Genealogy of Morals*. Translated by Douglas Smith. Oxford: Oxford University Press, 1996.

Nietzsche, Friedrich. *Thus Spoke Zarathustra: A Book for Everyone and No One.* Translated by R.J. Hollingdale. London: Penguin Books, 1969.

Nietzsche, Friedrich. *The Will to Power.* Translated by Walter Kaufmann and R.J. Hollingdale. New York: Vintage Books, 1968.

Ober, John David. "On Sexuality and Politics in the Work of Herbert Marcuse." In *Critical Interruptions: New Left Perspectives on Herbert Marcuse,* edited by Paul Breines., pp. 101–35. New York: Herder and Herder, 1970.

Olivera, Oscar, in collaboration with Tom Lewis. *Cochabamba!: Water War in Bolivia.* Cambridge: South End Press, 2004.

Paine, Thomas. *The Rights of Man.* New York: Penguin Books, 1984.

Parekh, Bikhu. *Hannah Arendt and the Search for a New Political Philosophy.* London: Macmillan Press, 1981.

Parekh, Bikhu. "Hannah Arendt's Critique of Marx." In *The Recovery of the Public World,* edited by Melvyn A. Hill, pp. 67–100. New York: St. Martin's Press, 1979.

Pearce, Clayton. "Groundwork for the Concept of Technique in Education: Herbert Marcuse and Technological Society." *Policy Futures in Education* 4, no. 1 (2006): 61–72.

Pippen, Robert. "Marcuse on Hegel and Historicity." In *Marcuse: Critical Theory and the Promise of Utopia,* edited by Robert Pippen, Andrew Feenberg, and Charles P. Webel, pp. 68–94. South Hadley: Bergin & Garvey, 1988.

Pitken, Hanna. *The Attack of the Blob: Hannah Arendt's Concept of the Social.* Chicago: University of Chicago Press, 1998.

Postone, Moishe. *Time, Labor, and Social Domination: A Reinterpretation of Marx's Critical Theory.* Cambridge: Cambridge University Press, 1993. http://dx.doi.org/10.1017/CBO9780511570926.

Reinhardt, Mark. *The Art of Being Free: Taking Liberties with Tocqueville, Marx, and Arendt.* Ithaca, NY: Cornell University Press, 1997.

Reitz, Charles. *Art, Alienation, and the Humanities: A Critical Engagement with Herbert Marcuse.* Albany: State University of New York Press, 2000.

Ring, Jennifer. "On Needing Both Marx and Arendt: Alienation and the Flight from Inwardness." *Political Theory* 17, no. 3 (Aug. 1989): 432–48. http://dx.doi.org/10.1177/0090591789017003004.

Robinson, Paul. *The Sexual Radicals.* London: Temple Smith, 1969.

Róheim, Géza. *The Origin and Function of Culture.* New York: Anchor Books, 1971.

Schiller, Friedrich. *On the Aesthetic Education of Man: In a Series of Letters.* Translated by Elizabeth M. Wilkinson and L.A. Willoughby. Oxford: Clarendon Press, 1967.

Schmidt, Alfred. *The Concept of Nature in Marx*. Translated by Ben Fowkes. London: New Left Books, 1971.

Schmidt, Alfred. "Existential Ontology and Historical Materialism in the Work of Herbert Marcuse." In *Marcuse: Critical Theory and the Promise of Utopia*, edited by Robert Pippen, Andrew Feenberg, and Charles P. Webel, pp. 47–67. South Hadley: Bergin & Garvey Publishers, 1988.

Schoolman, Morton. *The Imaginary Witness: The Critical Theory of Herbert Marcuse*. New York: New York University Press, 1984.

Shapiro, Jeremy J. "One-Dimensionality: The Universal Semiotic of Technological Experience." In *Critical Interruptions: New Left Perspectives on Herbert Marcuse*, edited by Paul Breines, pp. 136–86. New York: Herder and Herder, 1970.

Shepard, Benjamin. "If I Can't Dance: Play, Creativity, and Social Movements." PhD diss., City University of New York, 2006.

Shepard, Benjamin. "Introductory Notes on the Trail from ACT UP to the WTO." In *From ACT UP to the WTO: Urban Protest and Community Building in the Era of Globalization*, edited by Benjamin Shepard and Ronald Hayduk, pp. 11–15. London: Verso, 2002.

Shepard, Benjamin. "Joy, Justice, and Resistance to the New Global Apartheid." In *From ACT UP to the WTO: Urban Protest and Community Building in the Era of Globalization*, edited by Benjamin Shepard and Ronald Hayduk, pp. 389–94. London: Verso, 2002.

Shepard, Benjamin. L.M. Bogad, and Stephen Duncombe. "Performing vs. the Insurmountable: Theatrics, Activism, and Social Movements." *Liminalities* 4, no. 3 (Oct. 2008): 1–30.

Siegel, Jerrold. *Marx's Fate: The Shape of a Life*. Princeton: Princeton University Press, 1978.

Siemens, H.W. "Action, Performance and Freedom in Hannah Arendt and Friedrich Nietzsche." *International Studies in Philosophy* 37, no. 3 (2005): 107–26.

Sitton, John F. "Hannah Arendt's Argument for Council Democracy." In *Hannah Arendt: Critical Essays*, edited by Lewis P. Hinchman and Sandra K. Hinchman, pp. 307–29. Albany: State University of New York Press, 1994.

Slater, Phil. *Origin and Significance of the Frankfurt School: A Marxist Perspective*. London: Routledge & Keegan Paul, 1977.

Sorel, Georges. *Reflections on Violence*. Translated by T.E. Hulme and J. Roth. London: Collier Books, 1950.

Tassin, Etienne. "'*sed victa Catoni*': The Defeated Cause of Revolutions." Translated by Jérôme Melançon. *Social Research* 74, no. 4 (Winter 2007): 1109–26.

Torgerson, Douglas. "Farewell to the Green Movement? Political Action and the Green Public Sphere." *Environmental Politics* 9, no. 4 (Winter 2000): 1–19. http://dx.doi.org/10.1080/09644010008414548.

Torgerson, Douglas. *The Promise of Green Politics: Environmentalism and the Public Sphere*. Durham, NC: Duke University Press, 1999.

Van Heertum, Richard. "Marcuse, Bloch and Friere: Reinvigorating a Pedagogy of Hope." *Policy Futures in Education* 4, no. 1 (2006): 45–51. http://dx.doi.org/10.2304/pfie.2006.4.1.45.

Van Heertum, Richard. "Moving from Critique to Hope: Critical Interventions from Marcuse to Freire." In *Marcuse's Challenge to Education*, edited by Douglas Kellner, Tyson Lewis, Clayton Pierce, and K. Daniel Choi, pp. 103–16. (Lanham, MD: Rowman & Littlefield, 2009).

Villa, Dana. *Arendt and Heidegger: The Fate of the Political*. Princeton, NJ: Princeton University Press, 1996.

Villa, Dana. "Beyond Good and Evil: Arendt, Nietzsche, and the Aestheticization of Political Action." *Political Theory* 20, no. 2 (May 1992): 274–308. http://dx.doi.org/10.1177/0090591792020002004.

Villa, Dana. "Hannah Arendt: Modernity, Alienation, and Critique." In *Hannah Arendt and the Meaning of Politics*, edited by Craig Calhoun and John McGowan., pp. 179–206. Minneapolis: University of Minnesota Press, 1997.

Villa, Dana. *Politics, Philosophy, Terror: Essays on the Thought of Hannah Arendt*. Princeton: Princeton University Press, 1999.

Werz, Michael. "The Fate of Emancipated Subjectivity." In *Herbert Marcuse: A Critical Reader*, edited by John Abromeit and W. Mark Cobb, pp. 209–23. New York: Routledge, 2004.

Wiggershaus, Rolf. *The Frankfurt School: Its History, Theories, and Political Significance*. Translated by Michael Robertson. (Cambridge: MIT Press, 1995).

Weber, Shierry M. "Individuation as Praxis." In *Critical Interruptions: New Left Perspectives on Herbert Marcuse*, edited by Paul Breines, pp. 22–59. New York: Herder and Herder, 1970.

Woddis, Jack. *New Theories of Revolution: A Commentary on the Views of Frantz Fanon, Régis Debray and Herbert Marcuse*. New York: International Publishers, 1972.

Wolin, Richard. *Heidegger's Children: Hannah Arendt, Karl Lowith, Hans Jonas, and Herbert Marcuse*. Princeton: Princeton University Press, 2001.

Wolin, Sheldon. "Hannah Arendt: Democracy and the Political." In *Hannah Arendt: Critical Essays*, edited by Lewis P. Hinchman and Sandra K. Hinchman., pp. 289–306. Albany: State University of New York Press, 1994.

Yar, Majid. "From Actor to Spectator: Hannah Arendt's 'Two Theories' of Political Judgment." *Philosophy and Social Criticism* 26, no. 2 (Mar. 2000): 1–27. http://dx.doi.org/10.1177/019145370002600201.

Young-Bruehl, Elisabeth. *Hannah Arendt: For Love of the World*. New Haven: Yale University Press, 1982.

Young-Bruehl, Elisabeth. *Why Arendt Matters*. New Haven: Yale University Press, 2006.

Zaretsky, Eli. "Hannah Arendt and the Meaning of the Public/Private Distinction." In *Hannah Arendt and the Meaning of Politics*, edited by Craig Calhoun and John McGowan., pp. 207–31. Minneapolis: University of Minnesota Press, 1997.

Zerilli, Linda. "Castoriadis, Arendt, and the Problem of the New." *Constellations* 9, no. 4 (Dec. 2002): 540–53. http://dx.doi.org/10.1111/1467-8675.00302.

# Index